SEASO

SEASONS OF CHANGE

Busking England

Tom Kitching

Scratching Shed Publishing Ltd

BORN in Macclesfield in 1983, Tom was educated at Broken Cross Primary and Henbury High School. Not academically minded, he spent his time writing and learning the fiddle. After two attempts at his A-levels, he studied Politics and Social Policy at Loughborough university. A finalist in the BBC *Young Folk Award*, he soon joined a band, 'The Fox Hat', who specialised in playing Fairport Convention covers extremely loud to shell-shocked pub audiences.

In need of work, he joined ceilidh band Albireo and formed a duo with university friend Gren Bartley, signing to Fellside records and touring the folk clubs of England. In 2010, he founded the band 'Pilgrims' Way', who were nominated for a BBC folk award and have since played at almost every English folk festival. His celebrated 2015 solo album, *Interloper*, received impressive reviews, including being awarded five stars and a place on the *Sunday Express* albums of the year list.

Tom has worked with celebrated singers including Gavin Davenport, Zoe Mulford, Jon Loomes, and Elfin Bow, and is a staple of the English country dance scene both as a musician and a dance caller. He has played on over twenty-five albums and performed at well over 1,800 gigs.

A passionate supporter of Salford rugby league club, he has a one-thirteenth share of a historic wooden oil tanker, enjoys chess, and vegetable gardening. He is chairman of the Stockport and District Formation Mild Drinking Squad and lives in Chorlton with two housemates and a boa constrictor.

Selected discography:

Rushes – Tom Kitching and Gren Bartley. (Fellside Records, 2007)
Wayside Courtesies – Pilgrims' Way (Fellside Records, 2011)
Interloper – Tom Kitching (Fellside Records, 2015)
Binary – Albireo (2017)
Stand and Deliver – Pilgrims' Way (Talking Cat Records, 2017)

First published by Scratching Shed Publishing Ltd in 2020
Registered in England & Wales No. 6588772.
Registered office:
47 Street Lane, Leeds, West Yorkshire. LS8 1AP
www.scratchingshedpublishing.co.uk
ISBN 978-1999333935

A catalogue record for this book is available from the British Library.

Typeset in Warnock Pro Semi Bold and Palatino
Printed and bound in the United Kingdom by

Trecerus Industrial Estate, Padstow,
Cornwall PL28 8RW
www.tjinternational.ltd.uk

To Jude Gregson and Chris Spence

Two teachers who went well out of their way
to encourage me in my writing, despite my apparently
limitless academic mediocrity.

For more information on Tom Kitching and the Busk England project, including the album that accompanies this book, *above*, visit: www.tomkitching.co.uk

Contents

Acknowledgements

THE list of people who have helped as I've gone along, be it with advice, a bed to sleep in, a sight to see, a well timed sausage roll, a few quid to keep me going, or even a useful criticism is considerable. It's humbling to write it down and see how many people I'm indebted to after two years. Thank you all.

Simon Stephenson, David and Pam Walker, Cheryl and Edward Frank, Andy Knight, Owen Woods, Jess Bhavsar, Tony and Yvonne Moore, Jess Morgan, Mick and Penny Verrier, Vicki Swan, Jonny Dyer, Oscar Cainer, Kaeridwyn Efetlya, www.grenbartley.com, Jude Rees, Lucy Thompson, Richard Wood, Bob Mayow, Mary Kipling, Kim Osborne, Mike Wild, Edwin Beasant, Heather Sirrel, Elspeth KanaanBrown, Rachel Hill, Ben and Tanya at Pebbles tavern, May Fairweather, Colin Cross, Keith Adams, Ruth Burrows, Steven Troughton, Helen Lonsborough, Marc Cragg, Ray Butler, Loraine Grainger, Jamie Lomas, Samanta Alvarez, Debra Hannis, Eunice Kitching, Fruzsina Rakoczy, Robbie Sherratt, Pippa Jones, Sarah Field, Brian and Sue Kendrick, Steve Shaw, Heather Wood, Joan Crump, Mike Wild, Joe Grint, Mal Robins, Sophie Parkes-Nield,

Acknowledgements

Hazel Mayow, Liam Markham, Rebekah Parrott, Daisy Black, Peter and Sarah Crowther, Rhianwen Davies, Becky Gilman, Hannah James, Howard Jones and Sean Bechhofer.

I'm very grateful to the Arts Council for their lottery grant, which allowed me the time and space to create both this book and the album that accompanies it.

I'm especially indebted to my good friend Paul Sullivan, who mentored me in turning forty-six diverse blogs into what I hope is a coherent and flowing book, mostly over a glass of wine and with Jethro Tull on the turntable.

I always feel I owe a great thank you to my parents, David and Shirley, who have never attempted to divert me away from a dubious career in the arts when there have been plenty of times when they would have been entirely justified in the suggestion.

I'm grateful to Tony Hannan and Scratching Shed for giving me a chance to have this published, my first attempt at a book, and to Dave Hadfield for putting us in touch with one another.

And finally, to my girlfriend, Bridget Slater, who has expressed nothing but support and encouragement throughout.

Introduction

THIS isn't really a book about busking. Granted, a great deal of busking takes place, but really it's a book about England.

I woke up the morning after that referendum with a sinking feeling that I really didn't know the country as well as I'd thought. Thirteen years as a professional musician, travelling up and down, performing at folk clubs, arts centres and festivals had given me a false sense of familiarity with this rich and varied land, but the truth of the gigging life is how superficial your visits are, and how self-selecting your audiences can be. You turn up, do the gig, meet a bunch of people who look a lot like you but older, perhaps stay over at a Travelodge, and then go home again.

This isn't really a book about Brexit either. In fact, that's the last time I'll use that word. It's too emotive a subject, where views are too entrenched to make it any use for asking deeper questions about identity. I wanted to bypass that and get under our skin. This is a book about who we, the English, are. What we do, what matters to us.

I wanted to ask if there could even be such a thing as

England, other than the people and places within the line on the map? What, if anything, unites us as one people?

Fired with a need to know my own country better, I drew up an exhaustive list of the tools at my disposal. A fiddle, a list of contacts from over a decade of gigging. A tired Volvo stuck in limp mode. That seemed to be about it.

I also found myself to have arrived at the age of 34 with no children, no mortgage, no nine to five job, and no relatives who needed caring for just yet. I could just wander off and nobody would really notice for a while. I certainly wouldn't be letting anyone down, no more than usual at least.

Life hadn't quite worked out as I'd thought, and many of the little accumulations of value and stability that my friends had been busy achieving had somewhat slipped through my fingers. Perhaps I'd let them. I've no doubt that I know many people who have the talent and skills to carry off this project extremely well. The difference was that I had the freedom to do it where they were all tied down in one way or another. People told me I was brave to set off for a year's busking. I wasn't. It was the path of least resistance. The thought of a year or so to myself, busking anonymously around England, making notes, making friends, seemed deeply romantic. My parents, seeing I was determined to go, sorted me out with some new boots.

Busking was to be simply a means to an end. I wanted to visit as many corners of England as possible and, without any other income, this was how I was going to fund it. I set a few rules. It wasn't to be a search for the most lucrative pitches but to make enough overall that I could explore, meet people, take time. I wanted to be free to busk wherever looked or sounded right, without the pressure of having to make money every time I took the fiddle out of the case.

But busking did become a huge part of it. The busker has a remarkable view of the world. You watch the same street for hours, and see it change over the day. You see different days unfold in the same town. People get to know you. Most of my best insights occurred on the second day somewhere, when you'd become familiar and comfortable.

The musician is trusted with secrets and stories. If I'd turned up as a journalist, people would have worried, clammed up, kept it clean. Musicians cause people to relax and tell it how it is. The fiddle was not just my source of income, it cracked places open for me in a way that a notepad never could.

I wrote up each place I visited for my blog. That's all still online and will remain so, usually with a few photographs if you feel the story needs a little visual colour. A few of the locations have been moved chronologically for the sake of making the book more coherent, but the blog is still in the original order if you want to cross reference.

I was constantly humbled by the support I received as I went around. In the whole project, I only needed to pay for a room to stay in on four occasions. Other than camping out in the back of my car for two nights in Cornwall, I was accommodated by a wide variety of people, from friends, to musical acquaintances, to strangers who simply wanted to help.

I was provided with no end of suggestions for places to go and things to do. People sorted me out with meals and drinks. I performed a number of house concerts as the trip went on. It would not have been financially possible without this support, and I'm truly grateful.

Blogging gave me an instant feedback mechanism as well. At one time, you'd have saved up all your notes and finally brought out a book and, if it was controversial, you'd get it all at once. For me, people were reading up each visit after it happened, and were able to weigh in with information I'd missed, mistakes I'd made, and offer suggestions. I was being lightly edited in real time. On one occasion, I managed to genuinely upset a community with what I wrote. I was then able to go back and address this in a way that had I just published a book at the end

I would not have been able to do. That particular episode ended up being one of the most interesting and educational points of the whole trip, and I hope that a potentially damaging situation ended up becoming a beneficial one for both parties.

I consulted widely for advice before I began, being frequently told that travel writing required a great deal of forward planning to arrange the activities you intend to do and to set up the meetings you need to have. This was only partially true in my case. It quickly became clear to me that my journey was not about the exceptional but the mundane. Museums and great events would not help me half so much as just being in a street on market day. Announce you are coming and suddenly everyone is on best behaviour. People strive to show you the very best of it, spin a narrative. Just turn up and play and you see a place for how it is. Nobody suspects a busker of an ulterior motive. I rapidly became most interested in day to day life. I just wanted to see and meet normal people doing normal things.

But I knew little of this when I set out in early April for Berwick-upon-Tweed with a bag full of clothes and a fiddle. All I really knew is that I'd be learning on the job.

Tom Kitching,
January 2020

BEWAR
CCTV
ANTI CLIMB PA
BARBED WIR
IN USE

Berwick-upon-Tweed

I HAD to pick somewhere to start. I knew what I wanted to do, but needed some sort of logical order to do it in. Countries don't necessarily have beginnings and ends that fit the narrative of a book. This wasn't a straight-line journey from A to B via a sequence of other letters, but a scattergun exercise where a suitable representative sample was required, geographically, culturally, socially, economically. Chile might be doable in a straight line, but England was not. Ahead of me was the Midlands, East Anglia, the long peninsula to Cornwall, London. In the end I chose Berwick-upon-Tweed as much as anything for its lack of Englishness. I'd be learning what to do, just as Berwick was still coming to terms with being in England.

It felt right, too. The most northerly point in England. If England begins anywhere, it's here, in this ancient border town, where the concentration of centuries of defensive effort have rendered the border far more tangible than anywhere since Hadrian delineated an earlier iteration further South.

The main street was subdued and grey. Drizzle fell with a pillowy softness that suggested permanence. I walked around the town centre. A night club was bolted and closed for now with signs outside that said things like 'You may be subjected to random searching' and 'Top Brands only! Carling, John Smiths, Strongbow.' In the market place, an electric information board was slowly flashing the message 'We appear to be having some trouble with the sign.' The wetness hanging in the air muffled the town.

The centrepiece of the main street is the town hall, a huge but narrow building that blocks the flow of traffic like a giant log jammed in a narrow river, accumulating detritus into a new island. From this obstacle projects a tall tower, visible from miles around, a call to market.

I found myself stalling for time, nervous to actually begin busking after all the planning I'd done. The town was quiet after

Easter. Maybe nobody would like me. Maybe I'd be moved on. Procrastinating, I went into W.H.Smith's for a bottle of water. An old man in front of me in the queue delicately handed a lottery ticket over to the assistant. She scanned it before saying 'It's not a winner,' to which he replied 'Aye,' and shuffled out into the rain. I stared at the Guide Dogs for the Blind charity statuette with the coin slot disturbingly located in the top of the dog's head and persuaded myself to begin.

Perhaps later in my trip I'd not have bothered on a day so wet and empty, but I was new to it and knew I'd have to start for my own confidence.

The wet weather left me with few decent options. One side of the road had a narrow pavement, whilst the other was broad and spacious. That would have been the side to choose if the weather had been nicer, but all the shops that side were occupied, and there was no shelter. Instead, I chose the closed down Clarks shoe shop on the narrow side of the street, as it had a dry and recessed front door to play in out of the rain. I started up.

A smattering of damp people came past. The road was quiet, and the tall buildings caught the ring of the fiddle nicely. Reckoning that people would hear it easily from well up the road, I relaxed into it. Coins began to appear in my case, parents handing them to worried looking children to drop off. I continued. Someone shouted 'Bell End!' as they went past. Most seemed to be okay with it. After a while, a pair of drunken men appeared and dropped 50p in my case. Having bought my time, as far as they were concerned, one of them then proceeded to sing 'The Fields of Athenry' at the top of his voice to the tune I was playing, utterly untroubled by the differences in key, pacing, melody, and rhythm. His friend filmed this on a phone. I quickly ran the sums in my head, and calculated that they had two minutes before they were out of credit. Fortunately, they didn't know any of the verses and twice through the chorus was enough, and they left me to continue with a big thumbs up.

I'd imagined that the busking pitch would be a place for contemplation, philosophy even, where my mind could soar and crunch through difficult issues. In reality, it was over two hours into my performance before I finally figured out that the giant balloons in the window of the card shop across the way from me didn't spell out 'I.S.' but were actually '21' facing the other way.

Still, it could be worse. I watched the other street performer, the traffic warden, as he wandered up and down, not quite catching anybody parking in the loading bays. He seemed to always be at the wrong end of the street, lacking the killer instinct to actually ticket anyone. They too must pray for good weather to draw larger crowds and more cars than Berwick has parking capacity. On a wet day, nobody needed to take a chance and he looked thoroughly miserable. At least I could make a collection for my performance.

At about 5pm, Costa coffee rescued the optimistically placed and entirely unused chairs and tables from the sodden high street and called it a day. I decided to do likewise. I had no idea how much I'd made but it felt like a pleasingly heavy pocketful.

I walked up to the massive walls that surround the parts of the town that don't end at the water's edge and scaled one of the gun bastions. Built during the reign of Queen Elizabeth I, they cost an extraordinary £126,000, reputedly the most expensive project of the age. This grotesque expenditure was considered entirely necessary to keep out marauding Scots and once and for all end the regular changing of hands the town had been undergoing. Looking out north of the Tweed, there seemed little prospect of a Scottish invasion today. Indeed, one might have been welcomed. It would at least have given the traffic warden something to do.

As I was standing on England's most expensive wall, I decided to use my phone to book what claimed to be 'Berwick's cheapest hotel room'. It proved to be a box-room with a small skylight out of reach and an ingrained smell of deep fat fryers. At least the bed was comfortable. I counted up the coins: £37 in two hours, twenty minutes. If I could manage that on a wet afternoon in Berwick in a bad pitch, then I'd probably be okay.

I set out for dinner, hungry from the cold, passing a hair salon that had the leftover signage for the Anglo Scottish Fish Producers Association directly over the word 'Hairdressers'. It was a pleasing combination. Further down into town, the cockle shop's window assured me that their Berwick cockles were 'entirely different from imitations'. How do you imitate a Berwick cockle? At my table for one, I watched a family on holiday begin their dessert course. The father was presented with a giant ice-cream dish with two flakes. The little girl looked at it in astonishment before slowly turning to her father and asking; 'Are you afraid?'

I concluded my evening with a pint in the Barrels Ale House and read the local paper. There was an artificial insemination pull out and keep special in the agricultural section. I left it there in case it was of more use to someone else and instead read the events page. The family history society was hosting a discussion evening called 'Our favourite toy'. There was also a QI gong for health and a community ukulele group. I walked back to my hotel. In the dark, Berwick suddenly became much more Scottish. Pubs were marked with bright red Tennent's lager signs. Street lighting minimal. I climbed back into my deep fat fryer and fell into a weary sleep.

I returned to the main street at 9:15am. The rain was heavier than the day before. Fat, wet dollops fell with determination and certainty. It was market day. In practice, this meant a fruit stall at one end of the street and a donut van at the other. I bought a banana.

'Where's the rest of the market?' I gestured along the empty square to the distant donut van.

'It's been allowed to wither away. The donut van people run

it now and nobody else can be bothered anymore.' After a while, a fish van turned up to swell the market to three.

My alcove in the abandoned Clarks seemed dry enough, so I set up again. For twenty minutes I received nothing. Busking comes in waves, I was learning. Sometimes you get three people all at once trying to give you money, and sometimes nobody hands you anything for ages. The temptation is always to overthink and turn the near randomness of it into immediate cause and effect. If a tune gets you some money, you assume it to be a winner, and then find yourself surprised when it gets you nothing later. So I worried that the morning was just too miserable to succeed. The rain was relentless. Hands were in gloves and on umbrellas. Maybe I looked too warm and happy? I removed my hat. Immediately, the first money of the day arrived, and I took that to mean my hat was unlucky.

At 11:20am I packed down. The rain had got into my fiddle case much more than I'd realised. I needed to dry it out before I committed my fiddle and bow to the box for any length of time. Costa Coffee kindly allowed me to use their blue paper roll in return for the purchase of a small lemon tartlet, and I dried the case out as best I could, before lining around the instrument. It was time for my first appointment.

Having announced I was busking over England, a variety of offers began to come my way. Things to do, people to meet, places to go. My first offer was a ghost tour of Berwick, and I emerged from Costa to meet Edward and Andy of Frank N Knight tours. The rain had worsened further, bringing a biting wind with it, and so they started by asking me quite sincerely if I still wanted to do this. 'Of course', I said, so putting a professional face on it, they began with the story of the ghost in the British Heart Foundation stockroom.

With some of the most violent history in the UK, Berwick has no shortage of ghost stories. With screaming spectres, poltergeists, ethereal galleons, a zombie, burning corpses, poisonings, and what they reckoned could well be the oldest documented vampire tale in the world (1194AD), it seemed that every last phone box had its own story of bloodshed and retribution. Despite the weather, it was good fun. In driving rain and bitter wind, we climbed the walls and travelled round to the big lonely house behind the barracks, tall and desolate. It looked the part.

'When the artist L.S. Lowry came to Berwick, he was going to buy that house, but when he went in, and climbed the dusty stairs to the top floor...'

'Yes?' replied his colleague

'He discovered...'

'Yes?'

'To his utter horror..'

'YES?'

'It had dry rot. So he didn't bother.'

Nicely done.

The weather won and we went to a cafe, where the ghost stories carried on as we thawed with a warm drink. Slowly the conversation turned to a more general chat about life in Berwick. Ghosts are all well and good, but people here and now are more interesting to me. It'd been a tough Easter for the pair. The weather had been unremittingly awful and attempts to drum up custom for the ghost walk in the local holiday camps had failed, weather-weary tourists preferring heated pools and slot machines. We discussed the difficulties of making a living in the creative arts. Andy was trying to get work as an extra, a stand up, a ghost tour guide, anything he could turn his hand to, and he was good at it. But it was proving tough, and he really needed a sunny day. At least I'd earned something in my alcove that morning. You can see why so many of the youngsters head for the cities. It's hard to make it on your own as a young creative type. Berwick is becoming a place where the young leave, only to return at retirement, a living made elsewhere.

The main street was awash. Rain turned to plump, wet sleet. The wind blew it into the alcove, and busking was simply not possible. I walked and kept walking. From the high bridge across the Tweed, you can see the whole area. The railway goes round the town at a respectful distance, turning in a horseshoe, high up on viaducts and embankments. Beneath me, the in-rushing tide had met the falling river and ground to an uncertain halt, brown and mixed. This inspired me to buy a packet of humbugs from a shop on the Tweed dockside, and I asked the lady who served me what she thought of it all. She wasn't sure if she was English or Scottish and didn't really care. National identity just sort of peters out round here. People are from Berwick, and don't identify particularly with one side of the border or another. Kathryn Tickell once told me the anecdote of the small boy from these parts watching England v Scotland in the football, and deciding to support Scotland because it was closer. No wonder they call it the debatable lands. Berwick has changed hands so many times that it's stopped trying to decide which it is. The houses are a jumble of European pan-tiles and stout Scottish chimney breasts. Last time it changed hands, it was on the understanding that it could be governed by the English but not actually become English. This led to it having to independently declare war on Russia in 1853 during the Crimean war and inevitably being left off the peace treaty. Berwick was only formally absorbed by Northumberland and therefore England in 2001. Economically, it's part of an area that spans the border, and would prefer to ignore the border, were it not for political differences this forces. The school over the border at Eyemouth is now oversubscribed with Berwick kids. Berwick Rangers FC play in the Scottish league. My friend Cheryl lives in Berwick now but just a few years ago was the Eyemouth Herring Queen. Her world spans the invisible border.

The border wouldn't matter at all to the locals were it not for fact of devolved government in Scotland. A single economic and social community is subject to two significantly different sets of rules and funding priorities influencing decisions on schooling, housing, healthcare, differences met with exasperation by the locals.

It's certainly not about English or Scottish identity. The hard line on the map that shows me where England ends and Scotland starts exists only in law. England began to fade somewhere far south of here, and Scotland won't truly get going till much further north. Like the tide beneath me on the bridge, England and Scotland have met, mixed, and cancelled each other out.

That evening, I was invited to an open night at the microbrewery in Spittal, across the bay from Berwick. The brewery was in a desolate industrial unit next door to the abandoned dyeworks. I was told they were unable to demolish the works owing to pollution concerns, so it was slowly doing the job by itself, collapsing inwards. The tall chimney marked the end of the land, where the North Sea pummelled away at the spit of sand. It was bleak and very cold. The brewery was a single-story whitewashed unit, out past the last house. I opened the door and went into what felt very much like a knitwear rave. The building was packed, bare, dimly lit, and a sound-system was hard at work. Young, bearded men and colourfully dressed women were pouring strong beers. A wood stove in the corner really just served to illustrate how cold the rest of the room was.

A retired lady got talking to me. She'd ended up here with her husband, having gradually moved further and further north.

'They say you should look for the idyllic life. Well, bollocks!'

I mentioned I was heading to Darlington next.

'Darlington! Right, you should go to the snooker club and ask for Peter. Tell him Veronica and Mike sent you. Promise?'

I promised I would. No further information was given and we circulated.

Having dined on what proved to be the only haggis and

chips I'd find on my trip round England, I left for my overnight accommodation in Newcastle. Berwick had been just the start I needed. Generous, interesting, ambiguous. The only thing I'd really learnt about England here was how faint the ties were. Berwick was neither England or Scotland, it was just itself and didn't need to be anything else.

Darlington

I WALKED towards the middle of this handsome market town, through the park, past five consecutive mobile phone shops, the splendidly named Fatso's cafe, and along the raised main street, elegant banks and municipal buildings to my right, and the slope running down to the ornate Victorian market hall on my left. Like Berwick, the market had a significant tower, marking the centre of town both physically and spiritually.

The weather was sunny and warm and made a mockery of my choice of thermals. Spring was fully established and there seemed a number of places I could choose for my busking pitch today. I settled for a spot outside Barclays, half way down the main street. It was a slow start. Footfall was high, but coins were not plentiful. No matter. I'd vowed not to obsess too much on the amount of money I was making, but instead use the time to practice, compose, and think about the places I was visiting. The sun was warm, the day was pleasant, I had a coffee and a great view over the town.

After half an hour, a figure suddenly appeared by the benches across from me. A white-haired man of indeterminate age, wearing Elton John glasses, and a bright white t-shirt several sizes too big for him that read 'Stevie D' and 'I love music' where the 'love' was symbolised by a heart. Below these lines was a stave made out of colourful rainbows and unicorns. People flowed round him without seeming to see him. He didn't quite seem real. Having watched carefully for several minutes, he smiled and gave me a thumbs up. I glanced away and he'd vanished. Coins starting appearing in my case. As the morning wore on and my takings grew, I chose to believe that I'd been visited by a member of the fairy folk, and having passed their audition, been rewarded with good luck.

A small child came by and placed a single Haribo in my case. 'From each according to their means' I thought, and called 'Thank you, comrade!' Lunchtime was approaching, my stomach rumbled. Just like that, Stevie D was back.

'Are you about to finish any time soon? I'm having no luck around the corner.'

'I'm stopping for lunch now, it's all yours.'

I got myself a sandwich and a pie and sat a polite distance away. Stevie D was bringing his equipment over to my old pitch. It took several runs. First came a number of 'Guitar Hero' plastic guitar toys, then a considerable pile of maracas and tambourines, then the collection box, an empty ukulele case, and finally a large battery powered speaker, stand and microphone. Having completed his setup, he came over to me.

'It's been a terrible morning. My microphone won't work, every time I turn it on, it cuts my backing track off. And they won't smile, they just won't smile today. No.'

I commiserated and he went back to his pitch, ready to give it another go. The backing tracks played, mostly classic 60s pop songs, and he sang along, shaking his tambourine vigorously. With no microphone, I couldn't hear a word of what he was saying, but he made up for this by dancing all around the pavement and adding actions to the song. I'd still seen no evidence that anyone other than me was watching and the shoppers poured around his gyrating frame like a river round an island without eye contact or acknowledgment. Suddenly a bunch of kids ran over and picked up the guitars and maracas and I realised that only kids and other buskers could see him.

Now there was quite a scene. Children running around shaking maracas, waving guitars, whilst Stevie D danced and sang and drew their combined energy together into a magical spell that compelled adults to open their wallets and place coins in his case, their eyes blank and movements dreamlike. With the children's power drawn and focused, the walls between the worlds were made thin, and he could finally exert influence on the shiny coins going past him. A small boy picked up a single colourful maraca and ran off directly down the high street, never to return. I hoped maracas were plentiful and cheap in whatever world Stevie D came from. Maybe they grew as the fruit of some strange plant. An old lady on the bench next to me joined in with 'Sweet Caroline' whilst staring with empty eyes at the featureless wall across the way, her cigarette burning slowly away to an ashy twig in her hand.

I finished my lunch and left him to it. Down in the square, the army recruiters were at work, allowing the children who came to their stand to handle the replica guns. This initially shocked me, being unused to seeing schoolchildren holding rifles, but I conceded that it was at least honest, and better that than bribery with toys and sweets. To my surprise and minor alarm, I was still young enough to join up, being just under 35 years old. I noted down the financial incentives. £300 on signing up, £1,000 on completion of phase 1, another grand on completion of phase two, annual bonuses, sports and cultural organisations within the army. A tempting offer to a young person in a job hungry ex-industrial town. No wonder the army has such a strong presence around the North East.

The soldier running one of the stalls was happy to chat to me, and proud of his service. Said he'd joined up from school and seen the world. He also told me that the 32nd Signals had a band that met on Tuesday evenings and I'd be welcome to join them.

Darlington was also a town of poppies, many people still sporting them now in early April, far from Remembrance

Sunday. They were on lapels, on zips as toggles, attached to mobility scooters, and also to be found more generally in the artwork around town. Here, the poppy was morphing away from remembrance into a more general symbol. It would be something I'd be able to explore in much more detail later on.

At about 4pm, Stevie D packed away his plastic guitars and his remaining maracas and went back to whatever Elven reality he'd slipped in from.

'I save it all up and when I've got enough I make a trip to London and busk there for a day or two', he told me as he headed away.

I did a last hour of playing on the main street. The weather was still warm and sunny. A small girl threw Wotsits aggressively at pigeons, her choice of edible projectile ensuring a target rich environment. The hour went well, and I later found I'd made a total of £66 across a little over four hours.

The sun was still shining as I made my way back into Darlington the following morning. The lady in the coffee shop where I'd had my breakfast had been so taken with my project, she'd returned my tip to me with a story of how she planned to travel to Turkey by land. The mood felt good, and I decided to busk for a couple of hours before lunch and then explore more widely in the town. I didn't do as well as the day before, but I raised £20 before going to the railway museum. I'd largely wanted to avoid museums and stick to the present day, but I had a particular personal connection with this one.

Darlington is a serious railway town. The Stockton and Darlington railway is in many important regards the first proper railway in the world, built for transporting coal from the nearby mines to industry and the river for export. The town developed a large industrial and engineering base, with a good number of significant companies across several fields. My own personal interest in the museum was the locomotive 'Derwent', constructed in 1845 by William and Alfred Kitching, distant ancestors of mine. It stands next to the globally famous 'Locomotion', and it seemed right to me that it should be there, playing the support act to the main attraction, in fitting parallel to my musical career. I affectionately patted it when I felt there was nobody around to enforce the 'no touching the exhibits' rule and felt we understood one another.

In the entrance hall, I got chatting to the museum staff. The older fellow felt that the town had lost a great deal over the years, stuff that couldn't be brought back. Works were closed, and much of the industry had gone. Skills left to fade away, untaught and taken to the grave. The youngsters had never known it any other way, and didn't share the same sense of loss. To them, this was how Darlington is.

Following the advice given to me in Berwick by Veronica, I found the snooker club on Corporation Street and decided to see if her lead would get me anywhere. Darlington Snooker Club is a fine spacious upstairs room just outside the town centre. I got a pint of mild and began starting a series of awkward conversations. Although it was early afternoon on a weekday, the tables were nearly all in use.

'Oh. Veronica emailed to say you'd be coming. Have a seat.'

There were a few of us in the bar. I gently probed a few questions about the area and employment.

'There's apprentices, shift workers, charity workers.' he said gesturing to the tables, 'People work all sorts of hours. There's still Cummins engines and Cleveland bridge builders here. But the biggest employer is EE.'

The man behind the bar told me he wasn't proper Darlington as he'd lived out of the town for a few months before his first birthday.

'It'll invent itself again, Darlington. Anyone who needs work before that'll have to move for it, mind.'

He didn't offer an opinion on whether this was a good thing or not, but he seemed a sunny sort of optimist.

Darlington

There are jobs in Darlington though. As well as the remaining engineering firms, the student loans company is based here, but the biggest employer is EE, sustaining 2,500 jobs at their call centre on land no longer needed by Cummins engineering in the east of the town. I decided to go and have a look.

There are a series of smaller buildings alongside one huge one. This is their main call centre. It's a giant alien oblong of silver metal with no windows, one of those buildings that lacks the features to give it scale. The sort of place Dan Dare would have regarded with stoic concern. The reception was in one of the peripheral buildings, so I went over to see what they had to say. The man on reception did not know what to do with me, having never had a visitor who wasn't there looking for work before. When I explained why I'd come he took on a worried expression and directed me to a website with job application details on it, but I told him I really didn't need a job and was just here to see the place. This was dangerous new territory for him, and not covered in training. I asked him how many people worked here. He told me he couldn't answer for 'Data protection reasons.' This amused me so I asked lots of other questions that also all fell foul of data protection reasons as well. It was clear that he just wanted me to go away, so I got chatting to the security guard instead, who was much happier to talk.

He said they were a good company to work for and he enjoyed it, having moved up from London to take the job. Darlington was a good place to be, and he felt the town benefited from EE being there. They handled personal accounts and corporate stuff there too. I thanked him and strolled up to the main building. One side was mostly glass, but not transparent from the outside. The other sides were all dull grey metal. The area around the buildings was red brick and blue tiles in a semi-formed landscape, as if a municipal swimming pool had been buried for millions of years and metamorphosed, before being gradually exposed, cool, twisted and congealed.

This was a factory, just like the mills, mines, and forges that were closed and demolished. Staff on three continuous shifts just as the coal mines had been, ensuring the phones would always be answered. An employer of vast numbers of people. But this industrial colossus didn't make a mark on the landscape in the same way. Data doesn't leave spoil tips or slag heaps or cause subsidence. This building could come down in a few short days and there'd be no trace it had ever been there.

When the automation takes these jobs, what will the modern Luddites be able to do? You can't smash the spinning frames when the machinery is all digital. Unplugging the terminals won't help either. The important stuff will have disappeared down a cable before anyone realises they're even at risk. All they'll have is a redundancy notice and an empty shell of a building, already stripped of value without them having physically removed a single item.

Right now, that feels like a problem for the distant future in Darlington, where youngsters can still pick up a decent pay packet without having to leave town. It's done a lot better than some places round here, still big enough and diverse enough to be worth investing in

Considering all this, and with the blank, massive building in front of me, I sat outside with my fiddle and wrote a tune. I'd rather expected security to take an interest in me at this point and move me on, but I was left to it. The sky turned grey, and the building became as one with it.

Kielder and the North Tyne Valley

IT was a Sunday. The weather was good and busking in town centres when most of the shops were shut seemed a waste of time, so I set out for rural Northumberland. I drove inland from Newcastle to Hexham, and then up into the emptiness beyond

Bellingham. Just before the Scottish border, you get to Kielder. Kielder is a tiny village of just a couple of hundred people at the far end of Kielder Water, Britain's largest artificial reservoir by volume.

I parked at the visitor centre car park – £1.50 an hour or £5.00 all day, 'Parking charges are enforced at all times' warned the large sign – and headed past the mountain bike shop. The man outside gave me a cheery hello.

'Are you going to play that here?' he said in humour, pointing at my fiddle case and gesturing to the front of his shop.

I asked him if he lived here. He said he did. Was it good?

'Yes.' And he paused. 'Until the midges come.' And he visibly shrank at the thought, losing interest in the conversation and heading inside.

The village has two halves. I went to the high part, which comprised one street leading up to the disused railway line. It was neat and clean, and the houses were all well-tended, with a communal garden feel to the frontages. One house had little fake trees outside, made out of bits of chipboard roughly screwed together. The village shop was shut for Sunday, as was the community garage. This was the busiest day of the week for tourists, but old traditions die hard.

At the top of the street was the ghost of the railway. Built by the North British Railway Company in 1862, this railway represented an almost comically futile attempt to outflank the East Coast main line with an alternative route between Newcastle and Edinburgh. Heading west to Hexham, the line turned north, dividing at Reedsmouth, passengers for Edinburgh would then head up a slow and twisty route through the fells to Riccarton, a desolate junction whose 100 or so residents existed solely to serve this folly of a railway, before heading through the borders on what was known as the Waverley route. The fastest services took over four hours. It was a vanity project with no chance of success and had been abandoned a good ten years before Beeching had chance to force the matter.

The railway is fading back into the landscape now. The community garage, not a new building itself, is standing where the station once stood, and the trackbed heads into a tangle of undergrowth, identifiable by the line of trees that have colonised it, and the occasional in-filled bridge.

It was quiet, in the sense that the sounds of mankind were missing, and instead the true silence of birdsong was all around. I saw a front door with a post-it-note on. Intrigued, I stepped up the path and read it: 'The key is under the pottery pig round the side'.

It's that kind of place. Kielder is England's most remote village. I met Jessica, a lady who'd lived here for decades. She said the character of the village had changed a great deal. There were now only seven people left in the village who worked the forest. At one time it had employed most of the locals, but the forestry commission largely brought in outside contractors now. She told me the school only had fourteen pupils left.

'I remember when the mums sat on the steps outside every house watching the kids playing in the street.'

There'd been four snowfalls big enough to cut the place off for a while that winter. The old couple who needed home-help couldn't get it, so the cafe had sent meals round every day free of charge. It was a good community, she said, but lots of the houses were weekenders and out of towners now, and it wasn't as vibrant as it once was.

'But our Ospreys are back!' she said with a smile. 'Y'know they just returned yesterday to the forest to nest.'

I was impressed and somewhat envious of her connection to the land. I wondered if she'd seen them, or heard their calls.

'How did you find out?' I asked

'Facebook!'

We talked about the red squirrels and the newly reintroduced water vole, or 'Ratties' as she knew them. She'd heard that they wanted to reintroduce the lynx too, but she thought that a bad idea. I thanked her for her time and headed back towards the car park. There was a maze by the visitor centre, presumably to trap people who'd only paid for an hour's parking. The lower village has a Scandinavian style wood pellet communal heating system run from a central boiler house. Two local girls were zooming round in a two person tricycle, free to play in the streets. I wondered where the other twelve kids were and what sort of childhood they had up here.

The thing about England's remotest village is how remote it isn't. It's an hour from Hexham, and ninety minutes from Newcastle and Gateshead. That's not a trivial distance, but in global terms, not really remote at all. It's no great effort to get there. The place was heaving with people out for a stroll in the woods, visitors to the centre cafe, and thousands upon thousands of cyclists. The entire area around Kielder has over one hundred miles of designated bike trails, and the car parks were full to overflowing with cyclists of all shapes, ages, and sizes. There was probably a greater acreage of lycra per square mile here than anywhere else in the UK. There was also a long queue for the car park ticket machines, the toilets, and the cafes. This wasn't remote, this was urban without the buildings.

Nor is it in any real way a wild place. The vast ten mile reservoir is man-made, held in by a dam so big it feels like an outcropping of geology. The enormous forest that surrounds it, covering nearly two hundred square miles, is also man-made, and carefully managed. It is a huge industrial landscape, maintained and curated to provide water, timber, and leisure. The first trees were planted on a government scheme by unemployed coalminers and shipbuilders in the 1920s and '30s. Their camp is now inundated at the bottom of the reservoir. The object was to create a national strategic timber reserve. I wondered how the men of the great depression would react to being told that what they were really creating was England's first national strategic lycra reserve. In recent years, diversity and tourism have become more of a concern, and felled areas are re-planted with a much greater breadth of species to create more natural habitats for the future.

It is a beautiful place though. I pulled off the road at a spot marked 'Viewpoint', and climbed up to it with my fiddle. I found a large rock with a good view across the reservoir and wrote a couple of tunes, inspired. The country was still dressed in the faded oranges of Autumn. The hills were rough shields, unjagged but muscular. A bird in the bush behind me was singing its spring-song over and over. It sounded for all the world like 'PeepeepeepeepeepeepeepeepeepeepeeTalkSport Radio!', and once I'd heard that, it couldn't be anything else. By the road was a public call box, cocked back at an angle, mossing over. Rivers of motorbikes roared past in the delirium of this warm spring Sunday.

I headed down the North Tyne to Bellingham, pronounced with a soft 'G', and had my lunch in the Fountains cafe, situated in a rundown building that had variously been the workhouse, municipal offices, and the library. The cafe was the only part of the building still in use. There were three women working here. We chatted about life in rural Northumberland. They represented three different generations. One lady was just out of school and hoping to go to university to study to be a nurse. She hoped to go to Liverpool or Manchester. She felt there was nothing here for her here and couldn't wait to get away. The next lady was a mother and was upset that the local middle school was under threat of closure. We talked a lot about this. The council wanted to amalgamate a number of smaller middle schools into one big one in Hexham. This would mean well over an hour's travel each way for many students from the outlying districts, and there was considerable local opposition to the plan.

'The banks have both closed. We get the Lloyds van for three hours on a Wednesday. Now the middle school might be shut. Think how early a kid from up here will have to get up. They'll get home tired and that's before they have their evening meal and do homework. Nobody will want to bring a family up here soon.'

She felt it was a sort of accidental social engineering. Services had been cut back, so fewer families were able to grow up here, leading to services being cut back further. Rather than responding to dropping demand, reduction of services was driving it. The number of children growing up in the rural communities was falling away as it became a harder and harder place to raise them. Villages were hollowing out, with weekend second homes and holiday lets soaking up the slack.

The older lady told me she'd had three children but they'd all moved away for work.

'They come home for the holidays, but they'll never come back for good.'

Even all these centuries, the flow from the country to the city continues. As Graeme Miles wrote in his song 'Drift from the Land':

> Well you can't blame young hands throwing the towel in,
> They'll be much better off making iron and steel,
> But the drift from the land it will always continue,
> Till the money gets better for the man in the field.

Iron and steel are mostly gone, but the young still leave, pulled now by service jobs and the promise of more vibrant communities.

The building was now for sale, and the cafe staff had no idea what would happen to it, but they weren't confident that their interests would be taken into account by the council as they moved the property on. I paid my bill and walked around the small village centre. There was a notice board with a letter appealing for more young girls to join the brownies, and the dates where the flying chippie and the bank van were visiting.

Bellingham was ceasing to exist as a town. The services that made it self-sufficient being whittled away until it was forced to become the remote appendage of Hexham, miles down the valley. As I'd left the cafe, the middle lady had told me one more thing.

'It's not just the shops and schools. When I was a kid, we went out the back onto the land and helped the farmer with his sheep. All the kids did. We got a bit for it too. It's not allowed now. The kids can't learn about the land the same way.'

Up the road was the visitor centre, by the old railway station. Two carriages were trapped on a lonely and disarticulated bit of track, now being used against their will as a restaurant. Diners sat at the windows, oddly framed on a train that would never leave the station and broadside to the car park entrance. It was an uncomfortable sight. In the visitor centre, the two women on duty jumped when I walked through the door. It was clearly a quiet afternoon. They took a more positive view of the town, and reckoned that everyone came back in the end. They'd just had the Easter egg hunt.

'Some of the girls are the granddaughters of the girls who started on the first Easter egg hunt.'

'They must be close to finding it by now', I offered in return.

This went down well, and I left with a souvenir for my girlfriend, a decision that allowed one of them to finally be able to train the other on the correct and safe use of the card machine.

I drove in a vague easterly sort of direction, just enjoying the shape of the land. Northumberland must be the most beautiful county in England. A drystone wall had a line of daffodils all along, each one facing exactly away from the shade of the rock. I saluted their guard of honour. In the field on the right, a magnificent erratic sat alone and unimproved in agricultural land. I could see snow on the distant Cheviot tops.

Kielder and the North Tyne Valley

'You could manage this forest!' said a sign. The road became gated, with each gate painted in the colours of the nearest farm. I passed the spoil tips of a quarry, and crossed the abandoned railway again, as we both flowed out of the moorlands and towards the coast. Oranges and browns striped the hillsides. Tufts of reeds grew in the village street verges, and white lambs in countless fields knew of no other England. The fat-trunked trees were bare but ready to burst with life. The land was ready for spring's warmth. I was ready for a pint.

I was staying with old friends in the magnificently named village of Hartburn. They have the most eccentric of houses, like a castle shrunk down to the size of a normal dwelling. David was out the back, polishing his steamroller. It's the very same engine that was used to build the road network in this area, now fittingly using the very roads it created to bear David to the pub in the summer. The landlady has become grudgingly accustomed to it being parked outside on Sunday afternoons, simmering away whilst refreshment is taken.

We chatted over tea in their living room, under a large and brooding oil painting of a pylon. David decided to take me down to the local pub where the Northumbrian farmers meet up in the evenings.

The Ox Inn was dimly lit in a homely sort of way. There were indeed a number of farmers enjoying a pint after a long day at work. I sat in on the edge of conversation. It was lambing season and they were about half way through. That meant about seven hundred delivered so far per farm. Discussion was detailed, and concerned feed prices and quality, designations of types of path across land in terms of subsidy applications, and I soon gathered the extent to which a farmer's life is one of hard and lonely outdoor work, followed by labyrinthine bureaucracy and paperwork. This spring, the wet weather had made things even harder than usual. Their pints were very well earned. A farmer never really finishes work for the day.

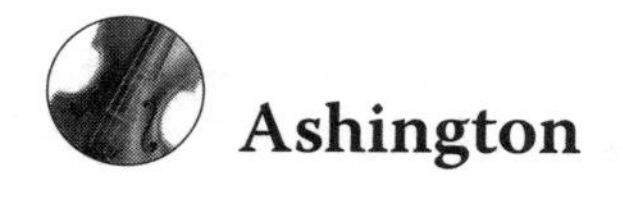

Ashington

ASHINGTON was ghost-white, sat today on the edge of the sea mist where it broke against the sunlit land and dissipated. The tideline was half way down the main street. I was to find myself busking with tall, rolling clouds falling heavily down towards me from the left, breaking up and dispersing before they hit, and glorious sunshine streaming in from my right. The roundabout on the outskirts of town had a sculpture of a miner drawing back a bow; his arrow a shovel. Heading into town was a large shire horse, bare back ridden by a flame-haired young woman in animated conversation on her phone.

Ashington is the world's largest pit village, with a population of 27,000, it exists simply because of the coal mining industry. When the mines were working, eight of every ten men in this place worked in them, and everyone else in the service industries that grew around them. It even has its own dialect, the famous Pitmatik, to mark it out from the Tynesiders and the rest of Northumberland. The lady in the coffee shop was from Essex though, and assured me she 'Couldn't speak posh, even if she had electrocution lessons.' She told me that Ashington is the butt of all the jokes from the rest of Northumberland. Meanwhile, Ashington folk make their jokes about the people of Newbiggin-by-the-Sea. I imagine there's one poor sod in Newbiggin, sat in a shed, who's drawn the short straw and is the final butt of Northumbrian jokes. The coffee shop staff liked the sound of my project, and said I could have a cup for free if I mentioned them. And so at Mojo coffee on the main street in Ashington, I began the long process of abandoning my artistic integrity. Thankfully the coffee was good, so my sell out wasn't all in vain. I started up with my fiddle outside the closed down greengrocers. The morning was warm. One young lad pretended to give me money each time he went down the street, making more and more extravagant gestures with each pass. By the end, I was quite looking forward to seeing what he'd do next.

Lunch came from the sandwich shop. A large cheese and ham roll and a high quality steak pie came to £2. I had a pocket full of silver, people had been generous. The locals were happy to chat. There was a new paint factory on the edge of town, which was providing a few jobs. They felt this was a step in the right direction, but nothing more, but everyone seemed fond of the place. It was, after all, home.

I picked a direction and walked. There were three Working Men's Clubs in a row, the Hirst Progressive Social Club, the British Legion, and the New Hirst and District Social. In the mist, Ashington seemed endless, like walking between infinite mirrors. A grid system of miner's houses, I passed alternate front and back rows, their repeating shapes fading into a focal point of chimney stacks and sturdy out-houses. The estate had CCTV every hundred yards. There was hardly a soul away from the centre. Against expectations, I reached the edge of town. The repeating houses gave way to a vast set of allotments, gone to seed, planted with pigeon lofts and portacabins. Each one an heirloom to be cherished.

I headed in a roundabout way back to the town centre. Above a front door, a large sign read 'No religious or political lunatics welcome here!' I wondered if anybody had ever self-identified as either of those things. There were very few people on the back streets. The place felt sad, sucked of energy. And no wonder, with the entire town's prosperity bound up in the coal trade, the gradual demise of the numerous collieries had taken the town down. Ashington has been hammered, through no fault of its own.

The main mining museum is at the former Woodhorn colliery site, where most of the main colliery buildings still stand, including the winding gear for two shafts. It's tidied up now, of course. In my experience around the world, a working colliery is a very busy and scruffy place, full of hum, and the tranquil and well-ordered serenity of this site has a melancholy power through omission. Like the town, the colliery is sleeping, robbed of action.

Inside the new visitor centre, one can take a trip through a virtual coal mine. It's well done, with sudden darkness, a superbly well designed soundscape, and the right amount of information and confusion. But for reasons of safety, they cannot replicate what it must really have felt like to be underground. When I was 13, I went to the coalface of a small pit in Northumberland, in what was definitely one of the most powerful and legally dubious experiences of my life. There'd been an extremely unofficial open day, and my father had taken me along, not realising that this involved a trip underground. The miner running it looked at me for a moment, and sorted out a helmet and lamp and made me promise not to tell anyone. This was a drift mine, so we walked into the hill, rather than down a shaft, and even at 13, I stooped my way down the tunnel for nearly two miles to where they were mining an 18 inch seam by hand. The miner in question had moved up from the Lancashire coalfield when his mine had closed, unwilling to give up the work he loved so much.

He'd told us that it wasn't so much the ceiling coming down as the floor coming up, that sometimes the pressures just caused big bits of coal to fire out of the coal face. Old roads led off to other workings, my imagination filling in the vast blackness. Darkness started where your lantern finished, and carried on beyond your reasoning. It's an experience I value extremely highly, and consider myself incredibly lucky to have had.

In Woodhorn, the tour tries, but they can't replicate the cold and wet air on your face that betrays the direction of ventilation. The uneven and treacherous floor, set with simple steel rails, endlessly pulled up and re-used, with the electric wire for the engine turned off to allow safe passage for walkers. The wooden beams splintering as the floor tries to reconnect with the ceiling. The need for composure and situational awareness in a labyrinth of miniature tunnels. The way the world smells like it's just been created when you walk out of the hill after hours with your senses compressed to your skin.

On the Durham mining museum website, which includes the Northumberland coalfield, they're trying to compile lists of those who died in each mine, when, and why. Each major pit has a list that runs to several pages. I don't know how a museum could ever capture the claustrophobia and constant fear of coal mining. Mines are fascinating and horrible places. Each with a roll of honour, now just a tomb sealed with a concrete cap, all other traces removed, spoil tips taken away for roadstone, buildings levelled.

Just a few miles down the road, at the Hartley colliery, the 1862 disaster was so disgustingly avoidable it caused a change in the law. To save money, only a single way into and out of the pit was sunk. When the beam on the pumping engine failed and fell into the shaft, it sealed the miners in. To make matters worse, it happened on a shift change, so both shifts were inside at the time. Two hundred and four men and boys suffocated, leaving just fifty-five employees of the mine alive. Being the only employer in the village, it left virtually every household bereaved, often several times over, and with no prospect of future earnings. Had there been a second exit, almost every victim would simply have walked away.

It was against such disregard for human life that the unions grew. They were more than just organisations to act for your conditions at work. They were an organisation to demand you be treated as a human being. Each of the collieries in Northumberland had a NUM branch, who had their own banner, a vast piece of cloth, ornately decorated with artwork and slogans that symbolised who they were and where they wanted to go. The banner was with you in life, would attend your funeral, a validation. In Woodhorn, the retired banners are preserved. Of two hundred banners that were carried in the Northumberland coalfield, just twenty-two are still active. The remainder are stored here, rolled up in darkness to protect them. At any one time, five hang from the ceiling of the main corridor. One might have thought that starved of direct context, the power would go out of them, but far from it. They are muscular and angry. Looming, brooding presences. 'Conveys Our Aims Literally – COAL' 'Let the lessons of the past serve the future!' It would be a cliché to say they felt alive, but that's how they were. Eyes on your back, cloth deeply infused with the essence of a community that had to fight for the most basic rights.

In the museum itself, the miner's strike is covered. Woodhorn closed in 1981, three years before this began. Indeed, a number of the Ashington collieries were already closed before this traumatic event even started. When viewed against the decline of the coal industry that was already well underway by 1985, the miner's strike was less about protecting the coal industry, and more of a last desperate gambit to change the direction of travel. On opposing walls, giant pictures of Thatcher and Scargill face off. Thatcher is merely known as 'Her' around here. Tasked with the impossibility of being both balanced in their views, and true to the deep resentment towards the Conservative government that did this to them, the museum doesn't try to run through either side's arguments, instead focusing on the suffering experienced by the mining communities in this time. The starvation, the cold, the hopelessness, finally the defeat and the acceleration of the closures. It is the right decision to portray it this way and makes the point so much more effectively than through direct argument.

The museum is largely staffed by young people. There are fewer of the old miners and their families left around now. The coal industry now sits on the border between contemporary reality and historical interest. The town has never remotely recovered from the loss of its entire industry. In common with most places so lazily labelled 'Crap Towns', it is, and it is not remotely its fault that it is. The lack of political interest in helping these places through the end of industry is still a giant cannonball round their necks. More than three decades on from the strike, the town has barely begun to shake off the effects. Down the coast in Durham, the council tried to wipe these doomed villages out with the dreaded 'Category D' rating, which forbade all development. I was interested to see how that had worked out.

The thing that most upsets is that these places are written off for no good reason. They are full of polite, friendly, intelligent people, who are ready to work. If just a bit more thought had been given to retraining and partnerships, it wouldn't have to be like this. Ashington is potential unfulfilled. At a time when it most needed support, it lost its railway station. A complete lack of joined up thinking.

Elsewhere in the museum is the Pitmen Painters exhibition. I had arranged to be given a guided tour, and it was excellent. What started off as an art class in the 1930s turned into a full-blown artistic movement. The coal companies were keen to support betterment for the miners, on the strict condition that they were not taught anything that could help them into alternative employment. I'm no expert on art at all, but the exhibition is first class. In broadly date order, you can see the development from the very naive first paintings, to the growth of a style both unique and powerful. They were the first British artists to have an exhibition in the People's Republic of China. Given opportunity, they learned how to produce something exceptional. When will Ashington next be given that opportunity?

In the cafe, there's a series of twenty large pages on the wall, telling the story of a young lad's first day down the mine. Drawn in the manga style by Nina Wakabayashi, this is worth the admission fee alone.

It was nearly the end of the day. I drove to Newbiggin-by-the-Sea. The fog was thick. A man on a bicycle lurched out of the mist with a giant netted bag full of horse carrots and a lump hammer. The beach nearly all washed away a few years ago, so a breakwater was built and 600,000 tons of sand brought up the coast from Skegness. The fog was so dense, I could hear the sea but not see it. A row of Coble fishing boats, flat-bottomed and high bowed, were at rest above the tide line. I drove to my accommodation via North Blyth, eight rows of houses on a spit of land, children's swings where the land gets too narrow. A huge undersea cable laying vessel was hidden in the gloom. The fog leant the whole day a strange and sorrowful air. One day I would come back here in sunshine and see it again, see what had changed.

Redcar

REDCAR was wet through and cold, rain slick to the pavement, mizzle drifting and lifted up on sudden gusts, filling hollows from below. The main street is one row inland from the sea-front, pedestrianised, wide, bleak. It was too wet to play so I got a coffee and walked for a while, letting my feet get the measure of this close-packed seaside industrial town. The drizzle was floating in fog again. Half of my experiences in the North East had been like this, street after street revealing themselves to me under sufferance, soft and blanketed, wet and running on red brick and flagstone. On the north edge of town, the blast furnace still stood, extinguished and cold, a dragon's nest looted and abandoned.

By lunchtime the drizzle had stopped falling, hanging loose in the cloud instead. I got playing. Change rolled in, the people of Redcar were very generous to me, the first busker they'd seen in months. A man went past in a Middlesbrough football shirt, camouflage-pattern shorts, and a policeman's helmet with a skull where the badge would be. Dress like that in the North and you're just a nutter. In London you're a fashion leader and heading for the cover of magazines. There's a wealth of untapped talent on these streets.

I was sharing the town centre with three representatives of 'Octopus Energy', who were out to attempt to sell the citizens of Redcar a new energy deal. I've always regarded the presence of salespeople to be detrimental to the financial potential of a busking pitch, but being here to meet the place and collect a few stories too, I set up where I could watch. It was theatre.

'Hello sir/madam, do you pay your energy bills by direct debit?'

Most ignored them, some got drawn into conversations, a few reacted passionately. One man shouted a violent torrent of abuse at the floor as he stormed through without making eye contact.

'Have a good day, Sir' came the reply, smile never slipping. Minutes later, they trapped a shopper and their small dog into conversation. The sale headed towards success. As the paperwork was filled in, the dog became more and more agitated, barking louder and louder, as if to say, 'It's a trap, don't do it!'

To my surprise, I made £31 in one hour and 20 minutes, and took myself to the independent bakers for a belated lunch. The North East is a paradise for baker's shops, of which Greggs, the breakout brand is merely the most famous. How was life on the main street in Redcar, now the steelworks has gone?

'Shops are closing, we've lost quite a few. We're barely hanging on ourselves.'

I ordered a custard tart and a coffee on principle.

'My son worked in the steelworks. He was lucky, got a job across the way in the other plant.'

But maybe the corner had been turned they said, without

really meaning it. It was just a thing you're supposed to say in these circumstances. I wished them the best and went for another walk. The rain was back. A group of young kids latched onto me.

'Will you be my new Dad? Dad's left us.'

It was a provocative statement, bold before the other kids, for their benefit. They were seeing what reaction the strange man with the fiddle would come up with. I was disarmingly polite. How did they like Redcar?

'Crap.'

'Why?'

'Nothing to do. It's dead.'

We exchanged a bit more banter and I headed back to the centre via the railway station. The large and ornate Victorian station building was closed and boarded up, eyes sealed to the decline of the railway's place in society. Tickets today were dispensed from the small cabin on the other side of the tracks.

On the seafront is the vertical pier. Seven storeys high, it has the external appearance of a helter-skelter, all bright colours in swirls round a cone. Inside, a man was making the best of mopping a sodden steel chequerboard floor. He faltered as I entered, a disturbance to the hermit-like peace of his out-of-season shift, and he quickly retired to a staffroom through a fobbed door to avoid me. I ascended the metallic staircase. Each floor had a glass-sided room off the path, overlooking the sea. Most were empty. One held the local radio station, deserted right now, but alert, waiting, two computers in screensaver mode, scrolling marquee charting the faceless and inhumane procession of time. The fifth floor was a small wedding venue. The empty chairs were set up for a ceremony. Two chairs faced me through the internal sheet window, whilst two thin rows faced back to the open side against the unbounded North Sea crashing in, brown and septic through the murk. There was no decoration to the room at all. The light was pallid yellow, the side walls plain grey fabric panels. The door was locked, but gloom oozed through the key hole. Fittingly, the top floor was abandoned, whilst the viewing gantry was closed for bad weather. I consulted *TripAdvisor*. 'A good idea in theory', read the first review. I descended again.

I resumed busking in the failing drizzle, bow done up tight to overcome the overwhelming dampness. A small child went past, almost buried by their burden of a twenty-four pack of Quavers. The kids I'd been chatting with came back through town on their bikes. They each gave me a few small coins and a nod. I was genuinely moved and thanked them from the heart. This was to be the way of things here. Even the toughest of characters regularly proved kind and warm to the music, given the chance.

A couple of gents turned up in my doorway and took the opportunity to light up cigarettes in the shelter. One was a busker himself and praised my music. He said he was about to busk his way around Italy. I suggested he might be lost. He laughed and flipped me a coin before thanking me for not using an amp.

It was damp, the wet was pervasive, the gloom pooled up in abandoned shop doorways and down alleys. The working day was drawing to a close. I let my focus on the world slip away and just played for myself as I'd promised, letting the fiddle ring. The cold and damp had sapped the bite out of the bow, so I drew slow notes out in rounded curves, shaping them until they were complete and full, before letting each go like soft arrows, seeing how they hit the frontages and rolled away down the street. It was a deeply personal time and I don't know how long it lasted, and I felt as close to my instrument as I ever have. Eyes open again, I'd gained a few watchers, stopped in their shopping, water settling on shoulders. They all came over and thanked me in clumsy words; and embarrassed, I felt more of a musician than I'd ever felt before, somehow delighted that my finest performance had been in such a time and place.

The day set like a Stygian jelly, leached of colours, so I gathered my coins and checked into my room. I passed a lawyers where the billboard proclaimed 'The fastest growing legal brand in the UK'. It was boarded up. The chippie had a tropical theme, with clownfish decorating the walls.

Inside my little room I left my instrument out to dry and hit the streets again, incognito without a violin case. The world is a different place with and without an instrument. With it, you're defined by it, 'Mate! Give us a tune!', without it, you're just a bald man in his thirties with bad dress-sense and too many low value coins in his pockets. There's nothing to latch on to. I dined in an Italian restaurant, paid in 50ps and £1s. I was re-reading my copy of J.B. Priestley's *English Journey*, from the 1930s, a similar idea to mine but better written and without the need to busk a living as he went. He didn't make it to Redcar, but then, few do. My great-great-grandfather did though, in the First World War. He was seconded for war work, although we don't know what. It's unlikely he had Carbonara with a glass of Sauvignon Blanc, paid for from the busking hat. I wondered if we'd have got on.

At the Cleveland Hotel, it was all happening. A big hotel on the edge of town, both Champions League quarter finals were showing and it was pool night. The A and B pool teams were both at home, and the two tables were surrounded by serious men and occasional women, deep in thought. I bought a pint of their own home-brewed ale and chatted to the landlord. I asked how much the closure of the steelworks had hurt the town.

'They're not steelworks lads these. Those were the cushy jobs, closed shop. Big houses on the other edge of town. No, these lads could never get a job there. It was the ICI chemical plant going that killed this town, but that didn't make the news because it's not iconic like steel. All those steel sods got jobs elsewhere.'

The pool mattered. You could see it. I've played league pool and it's never trivial, but every player here was deeply bought into it. The home teams fell to defeat and the table became open for play. I stuck my 50p down and waited. In due course I found myself against the local champion. He broke, nothing went down. I potted a yellow, only to see the white ricochet into another pocket. I did not get back to the table. The standard here was too good. You find meaning in what you can. They've taken our jobs away? I'll be the best pool player in Redcar. The Cleveland was home to a community. I shook hands, drank up and left them to it.

Back at my lodgings I wrote up notes and watched the rugby league highlights on my tiny TV. It was then that the food poisoning hit me like a train. In ten minutes I went from happy with the world to curled up round the toilet bowl wishing for oblivion. For hours it went on.

There's little in the world quite so awful as food poisoning, far from home, in a hotel room. For all the joys of the musician's life, these moments do make you question whether it's worth it. 'I'm 34', I thought, 'Far from home, doing what exactly? Giving adult responsibility another little shove down the road, pretending to be doing something important?' I curled up, unable to sleep, surrounded by half-filled cash bags of coins, a series of puzzles for the authorities to unravel after my now certain death.

Check out was at 10am the next morning. Not having slept, but having at least stopped the worst of the sickness, I packed my stuff and crawled into my car, moving out of the parking restrictions and stopping again, to sleep in the driver's seat. Hours passed. Around 2:30pm, nausea gave way to ache and hunger. I picked up my fiddle and walked to town. I managed a fruit smoothie. I couldn't possibly drive, so perversely and obstinately I opted to play instead. The weather was dry, the wind was down, so I picked a spot up the street, away from the relentless tentacles of Octopus Energy.

A mother gave coins to her three children to drop in my case. The middle one steadfastly refused, making the entirely reasonable case that I was no good, pocketing the coin for better investment elsewhere. This spurred me to improve. A loutish youngster gave me an earful as he passed, before rounding his bicycle, making a second pass and dropping 50p in. This was progress. I gave it what I could.

Cold and sore, I finally felt just about well enough to get some solids in. This was 4:30pm. In an hour and a half, feeling like death, I'd made an astonishing £42. Quite how, I wasn't sure, but it gave me back a little confidence in myself.

The Octopus crew were reaching the end of their day too. We met up and chatted. They worked out of Newcastle and took on a different town each week. The leader of the gang, at least on an unofficial level was called Lucy. She asked if I'd met the busker Stevie D.

'He always sings one for me. He says 'This one's for you, Lucy', and then he sings whatever he's going to sing anyway. He's a legend. Have you met him yet?'

So they could see him too. I said I had, in Darlington. Had they gone well today? Yes, they'd signed plenty up. On commission, this meant a good week for the team. Like the coal miners who depended on their marras to ensure the wages stayed up, this was a team who depended on one another to succeed. I promised Lucy she'd get a mention in my writing, which she was pleased about. She said she loved the work, just let the abuse of a few roll off her back, sign the next one up.

'We're helping them save money on their bills. We're helping people out. It's good work.'

They told me Middlesbrough would be worth a few tunes. I said I'd see. Tired of faking wellness, it was time to leave town. I waited at the level crossing for a Class 66 heading for Skinningrove to come through with a train full of naked iron oblongs. It danced heavily and without grace on the rail joints.

The final bogie came through and departed with a tick tock... tick tock... tick tock... and a flashing red light behind.

This was the end of the beginning. I'd go home, write it up, and get out for the next leg. Busking worked, I could make enough to cover my costs.

Cromer

THE road into Norfolk was lined by mature trees, canopies clipped square by the endless migration of road freight, mottling the sunlight with fresh, soft leaves. Spring was in full bloom now, and visitors to Cromer found themselves compelled by some deep, half remembered ancestral urge to enjoy the first ice-cream of the year.

A shop sold trinkets with a faux nautical theme. One item, such as you might hang in your kitchen contained an inspirational phrase within a lifebelt: 'Life isn't about waiting for the storm to pass, it's about learning to dance in the rain.' 'Thought no sailor, ever', I added for myself and walked on. After a long drive from Manchester, I needed a reviving beverage and found just the place in Grey Seal coffee, where a young fellow named Joseph was happy to talk to me about the town. He was a local and had set this business up six months ago. He said he hadn't seen a busker for a while, and wondered how I'd go. 'Norfolk people, they're... y'know...'

I said I didn't.

'Y'know... awkward.'

I took my coffee and wandered round for a bit. Cromer is a well-to-do seaside resort, town up on the cliff, overlooking a pier and promenade. It was early in the season, and the tourists were still thin on the ground. In the warm sun, the deckchair hire man dozed comfortably in a nest of unsold product. The pier was lightly populated, with just a handful of holidaymakers strolling towards the pavilion at the far end with a 'because it's there' attitude. I opted for a busking pitch back in town, on the main street, outside Boots and across from the intriguingly named Icarus Butchers.

It was to be an action packed session. Within a couple of minutes, I was singled out by a middle-aged fellow in a blue woollen suit, waving a camera around like a carton of all-purpose physical punctuation. His lapel sported a number of pin badges, including a poppy, a Union Jack, a Cromer carnival badge in purple, and more I didn't recognise.

'I'm a vlogger. Mind if I photograph you?'

'No problem', I replied.

With a skip of joy, he began. He photographed me from every angle, from across the street, from inside the shop, from behind parked cars. It was slightly off-putting, his exuberance turning a spontaneous busking session into a contrived performance. It looked so staged, I ceased to receive coins. After about 15 minutes, a heavily pregnant young woman turned up and greeted him.

'This is my daughter!' he told me proudly.

Between them, they seemed to know everyone who passed by, and my attempted busking pitch now turned into a large conversation about family news and Cromer gossip, as shoppers and parents were dragged into their sphere. The vlogger introduced himself as Andreas and asked if I'd now do a piece to camera for him. I obliged, and asked him where this vlog could be found. He said he didn't know yet, as he hadn't made one so far but I should search for his name in a while. With this, they made a generous donation to my busking pot and disappeared. I started up again, and was immediately drowned out by the considerable sound of a military jet engine going overhead. I looked up and all I could see to account for it was a single gull.

The busking pitch is always a great spot for people-watching, but in Cromer it's all about dogs. So many dogs. Greyhounds,

Alsations, Lurchers, Terriers, Salukis all came past. One small dog was impossibly long, tiny feet skittering at each end of a long hairy tube. It looked for all the world like a caterpillar that had been short-changed in the leg department. An Asian man came past with a Staffy which suddenly turned and barked at me. The man was mortified and immediately gave me £1.50 as an apology for his dog's rudeness. Dogs are so much a part of life round here that when you make a table reservation in the pub for dinner, you get asked how many people and how many dogs are in the party.

A German lady with two small kids stopped me to ask if I'd play the British national anthem to celebrate the forthcoming Royal wedding. This caught me off guard. I have a complicated relationship with this piece of music. Like the poppy, it's one of those things that means what you want it to mean, but where others too quickly judge what you mean by it according to their standards. I didn't feel like exploring this here and now so I said I didn't feel entirely comfortable playing it. This surprised her. I asked her how she was finding living in Norfolk with everything that had happened. She said it was fine for her but in the future it would be much harder to bring her family over for visits. Personally, she'd had no issues so far. As we chatted, her young son felt the need to drop a small coin in my case after each exchange like a gamer bribing their way through a conversation with a Non-Playing-Character in an RPG. I said 'It's ok, you don't need to do that', and he looked me straight in the eye and added another 5p.

No sooner had I got going again when a lady stopped me from playing an Irish jig to ask if I could possibly play her an Irish jig. I said 'of course' and played it again. This delighted her and she gave me a pound coin. Another lady passed and said 'Ooh I love a good fiddle', before returning 30 seconds later, upset. 'That came out really wrong, I'm SO sorry', before rushing off in a flutter, head shaking before I could reply.

This had all been in the first half hour. I looked at the growing collection of change, and realised that despite the interruptions I was getting somewhere. A small schoolboy came down the street with his mother, diligently holding a tiny violin case. 'Quids in here' I thought. Instead, the child clocked the music, fixed on me with an expression of horror, before turning to the parent with a look of pure betrayal that said, 'Is THIS what you want me to become?'

Mostly, though, I'd had a lot of smiles as people went past. I assumed that this meant that the good folk of Norfolk were simply a polite and friendly bunch. As I packed down at 4:30pm, I realised I had been standing in front of a large window poster for emergency contraception. It had been an eventful 90 minutes, and I was delighted to find I'd made £25, given how many times I'd been stopped.

Out over the sea, as the town closed and emptied of life for the day, a stunt plane was practicing. It rolled, climbed, stalled, fluttered before catching and picking up. It was odd to see such a fine display go unheralded as the town emptied of life. I suppose it's not like learning an instrument where you can just go and practice in the back bedroom. You've just got to go out into the sky and get on with it. People filtered past me, heading home, paying it no attention, and I felt like I had my own private air show. It climbed straight up, hiding in a cloud, before dropping dramatically back into sight, straight down towards the water, suddenly flattening out and heading out to sea, practice over. I headed for my accommodation.

The next day was wet. Busking was just not a possibility. There were no sheltered spots, and there was virtually no footfall anyway. Cromer was huddled around itself, staying dry. I put the fiddle to one side and explored. The pier has a theatre at the end. I walked all round it and dreamed of putting a show on inside. Past the theatre and built off the end of the pier is the new Cromer lifeboat station, ideal for a launch straight to sea.

Cromer

Back on land, I visited the Henry Blogg museum. Built around the motor lifeboat, the H.F.Bailey, upon which Blogg served the later part of his career, it's a monument to the RNLI's most decorated lifeboatman. Blogg won the gold medal three times, and the silver medal four times, a haul far in excess of any other person, partly due to his extreme ability and bravery, and partly due to the sheer volume of work that the Cromer lifeboat got through back in the day. The untopographic sea surface hides a number of deadly and moving sandbanks that can easily capture a ship. Once trapped, the waves will lift and drop a ship against the sand like an anvil until it breaks up. Besides these enduring hazards, there was also a battle in the Spanish civil war off Cromer, and several disasters during WWII.

Some of the details of Blogg's rescues were scarcely believable. On one shout, unable to come alongside a stricken vessel in towering seas, Blogg chose instead to drive the lifeboat onto the deck of the ship by riding a wave down, quickly pick up a sailor, before riding off on the next wave, not once but twice. The museum had next to no information on the man himself, as aside from his RNLI work, he fished for crabs, hired out deckchairs, and kept himself to himself, refusing interviews.

Still pouring with rain, Cromer wasn't bothering today, so I had little choice but to continue my journey around the museums. In the Cromer Museum, where I was the only visitor, one room contains the world's largest elephant. I think Cromer should make more of this. Discovered at Runton Sands, in exposed sediment from 600,000 years ago, the West Runton elephant is claimed to be twice as big as any living elephant. With 85 per cent of the skeleton, it's also by far the best example of its kind. If I had the world's largest and best elephant, I'd be telling everyone about it. I'd have a replica on every roundabout heading into town. 'Elephantopolis' I'd call it. But here it was, slightly apologetic that it had turned up in Cromer rather than somewhere more fashionable.

The exposure of the ancient elephant came about through the rapid erosion of the land. The sea is winning round here, eating back at the soft cliffs at an alarming pace. Cromer was not originally the seaside town, but was instead inland of a place called Shipden. Beyond the end of the pier is Church Rock, until recently just about visible at the lowest of tides, the remains of Shipden church, now several hundred metres out to sea. Down the coast, houses are regularly being lost and land is falling away. With the seafront heavily re-enforced at Cromer, and heavy erosion on the coast either side, Cromer is becoming a projection into the sea, a peninsula by subtraction.

I found myself staring out to sea and trying to imagine what had once been here. This was Doggerland, if you go back far enough, a vast prehistoric plain that ran through to Europe before the great flood, wet, lush, richly populated with animals and early humans. But the traces are still there, not just in the axe heads and mammoth bones that periodically surprise the trawlermen, but in the great forests of wind turbines far out to sea, their feet sunk into the sandbanks that kept Henry Blogg so busy. These white towers, in mega-clusters miles distant, mark the contour lines of an inundated land. The sea may be formless, but the land projects through it, still readable and tangible.

The rain continued to fall. I perused the Olive Edis collection, an early colour photographer, resident of Cromer, who had taken magnificent portraits of nobility and ordinary people alike. She had the great distinction of being appointed the country's first female war photographer in 1919. By about 3pm, it was clear that the rain was not going to stop, so I opted for a short drive to Sheringham and a ride on the North Norfolk Railway.

Sheringham greets you with a road sign; 'Sheringham, North Norfolk's Premier Seaside Town', which feels slightly contemptuous towards Cromer and Wells-next-the-Sea. 'I'll be the judge of that', I thought. Clearly some local rivalries were at play. Sheringham is the terminus of the North Norfolk railway, one of a large number of preserved railways across England. Alone in my carriage at the front of the train, I began to consider nostalgia, and why we English are so susceptible to it. The railway staff were in immaculate period uniforms, somewhat spoiled by the ubiquitous hi-vis orange jackets on top. The rain outside suddenly switched up a gear from steady to tempestuous, and a couple on the platform frantically fought a losing slap-battle with a reversed umbrella before belatedly realising the sensible course of action was to run for shelter.

England is a land of nostalgia. From preserved railways like this, to castles, forts, to the music of our youth, to the social norms that we've left behind. We want it and we love it. I have always adored steam railways, and now I found myself asking 'why?' They are slow, rattley, smelly, and you get a face full of black bits if you look out of the window. It's not even as if this railway is an accurate portrayal of the steam age either, with a large and spotless mainline engine slowly pulling four coaches tender first, through over-wrought floral railway stations with not a single pansy out of place. It's deeply idealised.

Before I could get too far into this avenue of thought, we reached the far end of the line and I found myself sharing a coach with members of the Meridian cycling club of Kent, out for a few days on the lanes of Norfolk. They asked me to play them a few tunes, so I obliged. The guard of the train turned out to be a Morris dancer, and having given a brief demonstration of his art in the corridor, sent the hat round for me. I made my fare back and some. It was a good end to a wet day.

Erpingham

I WAS staying with Jess, an old school friend living with her parents between overseas teaching jobs. I parked up at the village of Erpingham and was warmly greeted by all three.' I got a suitably formal 'How do you do?' and a handshake from her father, whilst her mother greeted me with a hug and 'Ooh, you've aged.'

Erpingham is a well off village about eight miles inland from Cromer. After dinner, Jess and I went for a walk to the pub, taking the long way round to see the whole area. The village is arranged around a large piece of common land, sodden from winter, low-lying and lush. I cannot resist the lure of a good laminated sign, and was drawn to the commons notice board.

> Thwaite Common Toad Patrol 2018.
> Toads moved to Safety – 1,509
> Frogs moved to safety – 414
> Common Newts moved to safety – 256
> Great Crested Newts moved to safety – 7
> Total number of amphibians moved to safety – 2,186
> Our number of Common Newts saved remains relatively high, being 256 set against a combined total of 287 for all twenty-one of the other Norfolk toad-watch sites.

The church is lonely and distant, divorced from the village and behind a low hill, the top of the tower just visible, ghost-like over the crown, so it is the commons that forms the spiritual heart of the village. As we walked around the perimeter, Jess gave me the gossip, the spectacular petty controversies of rural life. I heard about the naturist vicar, who was neither a naturist or a vicar, and the ongoing spat involving the lady with twenty cats, whose neighbour erected a large sign saying 'Sorry there's no beautiful flowerbeds, the cats have shit on them' before installing electric fences to stop them worrying the wildlife. These were removed after they were found to have cooked much of the local hedgehog population. I heard the controversy over the incomer whose first act was to build his own helipad in the back garden. A compromise was reached with the community which limited his total number of permitted flights.

He had a particularly large neon windsock, which was drawing complaints as it was considered not in keeping with the Union Jacks in neighbouring gardens.

The circuit continued. Gardens packed with impossibly perfect tulips, verges thick with the softness of yellow primroses. Pastel red brick and flinty knobbled walls. Dutch gabled thatch barns and pan-tiled roofs. Each with a trivial little story. It seemed to me there was a minor scandal to every house. Not so much *Midsomer Murders* as Midsomer post-it-notes. The village was largely a retirement community. Reasonably affluent people from all over had cashed in their savings to spend their later years here, and each had arrived with a grim determination to become heavily involved in community life. With people from all over the UK, there was a wide range of views about how things should be done, and the commons represented a cauldron into which all these competing visions were mixed. The result being that every time someone arrived and joined one of the numerous village committees, a new faction was born. The parish boundary was the event horizon. It was another world beyond that, alien and incomprehensible. The community focused inwards onto the commons, and relentlessly moved ever greater volumes of amphibians into their midst.

At the end of the walk, we made it to the pub, the Alby Horseshoes. We were greeted with a single welcoming bark by the publican's dog, a great shaggy bear of an animal grown sturdy on discarded pork scratchings. The pub served a good pint of Wherry, the celebrated local ale, and decades of back-issues of MG owner's club magazine were available for the drinkers to peruse. On the notice board, there was an advert for a function band. There were two contact names and numbers given, but one was scribbled out with a biro. I wondered if it had been a falling out or a deceasement.

In the other room, the local vocal group were practicing. The landlord told me they were 'The Wherrymen'. About half a dozen old men and a synthesiser, their repertoire consisted largely of wartime songs and music hall material. For the first time, I heard the Norfolk accent clearly, most noticeable in the phrasing rather than the pronunciation. Soft and languid, taking its time but always getting there. The synthesiser player decided to break it up, and followed 'Where have all the flowers gone?' by hitting the 'Disco' button and playing a spirited solo version of ABBA's 'Mamma Mia' to the backing track.

'They'll be as old as us now' I heard afterwards. 'They'll have to go on stage with their walking sticks too!'

They packed down.

'Are you practicing for anything in particular?' I asked them.

'Yes, we're performing in an old people's home on Thursday.'

It was 9:30pm and now being the last customers in, we drank up and let the landlord take an early night. The walk back took us down a narrow path, a 'loke' in the dialect. The trees felt fat with pigeons. Our passing in the dark put them up, sudden bursts of feathers against branch, awkwardly lifting bodies grown plump on so many bird feeders in so many floral gardens.

The village had recently celebrated the 600th anniversary of Agincourt, meaningful because Sir Thomas Erpingham, Lord of the Manor, had been in charge of the archers who proved so decisive. It had been a good career move on his part, and he'd been able to invest considerably in the village and church. In honour of the anniversary, a new village sign had been commissioned, with the central picture designed by the local school children. They had gone for the direct and historically accurate approach, and their approved design, standing proudly on the verge as you drive into the village features captured and executed French soldiers hanging limp and lifeless from branches. 'Welcome to Erpingham', it says underneath.

I was invited to attend coffee club, something of a village institution. On Wednesday mornings for an hour and a half, it's coffee, cake, and chat in the village hall. Everyone mucks in on a rota, and what profit they make on it goes to various good causes. It is hugely popular, with around sixty people attending each month. They were nearly all retirees, with just a few young mothers and children. I joined their table. It was a jolly mess of stickle-bricks and colouring books. A young boy was single-mindedly removing the heads from the stickle-brick characters and placing them disembodied on a large yellow sheet, like captives buried in sand, smeared in jam and awaiting the release of the killer ants.

The local school has pioneered a form of teaching called 'Flexi-schooling' aiming to be a halfway house between formal schooling and home schooling. So many children are home schooled in Norfolk that the school was on the verge of closing with just a dozen pupils remaining. Now providing the option to come to school on a split basis, it's completely full again and thriving, some children even reverting to full time as they enjoy the laid back atmosphere and outdoor focus it provides.

I made my way round other tables. I was introduced to all kinds of people, including the ebullient Dr Harrison (retired), who, peering over his glasses, expressed astonishment that I could possibly have been to a mixed comprehensive, and a couple who had recently been beneficiaries of the coffee club, as the gentleman was travelling to Cambridge for essential medical treatment, and couldn't otherwise afford the travel. They were genuinely emotional about the support they'd received.

Speaking to so many retirees, I was struck with how busy they all were. With a plethora of village committees and clubs to join and manage, open garden competitions, maintaining the common, indoor bowls, walking football, amphibian patrol, they were all operating at capacity. 'I know it's a cliché, but I don't know how I had time to work', I heard again and again.

Wealthy, successful people with a history of getting difficult jobs done were retiring here in numbers, and focusing their considerable talents and drive on the minutiae of village life. There were retired bomb disposal experts, successful businessmen, head teachers, people from demanding and stressful jobs, bringing a lifetime's experience in dealing with complex issues to bear on the village hall cleaning rota. Their drive was not being switched off, but diverted to the mundane. There were petty rivalries, factionalism, and conflict where there was no need, but also the organisation and commitment to work as a community to support those who most needed it. And there was no denying that the village was also exquisitely attractive throughout, perfect gardens and neatly trimmed hedges crowning the central wildness of the common land, tall grasses and the nervous pinpoint gaze of deer. You rather felt that every pebble, every little flower belonged on a list and had been assigned someone to care for it. Even the wildness was curated with care and diligence, animals collected and numbered, given their performance targets for next year. This was anarchy in the truest form, where no formal rules or governance were codified, but instead the risk of social exclusion, that harshest sentence of all, kept each new incomer on the straight and narrow.

Late that afternoon, I drove to the church of St Mary. It stands alone, the village reputed to have abandoned it when the plague came, fearful residents re-founding their village a mile away, by the common. It's a strange sight now, an unpulled tooth on a hummock of higher ground. The church and grounds were all suitably deserted, but the door was unlocked in case one felt the sudden need for private prayer. I let myself gently in. The considerable tower and much of the insides were built by Sir Thomas Erpingham in the aftermath of his unlikely away victory in the European cup. His father is buried here, with an exquisite brass effigy over the tomb. You can make a rubbing of it for a 'minimum donation of £5'.

I let myself out again and wandered round the back of the graveyard to see if I could spot any evidence of the missing village. The fields were deep ploughed and featureless. The ground beneath my feet had that graveyard softness of rich greens and long-unturned soils. Bees sang past my ears. Late afternoon sunlight fell through air where rain had been an hour before, dancing and sparkling on rich new green leaves. I felt the patient presence of so many of Erpingham's forbears, waiting, content in their idyll.

A car came spitting up the gravelled driveway. A hurried sound that stood out a mile in the reflective garden of death. I knew immediately what was happening. Somebody must have phoned the church warden to say there was an undesirable looking character poking around. I was well hidden deep in the jungle at the end of this barely tended graveyard and he did not see me as he rushed into the church, no doubt bracing to confront some ruffian. I saw him, though. It was the larger than life Dr Harrison (retired) from coffee club. Excellent. I made my way quietly down the side of the great flint tower, and as he emerged, relieved to seemingly be alone and undisturbed, greeted him with a hearty 'Good afternoon, Doctor!'

It wasn't fair on him, really, and he stuttered, trying to come up with a reason why he was here without explicitly stating that he was responding to a report of an undesirable character, come to steal the lead off the roof or perhaps make an unauthorised brass rubbing. We both knew what had happened though, and it was more polite not to bring it up, so we exchanged pleasantries instead until he felt able to go home again and leave me to it.

Erpingham is just one of hundreds of little places, out of the way, down a thousand twisting lanes across Norfolk. You learn to navigate by church towers. From any one church, you can routinely see five more, and each tower has a character and a place sewn in the cloth of the land. Later, I tried navigating from Holt to Erpingham by church tower, and managed easily. The land was starting to open up to me, and I felt the rhythm of it. When you are about eight miles from Erpingham, you start seeing the road signs for it, which continue until you are maybe three miles away. Then, you only see signs to places further down the road. It's as if when you get close, there's a collective loss of confidence about exactly where it is. 'It's around here somewhere. The rest is up to you.' I allowed myself the fantasy of believing this to be to do with the movement of the village after the plague, and the concept of Erpingham as a vague area that the village would be within, although nobody could ever say quite where at any given moment. Each time the mist lifted, you'd have the learn the roads again.

On my final evening here, Jess and I walked the fields towards two of the other churches in the Benefice, Alby, and Thwaite. The churches are so old as to feel timeless, but the hedgerows have long fallen to the plough, opening up the gaps between each tower to deep, curving views, speckled with clean, rain-washed flints, brought to the surface in the till. It's spring and the fields are still mostly low, fresh ploughed or seedlings in dense industrial lines. You can be a giant or a mouse as you wish between the rare boundaries. The sky is just as big either way.

In every direction, picture-postcard villages populated by brilliant and successful people spending their retirement and still considerable energies on creating communities whose social norms are stronger than law. Under the vast sky, an invisible and densely knitted matrix of committees, clubs, societies, and Parish councils furiously move the earth, one primrose at a time, back and forth, in an unending quest to sculpt Eden on earth.

Fakenham

IN 1998, Fakenham was famously declared the most boring town on Earth by the *Knowhere Guide*. This lent it a kind of magnetic irresistibility to me. Whatever else it was, in the here and now Fakenham was clearly experiencing something of a boom. You couldn't help but notice the number of properties undergoing renovations and improvements. You'd not be out of work as a scaffolder or plasterer in Norfolk. As my stride took me towards the church tower overlooking the market place, the path became shared by many others, busloads of pensioners pouring into the town like the match-day crowd heading to the ground for the big game at Geriatric FC. The turning circle was jammed with busses and minivans, and more were arriving every minute. Fakenham market certainly wasn't boring, filling the square and spilling out into the side roads, high quality fare too, food and drink, flowers, crafts. The sun shone, and Fakenham charmed me. Clearly the guide-writer had visited on the wrong day.

One old man walked past, jangling as coins fell from his trouser leg and into the street, clearly the tragic consequence of a pocket with a hole in. I gathered them all up and chased him, handing them back. He reacted as most people do to an unexpected conversation with me, with deep concern, before realisation set in, and his face turned into a broad grin.

I picked a busking spot just down one of the two main shopping streets off the market place. It was a good pitch, and just as well, as the rain in Cromer had seen me behind with my expenses for the week. Pound coins formed a pleasing scatter in my fiddle case. There wasn't much shrapnel, it was either a pound or nothing here.

In a lovely moment of karma, the gentleman whose money I had rescued earlier came by and returned the whole lot to my case with a big thumbs up. The sun shone, and I played with freedom, risking more complicated pieces, finding my zone with the fiddle. Some people stopped for conversations. The pace of life was good. After a couple of hours, a man emerged from the coffee shop across the way, and marched purposefully towards me. 'Here we go' I thought, expecting to be asked politely to go away as I was turning the ham green or something similar.

Instead he told me how much he was enjoying it and would I like a coffee on the house?

At lunchtime, I repaid the faith and bought a sandwich from them, before heading to Fakenham's most important attraction, the Museum of Gas. I'd read it was only open on Thursdays, but unfortunately, the information I had been lacking was that it was only some Thursdays and generally only till midday. Which was a great shame, as I knew from a previous visit that it is England's only fully preserved town gasworks, containing the last surviving retort, and a unique room showcasing the history of the Geyser boiler.

It's not that long ago that every town would have had a gasworks, where trainloads of coal were cooked to release the gas that households demanded. They were part of everyday life. The rise of North Sea Gas in the 1960s put them all out of business, and in a generation they were swept away, wiped from the map and completely forgotten. Fakenham's is the last standing in England. When I visited previously, my appearance at the door caused a sharp intake of breath and a panic to work out where the till had been put after the previous customer, weeks ago. It's the same problem with Queen Street Mill in Lancashire, the last fully operational cotton mill. It's just too close to home, it seems, and rather than being of historical interest, for many, it's still that place where Grandma lost her hearing and her fingers. Visiting it before its most recent closure, I'd been the only punter all week. The wrong kind of nostalgia perhaps. Similarly, the gasworks was not on the approved list of subjects.

We are a country so full of history we don't really know how to deal with it on anything other than a crude emotional level. Who decides what counts as important? Recent or unfashionable history struggles to find a space. People don't feel sentimental about more modern history yet, just resentful. Things have to survive a generation of being what people want to forget and put behind them before they become what people want to remember, and a great deal is lost before it gets there. I take my hat off to those slightly odd characters who recognise and preserve that which hasn't made it to the second stage yet. I often wonder which is to be England's first heritage motorway. The gas museum struggles to find its place in our collective national story.

As the weather was pleasant and I was doing well, I opted to continue busking. Picking the other shopping street, I played on, as the market finished at 2pm and was dismantled. For an hour and three-quarters I played, till fatigue started to get into my shoulders. I made a game of it, vowing to finish and pack up if I played a tune where nobody gave me anything. Even as the footfall dropped away to almost nothing, I kept receiving generous donations, and finally at 3:30pm, I called it a day anyway. I'd made a solid £19 an hour throughout the day, had some good conversations, and enjoyed playing.

I wandered for a while to see what I could find, but Fakenham was sleepy now. Without the energy of the market perhaps the *Knowhere Guide* had a point. I had clearly seen it on the right day. There was nothing left to do here, so I drove north to the coast and Wells-next-the-Sea for an ice cream.

Wells-next-the-Sea and King's Lynn

THE thing about Wells-next-the-Sea is that it can't decide if it's any good or not. Cheap amusement arcades stand alongside restaurants recommended by the Times. The main street was a mixture of high end delis and boutiques and total junk. I passed a shop called 'Never-ending Dreams'. It was closed.

The other thing about Wells-next-the-Sea is that it isn't next to the sea any more. All the land I'd seen eroded from the Cromer area has been gradually re-allocated to here by the tides, meaning that the sea itself is now over a mile away.

Whilst medieval villages might have moved and rebuilt themselves, the modern world is too rooted and invested to do that. Vast resources are used to keep channels open through the mud banks so that the water still makes it to the quay. After the obligatory row of rock shops, arcades, warehouses, the quay, the row of boats, there's a mile of land with channels cut through. It's bizarre and artificial. I had my ice-cream, and watched the tide arrive like it was coming up through a pipe. It's a sign of the modern world, where rather than react to the changing face of nature, enormous resources are expended to deny the change and keep things just so. How far out would the coastline have to go before they stopped? Wells-not-very-near-the-Sea? Wells-miles-from-the-Sea? Wells-well-Inland?

The next day I went to King's Lynn for a couple of hours on my way home. There were already several buskers at work. I watched one man play his guitar, in the shade of a doorway of one of the few empty units in town. After a couple of songs I gave him a coin. He was friendly.

'Do you want this pitch? I'm not here for long. I've got my mental health review at 1pm.'

I said I was happy to find my own pitch but maybe I'd be back near 1pm. He rolled a cigarette and I carried on around the corner. The best pitch in town was taken by a singer called Richard, who had the works, a full PA, a table of merchandise, and a series of wicker collecting baskets. He was wearing sunglasses and a smart jacket, and was singing light classics with an operatic voice. He was very good, if you like that sort of thing. Clearly many did, and he was doing a good trade.

'It's not busking this, I consider it performance. Difference is I have to apply for the licence to set up all this gear. I've spent years building up the relationships with the town councils so I can go all over.'

A lady came by and emptied the contents of her purse into one of his wicker baskets.

'I've sold over 20,000 CDs in my time doing this, but they don't sell like they did. People have changed in their habits, and they prefer songs from the films now.'

I tried by the new shopping centre, causing a big man in a black suit to put an arm round my shoulder and gently explain to me that it wasn't permitted as I was on private land. I tried again down the road outside Nandos. It wasn't open yet, but already a queue was forming at the door. At midday, when it should have opened, there was still nobody present, and people became quite agitated, and lots of phone calls were made. Things were getting tense, and threats were being made to take matters into their own hands, so I moved on again, not wanting to be associated with the great Nandos raid.

Norwich

ON the road from Boston I'd picked up a hitchhiker. Called Paul, he delivered cars for a living, and having dropped one off at Boston, had another to pick up at King's Lynn, a journey that would have taken three hours by bus. He was about 60, chirpy, and DJ'd at the weekend for a bit of extra money. He was pleased to have picked up the lift so quickly, and as I dropped him off he illustrated his gratitude by presenting me with a full sheet of knock-off McDonalds coffee loyalty tokens.

'I get them off the internet. Forty quid for two hundred cups, it's brilliant, here you are! Just make sure you don't put them on the card in the shop, I got chased out of one in Peterborough doing that. Thought my mug shot would be up all over the country after that. Anyway, cheers! Have a few on me.'

I wasn't sure what to do with them, having no particular affection for McDonalds, but not seeking to actively defraud them either, so I filed them away to consider later.

I arrived in Norwich in time for a late lunch. After an initial wander around, I selected the medieval area as the spot for my first busking pitch, at the bottom of the nicely titled Lower Goat Lane. Before I'd even played a note, I was aware of growing disquiet in the shop across from me. It was a modern looking place called 'Main Source', and it sold trainers, the expensive sort you definitely wouldn't dream of doing any training in. It was staffed, as these shops invariably are, by agitated young gentlemen in t-shirts whose slogans falsely claim a laid-back philosophy for their occupants.

'Fuck's sake', I heard, 'Get some beats on before he starts.'

Now I have a couple of golden rules on my travels, one of which is that if anybody asks me to move on, no matter how spurious their reasons, I'm not going to argue to toss. I'm not out to upset anyone. However, they hadn't said anything to me directly, and I decided that passive-aggressive rap music didn't count as being asked to stop. It was loud. I decided to play louder. My fiddle can project pretty well, and in the narrow streets I felt I had the edge. With only one door to let the music out, their sound system was not beating me. I let my tunes fit the bass beat of the music, and worked with it.

My refusal to give up made them more irate so they turned it up further. The searing volume caused all the customers to leave the shop, whilst I steadily accumulated about £10. This was a good game. I smiled at them. They grimaced, came outside and vaped furiously and impotently for a bit at no one in particular. Then they turned the music off. I packed up and wandered on.

I tried a few more spots around the city as the afternoon wore on, thinking about the next day, seeing what worked. Norwich has a large centre, with modern high streets and more bohemian areas. There's the beautiful Royal Arcade, set in delicious green tiles, the market, which comprises a vibrant square of colourful beach huts, and the forum, a huge modern building, spacious and considered, home to the BBC, the library, and a bunch of restaurants and council services. It's a nice place to be, and although I hadn't made a lot on the busking front, it was a pleasant afternoon.

I walked vaguely in the direction of the C of E cathedral, zigzagging my way to take in as much as possible. Heading along past the friary towards the river, I heard singing, and there busking on the bridge itself was a fellow called Chris. He asked me if I wanted the busking pitch, and I said I'd rather he carried on singing. I'd not heard an unaccompanied singer performing traditional songs on a busking pitch before, and he was good. He wasn't very loud, but his voice was clear and had carried right down the street to me. After a couple of songs I asked him about himself.

'I'm a climate campaigner. Well I am now. I was a teacher before I retired. I try to give as much of my pension away to charity as I can and make my living this way.'

He was bald, with a thin wispy beard. He wore hi-vis in a manner that suggested he was rarely out of it.

'I went to the Copenhagen climate summit without using any oil at all, either walking or rowing all the way.'

'A fine effort.' I offered a coin but he wouldn't take it.

'I've got to go now anyway', he said, 'I'm chairing a meeting of Norfolk against Fracking.'

I swung round past the cathedral and back towards the city centre. I passed one of the homeless of Norwich in the street and handed over a few coins. He was gaunt and twig-like from whatever combination of winter weather and other problems he'd been facing.

'God bless you.'

Poverty is a complex thing. It has many faces that I've met as I've travelled around. In China, poverty meant working every hour of the day so that you made just enough to survive. In Eritrea, it was not bothering to do anything at all because you wouldn't see any of the benefit if you did, somebody else would just take your work away. Both were awful and equally disheartening. One of the most damaging consequences of severe poverty is the loss of autonomy of choice. Being able to make decisions and choose a path in life is central to us feeling human and alive. When all meaningful choice is lost, one is simply at the mercy of fate, and it is dehumanising. To be human is to make decisions and have control over your life. When a homeless person cannot decide anything for themselves because they have nothing at all, or when an extreme political system removes all meaningful choice through state control, or a mine or factory owner pays in tokens only redeemable at the factory shop, then that is dehumanising.

'Oh they'll only spend it on drugs.' I sometimes hear, with regard to giving coins to the homeless. Some surely do. Perhaps I'd have said it myself once. Increasingly as I worked my way round the towns and cities of England, I was coming to the conclusion that I'd probably take drugs too. Anything to afford a momentary escape from the despair of being utterly abandoned by your own state, unable to reach the first rung of the ladder. And so I handed the coins over, and hope that in some small way, it gives people at least the freedom to own a decision in their lives, whatever it may be.

Meanwhile, back in the lanes, a car had crashed into a bollard, clearly pretty hard. The driver was standing outside looking at the mess. He was about 50, smartly dressed with two tie-pins operating at different levels. Not your usual boy-racer. His car was totalled. I bought a pie and chips from the Grosvenor chip shop and sat in the sun by the church to see if anything else interesting would happen. The police arrived and chatted to the unlucky driver, filling in forms. His predicament was catching plenty of attention. A very black man with a very white manbag came by and saw the mess, declaring loudly to all around: 'Well look at that! How has he crashed that in the city?' He then turned to me and loudly and repeatedly asked me to join him in his incredulity of what had happened whilst the poor driver looked on. The police car had 'Our priority is you' written on the side in friendly letters. I considered this to be a particularly high quality example of a meaninglessness slogan as I finished my chips, which were excellent.

I was staying with a friend through music, another Jess, a songwriter from Norwich. We went for coffee the next morning, walking into the city together. She lived next to a housing development converted from the hospital she had been born in. Norwich was too small in some regards, she said. If a relationship went wrong, you could never quite get away from it. The scene just wasn't quite big enough.

It's certainly a young city. Youthful types are drawn here, by the work opportunities and the liberalism of the place compared to the rest of Norfolk. There are endless coffee shops, craft shops, vinyl records, and art. Virtually every unit is in use. After coffee, I got to work on the main street. A smart and very upright older gentleman stopped me and informed me that whilst I was pretty good, I would be a lot better if I learned to read music. He'd been in the Royal Marines band as a trumpeter, so I should take it from him. However, he then gave me a pound coin, which seemed a fair compensation for his opinion.

A very old man gave me an old pound coin. A homeless couple sat cross legged in front of me, drinking Tennent's Super from cans. The sun shone, and they enjoyed the performance, applauding after each number. I wasn't making much, but it didn't bother me, as I was definitely reaching an audience. I tried an hour in front of the market. It was enormously busy. So much footfall, in fact, that people stumbled and jostled, and nobody reached for change, defending their space, heads down. Sometimes the quieter streets are better, where people aren't pressured and have time to really think about the music.

I had an excellent lunch in a small cafe outside the cathedral. It had rainbow flags flying outside, pointing at the house of God across the way, perhaps pointedly. Having eaten, I approached through an arched gatehouse that opens onto a green. I zipped my jacket up to hide my blasphemous heavy-metal T-shirt and entered the holy space. Peregrine falcons nest in the spire of Norwich cathedral. The gift shop offered a tempting book; *The Sparkling Wit of Prince Philip*.

I have a mixed relationship with cathedrals. They are undoubtedly magnificent, full of the highest quality craftsmanship, but I have never warmed to their purpose. I always feel like a trespasser, as if my atheism is a secret to be kept until I leave. To see such resources and skill diverted from where they could provide a material improvement to lives has always jarred with me. But they are hardly the only offender in this regard, and since they are built and complete, and mean a great deal to many people, it would feel wrong to resent them.

I rounded a corner, and there was a large school group, kneeling in a line towards a member of their class who was dressed in Bishop's robes and hat, mitre to his side. Their teacher was speaking the words 'The Bishop' as I arrived. I immediately and involuntarily replied in a gruff American voice with 'The Bishop!', recalling *Monty Python*'s sketch of the same name. This was met with a frozen stare. I mumbled 'We was too late…' and quickly carried on, having yet again completely failed to behave correctly in such a place.

I returned to the lanes quickly for another go at busking. I hadn't made much and needed something to pay for my food. I got stuck in. After a while, another homeless gentleman came past, stopped in his tracks, and latched onto me. He seemed to have been genuinely moved by the music, his emotion causing him to completely open up to me. It was a sad story, but I got no sense of him wanting anything other than someone to talk to. It wasn't a plea for money.

'Nice music mate. I'm homeless y'know. It's okay now, but it gets cold later. Lovely music mate. It's cold later, you get hungry... I'm homeless. They released me after thirty-two years, five months. Eighteen years after my tariff. I'm Paul by the way. Lovely music. Lovely.'

'I'm Tom, pleased to meet you.'

'Thirty-two years and five months, and now I'm homeless. I'm 63.' There was a pause.

'I'm a murderer. So, I'm sorry about that.' Paul told me. It was so matter of fact. This was his life, and what defined him. Paul the Murderer.

'Nice music, mate, nice music.' He kissed my neck and began to head off from me. He carried a rucksack with a sleeping bag hanging off the side. His front teeth were failing, his head bald and marked. Clothes ill-fitting and ragged. He smelled of alcohol, but his eyes were bright and sharp. He was a wreck. He'd never had a chance when they released him. What possible hope of re-integration did he have? Of course his story was impossible to verify, but he hadn't been after anything. He just wanted to tell me. I called him back, scooped up a handful of bits from the busking pot and handed them over. He lurched away towards the market.

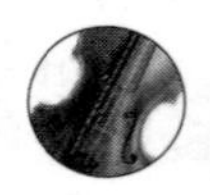

Harwich and Dovercourt

SOUTH of Norwich, a VW camper van was abandoned at the side of the road, broken down. It had wedding ribbons stretched across the cab. The evening was warm and dusty and summer was creeping into the landscape. I arrived in Harwich some two hours later, at the end of the light. Having been shown to my room by Mick, my host, he offered to take me around the town before sampling a well-earned beer in the New Bell Inn.

The town itself is conspicuous by its absence. Harwich, gateway to the continent, where fifty-eight Royal Navy men-of-war were constructed, home to the manufacturing and repair yards of Trinity house, whose former masters include Samuel Pepys, is basically missing. The main streets are a series of uncanny blanks, anonymous shuttered and curtained frontages, like someone has cast a spell of disguise upon the whole town. Look upwards and the town comes swimming into view, ghosts of awnings, faded shop names, disarticulated signs. The great storm surge of 1953 wiped a lot of the town out, burying most of old Harwich under sea-water for weeks. Pleasingly, a large electrical shop has survived the massacre, and trades solo at the end of the high street past the church, straight out of the 1970s, cookers, lights, toasters, and a vintage Bibendum statue, all in unequal rows. The post office is a recent departure, still bearing the signage. It's strange, to walk along a road that feels so very much like a town centre, but lacks the bustle and buzz.

On the shore, you can enjoy one of the finest views in England, across the Stour and Orwell estuaries to Felixstowe container port, by far England's largest port, conduit for over 40 per cent of our international goods trade. The astonishing mile and a half of continuous super-deep dock can rapidly service six of the world's largest container ships at once, each transporting a barely conceivable 18,000 shipping containers. Immense cranes on rails can run right up and down the length of the dock, the whole operation controlled and directed by computer systems. In the dusk, the lights of the yard lit it all up, and set back across the water the immensity of the shipping was reduced to toys you could hold in your hands, the countless containers too small to resolve as detail, just grains. The docks sang, ring of container touching down, whine of powerful electrical motors, sirens and horns, each disarticulated to any obvious event.

'Of course they come in full and leave empty', said Mick, 'We don't make anything anymore.'

I just stared. On the beach in the foreground, a large wicker whale built the previous year was now collapsing into the sands, powerless before the Mærsk titans across the way.

Harwich and Dovercourt

We walked round to the Lightvessel LV18 by the quay. Now retired, this was the last manned lightvessel in British waters, unpowered vessels sent to distant points of our territorial claim, to sit on station, a floating lighthouse. It was odd to finally meet one. I'm hardly the only person to have been soothed by the poetry of the shipping forecast on Radio 4, having a particular affection for Sandettie Light Vessel Automatic, and was pleased when Mick shouted out to the man in the gathering dusk to ask if we could step onboard.

'So long as you don't sing any bloody shanties', came the reply through the murk from a fellow called Tony.

The deck was a garden, pots and beds where ropes and chains had been. Tony told me that the group who owned it had decided to enter into the Harwich secret garden competition, and the floral consequences were before me. I promised to come back the next day to meet it properly.

The gloom had set in properly now, so we headed for the New Bell Inn.

Whilst much of the town might have dissolved in the flood, what is left are the pubs, a good dozen around the town, and mostly decent quality. With a pint of good mild ale, I listened as Mick told me about the mass U-boat surrender, the Kindertransport, and the ships full of giant cranes coming in from China to populate Felixstowe, like some sort of sentient robot sending bits ahead to build itself on a foreign shore, unstoppable and relentless, the new bloom at the end of a long runner. Harwich, with the view across the estuary had become the witness rather than actor in recent years.

I made my way to bed full of beer, and listened to the sound of globalisation through the open window, the music of the world carrying on flat warm estuarine water. Ants moving the food, eggs, and spoil of trade with a continuous singing urgency.

The next morning I felt a little untidy round the edges, so set off for a restorative breakfast. In the dockside cafe, I ordered an espresso to kick start my day. It immediately became clear that I was the first person ever to order an espresso here, as they were surprised by the small volume the machine produced, pressing the button again and again until they were finally able to present me with a large mug of the stuff. I drank as much as I dared.

Down the quay is the Harwich premises of Trinity House. Founded in 1514, this venerable institution is in charge of lighthouses, navigational aids, and providing deep-sea pilotage in British waters. In Harwich, they maintain their fleet of lightvessels, and make and repair navigational buoys. On the jetty, the rapid response vessel *Alert* was powered down and at rest. Lightvessels are no longer crewed, instead powered by solar energy and computers operated from base. One was in for repairs, and two more sat in the estuary awaiting tow to station. The factory manufactures navigational buoys of all sorts. By the road, sinker-weights were arranged in groups from two to six tons. Some had been painted like mushrooms or clouds. Piles of chains, massive and weighty were coiled up alongside. They wouldn't let me in, so I headed across town to the Redoubt, a Napoleonic era circular fortress overlooking the estuary. It wasn't open yet so I sat outside and wrote up my notes.

At 10am it opened, and as ever the only customer, I headed into the fort with my fiddle on my back. Around the rim, an odd assortment of historical artillery sat, trained somewhat ironically on China Shipping across the water, a symbol of our increasing impotence in the face of global capital. In the circular central courtyard, I sat and played my fiddle to nobody, responding to the strange acoustic within perfectly circular walls, and filling the space with ringing notes. Behind me, one part of the fortress had housed conscientious objectors during the First World War, their confinement graffiti still on the walls of their dismal cells. There were a lot of mannequins around the place, no doubt designed to imbue the place with a sense of humanity. Instead they only highlighted the emptiness of it, a series of bleak dioramas in period uniform. Each room had a few of them, frozen in time, succumbing to damp, emotionless.

One room had a display on the Kindertransport, ships of Jewish children sent out of Europe in desperation in the last days before Hitler closed off the escape routes. Unaccompanied, often speaking no English, these kids were warmly welcomed to Britain and given a chance to start a new life here. Some later went to Israel, many stayed, making a great contribution to the country. Speaking to my grandmother a few days later, she told me that one had come to her school in Hull, Tilde she was called, speaking no English, and within two years was winning public speaking awards. This welcome is the sort of act that could make you proud of your country. On a purely practical level, a refugee welcomed with open arms would surely be more likely to give much more back to such a country than one barely tolerated or even abused? Perhaps the sheer overwhelming complexity of arrivals to our country now makes it hard to comprehend the stories that send people here. There is no single compelling narrative to respond to, but a spectrum of migrants and refugees escaping regimes, wars, poverty, climate change, or just simply looking for something different. The simplicity of the Kindertransport story makes it an easy sell. In a fractured and confused world, compassion is harder to anchor.

I put my fiddle away, and exited the fort, politely refusing the chance to buy a plastic toy hand grenade. I needed to find somewhere to do some busking, or I wasn't having any lunch. Passing the 'PieSeas Chippy' I headed for the pier. My timing was all off, as the cruise ship had come earlier in the week, and the hot weather had given way to overcast skies and strong winds. A rare open shop, full of 'Antiques', had a sign that read 'Please come in and look around', but the mistrustful look on the face of the proprietor told another story. There was a bookshop, closed today, and so chaotic as to be impossible to tell if it was a going concern or if someone had decided to arm themselves for a future life as a librarian by entombing themselves forever in a pyramid of second hand biology textbooks. The pier was hook shaped and limited, a cafe at the near end, benches and sea spray at the other. Not only was footfall and weather against me, but the pier was being repaired, with workmen hauling lumps of scaffolding, tins of paints and tools back to a flatbed truck for removal. There was almost nobody else about. I set about playing anyway, being rewarded at least with a jig or two from the workmen. After an hour, despite only seeing about twenty people, I had miraculously made enough for my lunch, and the cafe threw in a pity coffee for 'keeping them entertained'.

But I needed a bit more or I'd be down on the day. I ate up and drove two miles to Dovercourt, part of the continuous conurbation of the Harwich region, and just slightly more of an active place on a day like this. Wind blew dusty and dry down the main street, full of plastic scraps and grit. Half the shops were boarded and derelict. I bought a sausage roll from the bakers, the worst I have ever eaten, pastry turgid and limp, filled with a sausage seemingly constructed on strict homeopathic principles. I started up outside Boots. A lady immediately came out and shouted at me to shut up and go away.

'You can't do that here! It's not allowed!', she roared, already full of fury before I'd even had chance to say anything. Was she already angry, or had my music just caused her to snap?

'I can, and it is allowed. But I'll move if you don't like it.'

'I'll call the police!', she continued, going for the jugular.

This caused me some difficulty. I'd vowed to always move on if asked, but I didn't like being told I had to when I was within my rights. I decided to move five yards to my right so that I was technically outside another shop. This seemed ok, so I carried on. It was clear that Dovercourt didn't get many buskers. A crossroads between two withering shopping streets, a couple of banks, a grim spattering of traffic, cars down on their luck. A gentleman on a bike stopped and gave me 50p. He was sad I'd been moved on. 'No wonder we don't get anything nice here', he lamented, before telling me about Dovercourt.

'No jobs now, the Channel Tunnel and Ryanair have taken all that away. All the rail freight used to leave from here, and it was a busy seaside resort. It's just London overspill now. Those who can't afford to live there and don't need to commute there. But there's not much crime, it's okay. My kids have both moved away for work.' He concluded on a sad note and rode off. 'But don't let me keep you from playing.'

An old lady parked right across the pedestrian crossing and tottered over to me to hand over a £1 coin. Having made £12 in an hour, astonishing in such a rundown place, I took my revenge on Boots by going to Superdrug for a new tube of toothpaste instead.

Dovercourt had much in common with the industrial towns of the North East, albeit at the other end of the country and having grown up to support another set of industries. It'd lost its industry and employment. But far worse than that, it had lost its identity too. It was just a shell. For all that Redcar and Ashington had been difficult and damaged places, they still felt like Redcar and Ashington. Dovercourt was dead, and lacked any sense of itself. It was the saddest town I'd seen. I could find no positive note to sound, and drove the two miles back to Harwich in a cloud.

I was invited onto Lightvessel LV18, and got the full tour. It had been used as the set for *The Boat that Rocked*, a film documenting the pirate radio station phenomenon that forced the grudging and uncomfortable birth of Radio 1, and was now filled up with obscure broadcasting and phonographic equipment. Beyond this, I got a sense of a tidy and well laid out ship. The cabins were nice, the corridors wide, the kitchen suitable. On station, it would have swung around on the tides on a single anchor cable, and therefore had a special window that the crew could reach out of to adjust the TV aerial. I blagged my way into the engine room, normally off-limits. Inside, six Gardner engines were installed in pairs of different sizes. They were not connected to any propeller, as lightvessels couldn't move on their own, but were instead to power the huge bulbs that marked their station.

In the top deck of the ship, the gang had built their den. A man-cave of epic proportions. Alan had brought a bouzouki so we played tunes and exchanged stories. It was approaching time to move on again.

I went for a final walk round town with Mick's wife, Penny and her daughter Zoe in the hour before Penny went to her folk singing group with Mick. They pointed out the distant proto nation of Sealand, a WWII defence platform now occupied as a sovereign nation by the hereditary Bates dynasty, a sovereignty claim completely ignored by all others, who tolerate it as harmless distraction. Then we found a Harwich rock. Colourful painted rocks are hidden all around the Harwich area, discovered, and moved on by other Harwich residents. I picked it up and pocketed it, in the sure knowledge that the right place to leave it would become apparent further down the line.

'Sometimes when you're in the main street, a ship goes past so big that it seems it couldn't be moving but instead the whole street is moving to the left', said Penny.

Mick then came striding round the corner to join us, a huge grin on his face.

'I have just found the most miserable song!'

Braintree

MY friends dropped me in town at 9:30am, promising to retrieve me at 6pm, and feeling like a little kid sent out to play for the day, I ambled around with a big grin on my face. Braintree seemed pleasant in a low-key sort of way, a broken crossroads of shopping streets, an arcade, a few supermarkets and pubs. I got myself a coffee and tried to figure out the best busking pitch. I chose a spot opposite the British Heart Foundation and fired up. Things were going well when an elderly gentleman with a stick suddenly appeared on the opposite side of the street and started bellowing at me;

'Awful din! Bloody awful! Why don't you go away and come back when you've learned to play! Doing my head in!'

My policy was to move on if someone asked me to, but I wasn't sure if he worked for the shop, was a customer, or just a nutter who shouted at everyone he saw. Sometimes it's hard to know. A bus came between us and when it had cleared, he was no longer there. I decided to carry on and see what happened, especially as coins were coming. Twenty minutes later, a slight and harassed looking gentleman came over from inside the British Heart Foundation to explain that the angry apparition I'd encountered was actually a volunteer in his shop and was so enraged about the music that he was violently tearing the stockroom to bits. Would I mind moving on for his sake at least? I said of course I would, but suggested grumpily that if his colleague had been polite and coherent, I'd have gone ages ago.

I moved up town, to outside Iceland and had a productive morning. A man brought me a box of grapes on the basis that I looked like I needed them. I saw myself in a shop window and concluded he had a point. I paused and went to Boots for some suncream. The weather was hot and still. By lunchtime, I had a heavy pocket of coins and set off for some food. Passing by the pub opposite Tesco, a bunch of lads who were sat outside enjoying a lager in the sun yelled at me; 'Oi! Give us a tune!'

To their surprise, I headed over and obliged. This delighted them. 'Mate, that's amazing. 'Ere, what do you want? Pint? Sandwich?'

So they sorted me out with lunch and a pint of lager, one of them nipping across the road to the supermarket, returning with the three manliest sandwiches on offer, as well as a fiver for my collection. They were enjoying the sun, although the more ginger of the three was suffering a bit in the uncovered street space. A lady joined them for a lunchtime drink between meetings. Conversation was risqué and bawdy. Periodically I'd have to play them another tune to earn my continued place at the table. They were delighted to have their own personal troubadour. All four of them were technically at work, and were either supposedly answering emails, taking their lunch hour, or on call. It seemed all was well in their world. I thanked them and headed back for my pitch outside Iceland.

As I played, a woman came up and dropped off a £1 coin, saying 'At least you're doing something. Not like that homeless man down there. He just sits there.'

I'd had this a few times, the suggestion that a bit of effort was what separated me from the homeless, and I attempted a gentle answer.

'Well, I'm very lucky to have this beautiful instrument and a family who gave me the chance to study it. I don't know his story, but maybe he never had chance to learn a skill like this. I imagine he can't afford an instrument.'

'But he could do something though? Not just sit there. Maybe he could draw something with chalk.'

The more I thought about it, the more this upset me. The poor fellow had nothing, and this lady wanted him to draw chalk pictures on the floor before he was worth her charity. I decided the best thing I could do would be to meet and get to the know the homeless person in question. On my next break, I headed down and gave him all my 50ps, saying I hoped my music wasn't spoiling his afternoon. His name was Robert and he was in a good mood, especially considering his circumstances.

'I've got a bank account over there.' He gestured at HSBC. 'I pay it in on good days. Trying to save up, but sometimes you've just got to eat.' This had been a good day so far, and he'd had a decent meal. 'You need more food and drink out here. Body needs feeding on the street. Just burn through it.'

Food is expensive when you can't prepare your own. He had a cheap phone stashed away, useful perhaps to receive a call one day. No prospect of putting any credit on it.

'I'm waiting for the shelter to have a space. I'm on the list, but every time I move up there's always another mother with children who gets priority.'

It was said without bitterness, this is just how it is.

'I'm not on drugs, I don't drink', Robert told me. I believed him too, but it was desperately sad that he felt he had to live up to a standard that few of the rest of us do. We expect the homeless to be far better people than us before we owe them anything.

I asked what his plan for getting out was. Get a hostel, sort out benefits, get somewhere to stay, get some clothes, apply for a job, earn his own money. It all seemed so reasonable and possible, laid out step by step. In reality, every step of it was going to be a slog against the odds, with dozens in the queue before him and a wall of bureaucracy to overcome. I wondered if he'd make it. He had more of a chance than many, but the odds were long.

Meanwhile, the weather was perfect, I was the only busker in town, and footfall was steady. Today was the day to make up for my poor returns in Norwich and Harwich, so I knuckled down and played and played, knowing that with a fair wind I could cover the week's expenses here and now. When my friend picked me up again I'd made £105 in five hours of playing. This took the pressure off, paid for my food and fuel for the week, and meant I could really get to know Braintree in the morning.

I returned early the next morning and had a really good explore. Braintree is a town of two halves, having merged with Bocking into one entity some years ago. On the Bocking edge of the town, a large and scruffy Victorian municipal building had been turned into an antiques showroom. These were antiques in the loosest possible sense. As they invariably do in these places, things had achieved the status of antiquity simply by avoiding landfill for long enough. It was all junk. I wonder if antiques shops exist not so much to resell old items, as to remove archaic rubbish from circulation, in much the same way that bookswaps exist mainly to filter out surplus Jilly Cooper and Dan Brown novels. There was nothing here I'd have wanted even if I'd had any money to spare. There were boxes of Perry Como and Jim Reeves records, a stuffed mongoose, leather flying helmets, cabinets of Toby jugs. Why is there such a market for this stuff? Who buys it? Where does it all go? Are we incapable of making a judgement of what matters, storing up old shite just in case it ends up being valuable and important? How much of the value of this stuff is simply a collective belief that because it's old, it must be valuable? Perhaps it's of the same school of thought that says old values were more wholesome, and old ways of life better for you, forgetting the racism, sexism, homophobia and illnesses. Antique shops like this are symptomatic of our inability to deal rationally with the past. It's always portrayed as a golden era where things were better, and this stuff is materially linked to that emotional feeling, objects that take us back to a better time. A better time that, much like these objects, was worse.

For most people, the golden age was when they were in their youth. They remember the time where they had freedom, fitness, and the world was a host of possibilities before them, and extrapolate out that it must have been the golden era for everyone. My maternal grandma always remembered her childhood as a golden era. She had rickets and then spent ten weeks in bed with flu, before leaving education at 13 to work in the mill, but it was still her golden era. In the antiques shop, I saw so much evidence of this harking back, comfort blankets of pottery and wood. I left empty-handed and confused.

Braintree

Back on the street I set up for an hour of playing. A youth approached me.

'Can you buy me some cigarettes?' He gestured at the shop across the road.

'No, I'm a bit busy.'

'I'm only two months away from 18.'

'No.'

'There's a few coppers in it for you.'

'Go away.'

An hour later, I decided I'd made enough for the session, and went in search of interest. I got chatting to Michelle, one of the security guards for the town centre. Now on my second day here, I'd become a familiar enough face that she was happy to tell me a lot more.

'This town centre's been totally rebuilt. The church was taken down and removed. They took up the gravestones and stored them. The glass factory was demolished, and they wiped out the old street lines. This whole shopping area is a new layout. There's tunnels right under the town you know. All connected up. I don't know the way in though. Here, I'll show you a few things.' She was enjoying the chance to show off Braintree to someone.

Upstairs at the pop-up vaping shop in the arcade was a significant piece of machinery, a crane and winch made of cast iron, unmovable, blocking out the top floor.

'It's listed, we can't move it. It just lives there', said the proprietor.

Out the back of the arcade was a closed off section behind an anonymous black gate. This was the gravestone store. Ripped up and cleared for the redevelopment, they had clearly not been able or willing to recycle or destroy them, so they were piled up in rows, like a very heavy reference book.

'Right, if you want, I'll take you to England's most haunted autoparts centre', said Michelle.

This was indeed definitely what I wanted. We went in. The owners were very happy to talk about it. Their ghosts included a 27-year-old woman and a young boy and girl, their identities having been confirmed by cross referencing against the gravestone store. One customer joined in the conversation in agreement, very matter of fact.

'Thing about this town is you never know where you're going to find an old bit. Sometimes there's a Tudor room in what looks like a new building. There's whole courtyards locked away, you have to work them out from where there's an obvious gap in the buildings. And there's tunnels right under the whole place. Council maintains them, on the quiet. They go right through from the White Hart to the church and there's a whole network of them.'

I asked if he'd been in these tunnels. He hadn't but he had it on good authority that they were there, and very old they were too. He was very matter of fact about the ghost situation. You put stuff down and it moves. Doors bang, there's steps upstairs when there's nobody in. Same with the autoparts people. They were quite convinced that it was haunted, to the point of it being mundane. Stuff moved around.

'It makes stocktaking a nightmare.'

That's how it was, and you just got on with it. It wasn't controversial, just a statement of fact.

'Sky TV wanted to make a programme in here, but they wanted us to shut for two days so we said no.'

I walked back to town, seeing it in a new light. Everywhere was haunted but it wasn't a big deal. It was common knowledge there were tunnels connecting it all together, although nobody had actually been in them.

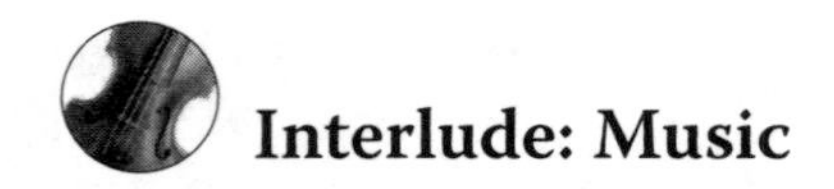

Interlude: Music

SOMETIMES, when the moment is just right, the act of busking ceases to be a performance and the world around you shrinks until it's just yourself, the instrument, and the acoustics. Then the context collapses, your experience becomes internal, and the boundaries between self, fiddle, and the sound weaken until your consciousness is floating somewhere in the middle of it all, no longer really commanding the movements but simply experiencing the totality of music.

Some of the most intimate and personal moments I've had with my instrument have arrived during these times, when hours of playing in public have washed away the last remnants of nervousness and self-awareness and let me reach a trance like state.

It can happen at the oddest of moments, a wet afternoon in Redcar, a painfully cold winter's day in Cirencester. Perhaps a fleeting ten minutes in an otherwise ordinary afternoon. It tends to happen when things are a bit quieter, when you're able to relax and just play. It cannot be summoned up and can slip through your fingers, evaporating in the face of a question from a passer by. It can last just a couple of minutes or for much longer. Weeks can go by without it happening at all, or it can happen several times in a day.

This is not to say I don't enjoy just playing the rest of the time, but these moments of total connectivity are the ultimate, the astonishing alchemy of everything you practice and feel. I wish I could bottle it somehow, to be opened at important performances, but I've never quite found the magic formula when there's an audience. The expectation and the pressure weigh down, I strive a little too hard and too heavy and my music stays earthbound and entirely plausible. I have a few friends in the music industry who do seem to find this place on stage, even when conditions shouldn't allow, their faces hitting a soft neutrality as consciousness moves out of the body and into the music itself. It catches you up and you too get a little hit of it. When people talk about being transported by music, this is what they mean, and those moments where you yourself are the agent of that magic are the most precious in a musician's life.

The times where I have moved people the most have nearly always been when I wasn't really aware I was playing for someone. I did it at Redcar when the weather had emptied the street, and instead of fighting the damp I found a way to include it in the sound, the lack of grip of the bow, the soft, fat acoustic, all became part of the spell, and I emerged from this to find I'd stopped shoppers in their tracks across the road and genuinely moved them. I could not have done it if I'd known they were there, and I could not then repeat it.

I took up the fiddle aged eight after a couple of failed attempts at other instruments. For some reason, it stuck, although barely, as I was not the type to practice much. I had several strokes of good fortune. The first was that my parents valued a music education and had the resources to pay for it. Many of my friends from the council estate were not as fortunate, their families unable to afford the tuition and equipment, I now realise. Struggling with my teacher, who took a strict classical view, I was about to give up, and had a letter in my pocket for her to this end, when I found out that a new teacher was taking over at school. I carried on.

Having made little progress by the age of 16, I suddenly discovered that the fiddle was the key to the pub, allowing me access to pub sessions and beer, and a period of near total obsession followed. I was failing my A-levels and fell deeper into the instrument as respite. Finally I was good at something! It's a pretty intoxicating feeling to suddenly have a talent, however minor, having displayed no previous evidence beforehand.

I moved into my second session at 18, at the George Hotel in Buxton, and fell under the wing of a remarkable musician, Sean

Heeley, to whom I dedicated my first solo album, *Interloper*. A small, round fellow with masses of curly hair, he was a genius on the fiddle, especially between three and eight pints down, a short window on those formative drunken nights. He had terrible stage fright, and couldn't perform to an audience, devoting his life instead to social music making. Was he a good influence on me? Yes and no, but he was a great mate, and his fiery, true playing has underpinned my style ever since. He passed away a few years ago, aged 59, and I still miss him. Generous to a fault, quite literally, and a firebrand socialist, I wonder what he'd have made of this project. I imagine he'd have given it a mixed review, but I owe to him the understanding that music is always social and deeply connected to societal issues. It cannot exist without that context.

Rather than detail the rest of my musical biography, I'll just include one more important influence. At the age of 21, I was invited to the Hexham gathering by David Oliver of Folkworks. Through this organisation, over the next few years I met and had the opportunity to learn from the great Scandinavian fiddlers, especially Emma Reid, whose incredible tone, and rich, living style has always been the gold standard for me, and Sturla Eide, whose bright ringing sound is so alive and fulfilling. Although still an English fiddle player at heart and in repertoire, these styles have inspired me and guided my tonal approach. I recommend listening to their albums.

Busking has been a deep experience for me. Rather than just playing the tunes I know on the street corner, I've searched for spaces where the sound is just so, the acoustic supportive and challenging. I've learnt a lot about my fiddle and my music and grown into the project. I quickly became so much more aware of the value of the space I play in and the qualities that a sound needs to turn heads and stop people on their way past. It's a constant feedback loop, the people of England my focus group. An audience with no preconceptions or existing knowledge of traditional music, who must simply be won over through the music speaking to them personally.

I'm grateful for each and every coin and conversation. It's been the most interesting time in my life so far.

West Bromwich

WEST BROMWICH is a long thin strip of a place, a straight line mile from Victorian clock tower to ring road, a town-centre on the move eastwards. I popped into Wetherspoons to use the facilities. The first table had four ladies sat by their fully loaded and migratory Wilko's shopping trolley. On the main street, aggressive beggars were being confronted on by the police. Homelessness and begging has many faces, but these gentlemen were getting right up to people and demanding money in a scary sort of way. It was definitely a world apart from what I've seen elsewhere. Another homeless man's dog broke free and ran barking furiously down the road. He ran after it in desperation, struggling with a terrible limp, rags flying. West Brom was a tough place, even in the warmth of a bright early summer's day.

Picking the right busking pitch is not always easy. Sometimes there's just nothing that looks quite right. Perhaps there's a spot that looks perfect until you notice the pigeons resting above it, ready to offer their unique critical appraisal of your work. I walked up and down the main street. The busiest part was right at the east end. A wide street with market stalls down the middle, flanked by two stories of grotesque 1960s concrete. One end had a Cash Generator facing a Cash Converter, both with speakers outside blasting clashing music at each other, like opposing regimes conducting a propaganda war across a demilitarised zone. No chance of busking here. The other end of this section was very crowded, but I picked a spot by a big empty unit and gave it a go.

West Bromwich

The street was a colourful jumble of people and cultures. This part of the Midlands is amongst the most ethnically diverse communities in the UK. I saw a huge range of clothing and skin colours, from bright African cloth, Jamaican, Muslim, Sikh, Polish, and white English people too. There were many more I couldn't recognise, and plenty who chose not to give it away by their clothes. I wondered how I'd get on. Would one ethnic group be more or less likely to engage with the busking than another? It would be interesting to see, in a not terribly scientific sort of way. I got stuck into my music.

Almost immediately I was set upon by a great big smiling Asian chap. He thought I was brilliant, and insisted on taking selfies alongside me, as well as directing a narrated video. He said he was called Rakka and he couldn't stop going on about how much he was enjoying it. He gave me an apple.

Slowly coins came my way. There were plenty of contributions but they were mostly small change, a reflection of the total lack of wealth of the area. I also started to collect more apples. People were leaving me bits of fruit in lieu of having any change. Another fellow came up and introduced himself as Kamal and asked if I'd play a sad one. I racked my brains, and gave him a heartfelt rendition of 'Nathanial Gow's lament upon the occasion of the death of his second wife', which was the most depressing tune to spring quickly to my mind. Kamal was delighted by this and pressed a fiver into my hand, before taking a business card with a view to buying a violin and contacting me for lessons. I haven't heard from him yet.

By 4:30pm the street activity had died back to nearly nothing and I packed down, looking forward to a really good day here tomorrow. The church near my car had a large crucifix outside by which someone had graffitied 'God is the cross man'.

The next morning I parked at the far end of town and walked the full length of the street, trying to understand the evolution of modern West Bromwich. The Farley clock tower feels like the beginning of town. Erected in 1897, it is now somewhat divorced from the bustle of the market street which is best part of a mile away. It was, however, next to the YMCA coffee shop, into which I dropped to recharge my mug. I was served by Paul from Chicago. He'd married a West Brom lady and moved here. He said he liked it in West Brom.

'It's just as friendly, but poorer here', he told me.

The street slopes gently uphill, and you soon pass the first of half a dozen Polish supermarkets, some of which are very large indeed. There's probably a greater length of sausage in the West end of West Bromwich than anywhere else in England. I continued uphill, and although the town hadn't really got going yet I was soon in what must once have been the centre, arriving at the town hall, church and the library. Alongside them several large office buildings stood derelict and boarded. Many of the smaller buildings were not just closed as shops, they clearly hadn't been shops for a generation. The town itself has moved away from the furniture of civic organisation, like the church at Erpingham, abandoned by its village due to plague and left quietly alone. Further along the road are the banks, nearer to the action but still isolated, not quite able to justify relocating again to the centre of action.

Finally then, after another a few hundred yards later the town really begins. The main street is busy, although the shops themselves speak to its poverty. Pawnbrokers, pound bakers, independents, charity shops, discounters, newsagents pushing the lottery 'Get rich quick. Play Lottery Here', and the market stalls sell fruit and vegetables, very cheap clothes and shoes, and fabric for those who must simply make their own. Running off this street are two arcades, one, the older of the two, leads to an indoor market with more of the same, as well as a record shop so overflowing with vinyl it was impossible to peruse as the stock was solidly jammed together and immovable on shelf after shelf.

The other arcade was new, and whilst still having far too many abandoned units, fed into a courtyard with some big high-street names. It was an odd change of gear. In a street with so many ethnicities it suddenly jarred to see huge window adverts featuring white people with the odd tokenistic black lady thrown in. Past these windows, all the colours of the world walked past, mostly unrepresented and uncatered for. The main street was theirs, but this arcade was not. The cultural boundary was invisible but stark and tangible at the electric doors. I made my way through the arcade, jostling for position when the route was bottlenecked by a significant blue outcropping of giant plastic Smurfs. West Brom was short of money, but not footfall. The streets were rammed with people buying the barest of essentials with the little they had, and shopkeepers trading on the slenderest of margins.

Round the corner was what had been 'The Public', a modernistic looking art gallery designed as a new centrepiece to restore prestige to the town centre. It hadn't lasted long, and was now a sixth form college. It's all very well intentioned, throwing money at a town's regeneration, but if the project is too ambitious like this, it's soon wasted. It had been a great gallery, I went round it before it closed a few years ago, but utterly in the wrong place to pick up the numbers it needed.

I pieced together the progression of the town. Immigrant families, mostly from India and the West Indies wanted to open up shops but couldn't afford rents in the main part of town, so they set up towards the east end. Slowly, as these communities grew, that became the thriving part of town, so much so that the new arcades needed to be established there rather than near the old centre. A later wave of Eastern European immigration then took advantage of the now unwanted properties in the West of the town to create a little Poland. Between the two, the town hall stood in the midst of empty, long abandoned shopping streets.

It was time to play a few tunes. There were a number of popup market stalls today, on top of the regular market. They were joined by a very angry and agitated black man with a lectern who had an important message about Jesus. Finding a spot where I wouldn't get mown down by speeding mobility scooters was very difficult, but I squeezed myself in outside Argos.

Frankly, there were too many people to make much money. As had been apparent in Norwich, if a street is really crowded people get their heads down, focus on avoiding collisions, and become defensive. Add to this an array of street sellers, foisting leaflets, trying to sell you a new electricity supplier, asking you to consider if Hell is real, and you do not have a recipe for getting people to appreciate your music. This didn't bother me. I was happy to play and watch what seemed like the entire world go by.

I became aware of another set of actors on the street. Four blokes, heavily muscled, dressed in white vests and shorts were working the space. They had large supermarket bags full of something that looked like small boxes, and were going up to people and trying to sell the contents. It appeared to be perfumes. A saw a few sales made. They weren't aggressive as such, but they went right up to people and blocked their paths. Big lads too. It all looked pretty dodgy to me, but I try not to be too judgemental without proof. Perhaps these weren't knock off or stolen goods, perhaps they had street trader licences. My scepticism was confirmed a little later though, when a pair of policemen appeared at the far end of the street and the lads vanished instantly, re-appearing when the coast became clear. Later on, they sold some perfume to the energy contract salespeople, which pleased me for some reason I couldn't quite put my finger on. They never asked me if I wanted any. Clearly I don't have the look of a perfume connoisseur.

In the middle of the market street are a number of long benches. Slowly these filled up with old Sikh men, each bringing their own special cushion. Forbidden by their religion from cutting their hair, these aged gentlemen all have a massive white beard and a stick, and I could only easily tell them apart at distance by the bright colours of their Turbans. But perhaps that reflects more on me and my lack of familiarity with the Sikhs. I was focussing in on the hair and the turbans, distinctive and unusual to me, and just seeing a group of people not like me, instead of individuals with their own stories meeting up for a chat. Perhaps they feel the same way about jeans and T-shirts.

Nonetheless, from where I stood it felt like a gathering of birds on an overhead wire. I'd look up and the order would have changed. It was clear they came here every day, and filled this space. There wasn't a huge amount of chat, as they shared their lives and enjoyed the view. It all seemed enormously peaceful and civilised.

I made a bit of money. There didn't seem to be any discernible pattern about who would or wouldn't contribute to the busking. I got coins from every ethnic group I could identify. Nobody was cross or annoyed. People here seemed very good at knowing how to share street space and tolerate what other people would like to do with it, much in contrast to some of the white English shop owners and employees who'd shouted at me to go away in other towns. Diversity helps you to share. Too much similarity leads to a negative response to someone out of the ordinary.

A Muslim gentleman went past in the full white robe, with a brightly dyed orange beard. A small child repeatedly pretended to shoot me with a plastic toy gun. I saw West Brom shirts and turbans, headscarves and camouflage shorts. In what was probably the most architecturally dismal street I'd seen in England, the colour and variety of the people more than made up for it and I was happy to play and watch.

My afternoon carried on much as before, too crowded, a few apples, a few pounds. It was time to throw myself deeper into the Black Country.

Smethwick

MENTIONED in the Domesday book, Smethwick has come a long way, and is now even less white than West Bromwich. I hardly saw a white face all day. Race and immigration have pretty much defined the place over the last century. Sir Oswald Mosley represented the town for Labour until he left the party in 1931 to form the British Union of Fascists. White worries about immigration were played to in the 1964 election when the Conservative candidate Peter Griffiths won on the astonishing slogan 'If you want a n****r for a neighbour, vote Liberal or Labour'. (My censoring of the word.)

The town today feels calmer. The Sikh community is predominant in the area, with Europe's largest Gurdwara standing prominent by Rolfe Street station. It looked entirely in place and English, concrete facaded, a little tired and just slightly municipal under its golden dome. Next along was the Tollgate centre, a failed attempt to breathe a bit of life into the town. An arcade running back from the road, the sign outside listed the amenities within, including Tesco. 'Proudly serving the local community. The Tollgate Shopping Centre. Now OPEN'. Tescos was long since shut and boarded up. A small number of local shops survived, including an Indian drum shop, packed to the roof with tablas, but most units were empty. Another attempt at regeneration that had failed.

I wondered if I should play here? This was not my world at all, but I'd come here to see all the different aspects of England, not just the bits that feel like home. The main street was not pedestrianised and had narrow pavements. In true Asian style, the shops happily spilled out onto the street, the best and freshest stock piled up on the pavement, a full palette of vibrant colours in fruit and veg reflecting back the brightness of early summer. Finding a spot wouldn't be easy. There were bookmakers, mostly filled with elderly Jamaican gentlemen, two banks, and a couple of very tired looking pubs with Asian names on the licence board.

I found a little section set back by a takeaway that wasn't open yet, right next to one of these mighty green-grocers. I decided to ask the proprietor if he minded me playing next to his shop. He didn't really understand the question. The street is everyone's to use, why would I even ask, please go ahead.

With a certain nervousness I'd not felt since Berwick, back in early April, I set up and played, my English tunes seeming so out-of-place and almost comical in this setting.

But slowly it worked, I settled in, began to feel at home, and people took an interest. I was clearly unusual. You wouldn't pick Smethwick for busking under normal circumstances, mainly because it's simply not very big, and nobody has much money. But people dropped off a few coins, asked questions, danced down the street. It started to feel a lot like normal. One can get too pre-occupied with the search for difference and miss the things that make us so similar. It's also true that I'm a bit weird by any measure, it's not like I naturally fit in in other places anyway, so being a bit weird here wasn't as awkward as it might have been. Cars pulled up with whole families in, father picking up ten bags of onions perhaps destined for a curry shop somewhere. Vast amounts of vegetables disappeared into the backs of Mercedes. Trade was wholesale as well as domestic. Children would wind the windows down to hear the strange white man playing tunes on their street. Some got out with little coins and smiles. All was well with the world.

Around 3pm, the shutters started to go up behind me as the takeaway opened for the day. I started to pack down, but the owner came out and said he was enjoying it and encouraged me to carry on. So I did. Eventually I called it a day and went to buy some fruit and vegetables from my neighbours. I try to spend much of what I take back in the communities, always buying food and drink from local shops. I filled a huge bag with all sorts of produce and took it to the owner. He half glanced inside and said 'One pound please.' It was a generous gesture.

As I drove to my accommodation, I recalled that this area was alleged to be a 'no-go zone' for white people like me, if certain alarmist sections of the press are to be believed. Well, there's no substitute for experience, and mine had been thoroughly pleasant. That's not to say that there aren't problems with integration. It's a complicated picture, and a few afternoons hanging out on the street are not the same as living in these communities, but some of the hyperbole at least bears no resemblance to the reality. Perhaps it's a matter of how you approach it. Turn up aggressively, looking for division to prove your point and you'll find it, as nervous communities push back against you. Turn up to make friends and play a few tunes and you get a big bag of free vegetables.

Dudley

I SEARCHED for a parking space where I could leave my car for a few days. Three shirtless lads headed into the park with a twenty-four pack of Budweiser and a large waddling dog off the lead. I walked towards the centre idly wondering why vaping shops are always so masculine. Devils, skulls, monsters. Dudley was another town of concrete and faded glories. A department store in a bleak building that had aimed at art-deco and missed was closing down for good. This was an England reducing to the unholy trinity of Essentials, Desperation, and False Hope, as represented by discounters, pawnbrokers, and fixed-odds betting machines. This is an England whose reserves have been sucked dry and whose meagre wealth has been burnt simply getting through the last decade. Whose valuables are pawned or eBay-ed away. A camel whose hump is spent and slack, hoping another unsurvivable shock isn't coming soon. An England that can't afford another economic failure.

Drawn as graphs, the recent economic shocks look much like the great depression. One reason it hasn't caused the same levels of mass suffering is that this time the country was generally richer, and more people in nearly all communities had some sort of reserve to draw on. Those reserves are gone now. Household debt is high, and the valuables are sold. There's a huge number of people who are now only a whisker away from missing the rent. The shops on Dudley high street tell that story.

I walked round the centre for a while. At the lights, a car drew up with tinted windows rolled down. Rap music was emerging at a considerable volume. The lyrics were 'f*cking n****r shit, f*cking n****r shit' over and over.

The centre of Dudley has a fixed market place where the road is widest and pedestrianised. I set up outside an empty unit and gave it a go. I could see a Muslim gentleman selling head dresses. He had his stock on mannequin heads, and was sat on a stool which put his head at the same level, making him seem like an animated part of his display. There was a flower seller, fruits sellers, clothing, and a cake stall. About half the available market stalls were in use.

I made a few pounds. People were generous, but often with just a few small coins. That made sense. The town was clearly very poor, and I was grateful for anything. As I was about to call it a day at about 4:30pm, a group of black teenage schoolgirls came by and dropped off a scrap of paper in my case. Intrigued, I picked it up before it blew away. It was a note: 'Love your music! Keep playing!' It was a special thing to get and I was genuinely moved. I wished I could have spoken to them but they had already gone.

The next morning I had a good wander round before starting to busk again. There was one sort of shop bucking the trend all over the country, and that was the quality coffee shop. It had been possible to get a decent cup of coffee just about everywhere I'd been, no matter how economically ruined the place had been. Dudley was no exception. With my coffee in hand, I walked to find the edges.

Dudley really does have a literal edge of town. Once you get out of the immediate centre, the views are excellent in every direction. Built right on top of the hill, this location is a legacy of Dudley's historical significance, having been a castle worth sieging in the civil war of Stephen and Matilda in the 12th century. Excavations in the castle grounds have also uncovered what are thought to be the world's oldest condoms, something they are very proud of. From here, you can see right across the Black Country, surprisingly green and leafy now, spaced out, town after town, not quite merging into one mass.

Dudley grew in importance in the industrial revolution, mining coal and iron, and fostering a whole range of industries. It had the good fortune to be at the heart of the burgeoning canal network, several of which wind around the base of the hill, including a two mile canal tunnel right through the heart of it. The railway has similar issues, being unable to climb the hill, and both of Dudley's stations are a good mile away on lower ground. It's an island, left high and dry by the falling economic tide. All the flows are with gravity, away from the hollowing centre.

I passed what might be the most derelict office block I've ever seen. Once called 'Cavendish House', letters had dropped until it was just 'Cave dis House'. Every window was smashed, and the site was fenced off. Apparently it was slated for redevelopment. But into what? What could be done that wouldn't be a waste of money in a declining town?

I'd seen 'The Public' in West Bromwich, a noble attempt to bring a major art gallery into a subsiding Black Country town, which had failed in a few years at vast expense. There's nothing approaching a coherent strategy to deal with our town centres. Just a willingness to let them slowly collapse on themselves, occasional unfocussed redevelopments throwing money like small and useless sandbags into an ever-widening breach. Single projects funded by endless short term programmes do not make for a strategy but instead waste a fortune without making things better.

The edge of town hosted straggler shops left behind by the falling waters like starfish on a beach. Quiet, without footfall, lone and scruffy proprietors stood on doorsteps, vaping to fill time and staring across at closed units. Military paraphernalia, second-hand household goods, a giant furniture shop looking like a small child lost in the woods, surrounded by urban wilderness. Smartly besuited, the manager was stood by the front doors too, staring out, hopelessly wishing customers over the horizon.

My walk took me through acres of empty pay and display, weeds emerging from tarmac, blinking into the unused spaces furthest from residual town, undisturbed, amazed at their luck. This must have been what a medieval plague village felt like.

Back in the centre, the market had all changed round today. Different stalls in the same spaces. A vocal lady forcefully shouted 'Six crusty cobs for a pound!' A shopper passing by turned to me and said 'God, what a big mouth.' They were all at it, a lady selling three peaches for a pound, a man selling two punnets of strawberries for one pound fifty. I bought three peaches and ate them, whilst recording the sounds of the market on my phone. The peach seller had the toughest hands I'd ever touched, a lifetime of fruit juice and lifting boxes.

It wasn't that there weren't shoppers. There were lots, but they couldn't afford to drive in, and when they got there they weren't spending much. The bus station was the busiest part of town. Frugality was the order of the day. Every pound had to achieve its maximum, pennies couldn't be wasted. Against this backdrop, I busked again, making a little change as time went by. The Sikh flower seller came by and said that whilst he didn't mind the music, perhaps I'd do better on the other side of the street. He paused, then flipped me 20p to prove his sincerity. I gave it a go. It didn't work. When I moved back, there was an Eastern European piano accordion player in my place. I gave him 50p. He was noodling without any apparent aim, but it was nice enough.

I busked a bit more at the other end of the street. Eastern European perfume-selling gangs were operating here too. A group of Down's syndrome people danced to the music for a while. I had to keep it really steady or they got too carried away in it. A woman wearing headphones gave me a pound. One young gentleman watched for a while, before handing me a fiver. This was a welcome contribution as I could now afford my lunch. I had a pork pie and a sandwich sitting beneath the statue of Duncan Edwards, the outrageously talented Dudley-born footballer killed in the 1958 Munich air disaster.

Dudley is also home to the Black Country museum, a collection of buildings and artefacts rescued from around the region and combined to create an entire village showcasing Victorian Black Country life. It's well worth a visit, and I have been many times. It covers a large area, and numbers of costumed volunteers bring it to life by manning the shops, the tram, the boats, the furnaces.

In common with my previous experiences of historical presentation though, it leaves me slightly uncomfortable, as by necessity, it can only re-create the best of it. It's one thing to walk around an authentic looking village with people in costume, but it's very hard to get across the devastating pollution that the area suffered and indeed got its name from, the diseases, the poverty, the patriarchy. It makes it seem like a thoroughly nice place to be, with decent fish and chips and a good pint of beer, and the simple pleasures of chasing an iron hoop down the street. This is not a criticism. A museum that infected children with polio and lost every fiftieth school group to an explosion of firedamp would not really be the solution.

But how to accurately teach history in a setting like this? In the boatyard, where repairs to the historic fleet would be made, you are shown around by a youngish Asian woman who plays the character of a boatyard employee. She is excellent, knowledgeable and engaging. She is also symptomatic of the problems museums have in properly contextualising history. This was not a place where women would work, and in that era Asians were basically unheard of in the area. But it is also entirely appropriate that the museum should represent modern Dudley in its workforce.

What is the right way to handle history? Does this sanitisation and inclusivity lead to rose-tinted views of what was actually often an awful past? Rose-tinted views that shape how we take decisions about our future? As in Ashington, at the coal mining museum, where the simulated pit experience in no way resembled the claustrophobia and danger of the real thing, as in Sheringham where the North Norfolk railway was spotless and floral, it all conveys a past where things were simpler and better. Having been to industrial regions in China on a number of occasions, cities where the sun doesn't shine through the pollution, where health and safety is a personal responsibility, incompatible with the pressure of making a living, it was never like this. The implied argument in Ashington is that things would be better if the coal mining jobs came back. A better argument would be for a future with neither the unemployment and purposelessness of today or the dangers and miseries of the past.

But museums exist in a market. Give people a miserable time and they won't come back. Make them happy and they take home the wrong ideas. The Imperial War Museum manages it, but certain subjects come with an expectation of misery. We've sanitised that out of other areas of the past. It is hard to see how it can be brought back. It is very much to our detriment.

The true museum of the Black Country is further up the hill. In Dudley town centre, where almost all the shops are independents and market stalls. Few cars, cash economy. Here you see both sides of the coin.

Stourbridge

MOATED by a three-lane ring road, Stourbridge is a concrete motte and bailey on the border of the Black Country. It only takes a couple of minutes to drive round it, clockwise being the permitted direction, but to breach the keep you must drive into the foundations of the towering Tesco, down the ramp to the rubberised floor of the sunken car park, before ascending to the arcade where Tesco has merged with the Victorian redbrick town hall to create a truly architecturally confused shopping experience.

Within the ring road are three smaller, older roads, oxbowed and narrow. Stourbridge is therefore now a fixed and calcified layout, redevelopments piling up against the ring road like jetsam on a tideline. The main shopping street runs towards Birmingham, narrow, unpedestrianised, tall sided. I walked up and down, and chose a slight widening outside Wilko's for my busking pitch. There was a coffee shop called 'Chemistry' a few doors down, so I went to fill my mug. A Dutchman saw my fiddle and paid for the coffee, whilst asking me what I was doing. This was, and remains a tough question to answer. 'Busking my way round England' is true, but misses the point a little. 'Discovering my country through street performance' makes me sound like a pretentious prick. Maybe I am. Anyway, I usually opt for 'Busking my way round with the view to writing a book'. If I was a better publicist, I'd probably be doing something else instead.

I began to busk outside Wilkinsons, next door to Coral. There was a slight niche in the pavement that set me back enough for people to pass without problem. I soon discovered that it was also the unofficial turning circle for mobility scooters as well. That was fine, there was space for all of us, if the scooters all used the litter bin as a roundabout. I even picked up a few high fives as they came past. A series of expensive cars parked on the road in front of me. I saw a Ferrari, a Lotus, an open top Audi, and an MGB GT all within the nearest few spaces. Each driver went through the same process upon arrival; got out, locked up, began walking away, paused and thought about it, then spun me a quid without making eye contact. Clearly they regarded this as some sort of insurance, or protection money. Fine by me.

Periodically, people came out of Coral for a smoke. They were always generous with my busking collection, each gambler absent-mindedly dropping a clatter of change as they lit up. I wondered if the average gambler just had a more transient relationship with their money that made it easier to surrender to a busker's case. I generally try to avoid picking cynical spots, near cash points or such. This felt a little uncomfortable until one young lad got chatting. He really liked the music, and stayed out for an extra ciggy. He was getting married soon, and wondered about hiring me to play at his wedding. He offered me a cigarette; I declined.

'Love the music. Can't beat the old tunes. So does the missus. She wants me to get married. I'm not sure, but she's pushing me towards it. Would you be free to play? She loves the old Irish tunes. If it happens, of course.'

I said I could be, if they both wanted, and gave him my card. He headed back in and did not emerge again in the remaining hour and a half I spent on the pitch.

The Dutchman who'd bought me a coffee now returned eagerly with a ukulele. He was very excited to show it to me. Having done so, he wasn't sure what to do next. He couldn't play it, and neither could I, and it existed between us, a comma in search of clauses to split. I said it was a nice ukulele, and he agreed that it was. Eventually I asked if he'd like another tune, and he said he would, which gave us a dignified end to what had been a difficult conversation.

The money came rolling in to my case. Stourbridge is definitely a well off sort of place, a world apart from Dudley, just six miles down the road. It's extraordinary how utterly the wealth and social class of an area can change from town to town in just a few miles. If you've got no money and no car, those six miles must seem an ocean. I could have walked to Dudley in two hours, and yet it felt like a different planet here. Artisan coffee shops, brew pubs, every shop a going concern. And far more white faces too.

Suddenly Dan Walsh came past, an acquaintance of mine from the music scene, and a very fine banjo player. He said hello, and asked me what I was doing here, before handing me a pound coin. I took this as an endorsement of my project. Shops began to shut. It was time to pack up. I counted up my takings. In two hours I'd managed £41, 3 yuan, and 60 euro cents.

I was staying with Gren and Julia, good friends of mine. After dinner Gren and I went for a game of snooker. I love snooker clubs. They're all so very gloriously alike in their utter mediocrity. When I was young, my grandfather told me that being good at snooker was the sign of a misspent youth. He was wrong of course. Despite wasting much of my youth in snooker clubs, I never became any good at all.

This snooker club was at the top end of the scale. Yes, it's still an indeterminate concrete cube on a gone-to-seed trading estate on the outskirts of town, with wall to wall Sky Sports in the bar, but the tables are level, the cushions responsive, and the rests still have all four rubber feet on the end. We settled in for a few frames.

As I missed my shots, the maleness of the place tugged at my attention. There were table after table of blokes, lads out together, father and son, old gaffers never missing the easy ones. But no women, other than the lady running the bar. I wondered, not for the first time why that might be. Around the room, gent after gent bent down to the table to inadvertently and collectively reveal a nauseating legion of hairy arse cracks. Once a place is gendered like this, it probably can't change without a concerted effort from all parties. There's a sort of gender inertia that's fairly difficult to overcome. I don't think anyone is trying to preserve snooker clubs as male dominated locations. They just are and that won't change unless a lot of people make a conscious decision to choose to do so.

After my defeat was assured, we returned to Stourbridge for a pint. The town was pretty much deserted now, a smattering of pubs stacking their many empty chairs and tables early so that the minimum wage staff with no emotional attachment to the business could get away quickly after last orders.

The next day, I resumed my spot, having had success the day before. It was a seriously uninteresting session. The world went by, nobody complained, and nobody stopped to talk much. I was left to my own devices, and slowly accumulated a pile of change. Gren and Julia appeared with their two small children, who were given coins of their own to place in my case. Wide eyed, they faltered, seeing me, a familiar face in an unfamiliar place, behaving oddly. 'And he is to be rewarded for this?' said their expressions.

Later on I walked back through the arcade. The lady selling home improvements needed only one telling glance to filter me invisible from the pool of potential clients. The busker winks out of existence once they pack up, disappearing down side streets or alleyways, anonymous and withdrawn.

Stourbridge cooked in the sun. The industry had gone here too, the glassmaking reduced to a single traditional cone by the canal eking a living from the curious and school groups. Another world-famous industry that was no more. But here, the town still prospered with newer money. On the edge of the Clent hills, escape to the country is easy. The town houses are tall and smart, and money has come in. Black Country Lite. Lattes and Skoda Yetis. The plumbing shop was selling vinyl albums on the side. Anyone wishing to deep-dive the Midlands could use Stourbridge as an acclimatisation station. I was coming the other way, after days spent in West Bromwich, Smethwich, and Dudley. I was ready to surface and head home.

Deal

SUMMER was in full bloom. I'd had a week's work at Broadstairs for the folk week, and decided to meander around the South Coast for a while afterwards, perhaps the part of England I knew the least.

Deal is a port without a harbour. A limb of the port of Sandwich, it thrived within the economic and administrative bosom of the Cinque Ports once, a confederation dating back to Saxon times, where responsibilities to the crown were traded for freedoms other towns didn't have. By the 1780s, this arrangement had degenerated into anarchy and smuggling, and in an era of much larger warships and shifting priorities the system had become a hindrance rather than a help to the government. Pitt the Younger sent men to smash and burn the boats and bring the town back into control, posting a cutter offshore to prevent any escape by sea. Thus broken and tamed, the strategic power of the area waned into the gentle seaside resort of today.

A vast sandbank out to sea generates a zone of calm water where generations of vessels have set anchor to ride out the storms that head up the channel. In the modern world, the action is much further out to sea, beyond the sandbank, where LPG tankers and container ships pass through the channel, blocky in the distance, the ragged edge of France visible beyond them. On the shingle shore, small vessels sit by their winches, waiting for the right day. Some had signs by them like the one that said 'Fishing Boat Club. Three new members wanted.' The three had been crossed out and replaced by a four. Some winch houses, stripped of their original job, had become floral instead, a decaying lump to hang baskets from and train vines and sunflowers up.

A disused fort marks the edge of the town centre, cannons in position, trained on the channel, ends plugged up with stoppers of bright red plastic, presumably to stop people using them as bins, laughably irrelevant, strategically trained across the world's busiest waterway, as it carries the planet's wares to the ports of Western Europe, departing empty or with scrap and German exports for the east. It is the aorta, the critical feed for the economies of the world, catastrophically torn open by floods at the chaotic end of the recent ice age, severing the physical connection between Europe and Britain, a geographic act of separation whose continued psychological consequences are still being determined.

Between the sea and the land is a broad walkway, almost entirely lined with hundreds of memorial benches, backs to the land, views trained on the shipping lane the cannons once covered. It is the modern way. In our 21st century England, benches represent an acceptable way of taking the dead from their designated resting places and bringing them back into society. The shore was a long and narrow mausoleum, each bench a personal monument with a small apologetic brass plaque excusing their continued presence among us. 'He loved this view.'

In creating this new kind of civic memorial, we have encouraged the dead to escape the graveyard and retake their place among the living. This is not so unusual in societies around the world. I wondered if it were symptomatic of the church's narrative of death losing its traction. We are no longer storing our deceased in preparation for the end times, but instead preferring the looser and more personal stories of past, present, and future. In Peru, the mummies of significant leaders were kept in storage for moments of great need and wheeled out into the countryside to encourage rains and good harvests. I'd seen them in the museum in Cusco, darkened with age and skin shrink-wrapped awkwardly onto their own bones. Perhaps the mummified corpses of Atlee and Thatcher could be brought out on a national tour to smooth our passage through times of national crisis. It seemed as good a plan as any I'd heard lately. I looked at the benches again, stretching into the distance. They seemed to me, then, as a continuing manifestation of something very ancient and fundamental. The comfort we gain from having the wisdom of the ancestors amongst us, but not so close their presence intrudes upon dinner.

I walked onwards into town, thoughts of death and memorial going round my head. I'm not sure I'd want to be turned into a bench when I've gone. Perhaps a miscast and unfitting manhole cover, in a moderately used suburban road, doomed forever to clonk metallically whenever a car drove across.

Deal, like so many seaside towns, concentrates its focus a couple of streets inland, benefitting from cover on both sides. It was prosperous, and there were no disused units outside which I could stake an untroubled claim. Instead, I plumped for a spot at the end of the long frontage of a chain clothes shop, in front of the zombified headless mannequins. It was a good morning, and coins began to rack up. An old lady walking with a frame made her way towards me with detectable purpose.

'Excuse me, but where did you train?'

This was a new question to me, and it took me a second to understand the implication that she thought I must be a classically trained player.

'Erm, the Harrington Arms, near Macclesfield.'

It was her turn to undergo a moment's confusion. Finally with credentials properly established, we had a good conversation. She'd trained at the RNCM, when it was just the Northern College of Music, (it didn't become Royal until 1973) studying viola. Remarkably, this was the exact same course and instrument as my girlfriend had taken there, much more recently. She said she was 84 and retired now, having survived cancer, been run over, and managing a bad leg and arthritis. Her family were scattered to the four corners of the world. She kept in touch via video calls on her iPad. She told me she could no longer play, due to her advancing arthritis. I risked a dangerous but heartfelt question.

'Was music good to you?'

It's a question I wanted to ask. As a comparatively young man looking at a lifetime of jobbing gigs, working hand to mouth, making ends meet or more often not, I do wonder how I'll feel when I'm old. Will it still feel like the right life to have led?

She thought about it carefully, and then answered with a firm certainty.

'Yes, it really was. Not always of course, but some of the students I got to teach were very good indeed. Great talent, and I always loved to help it along. No, I don't regret it at all.'

She said she'd assumed I must be a classical player from my tone. 'I heard you from a long way away. I looked but couldn't see you to begin with, I assumed you must be much closer. Your technique is very good indeed.'

This was a fine compliment, and with that she said goodbye and went to join a friend for a coffee, but not before dropping a £2 coin into my case. I was warmed by the conversation and settled in for the morning with growing confidence. A man sat down at the bench near me with a bright red parrot on his shoulder. He smiled and offered a thumbs up. The parrot screamed and honked at me when I played. It was a strange juxtaposition, to be appreciated and heckled from the same seat, but I didn't let it bother me. Parrots don't have money.

A window cleaner appeared, tasked with the windows of the clothes shop. I took this as time for lunch, and loaded up with items from the bakers across the road. The lady in the coffee shop was from Margate, and commuted to Deal daily to sell coffee to people like me. All round the town there were job adverts in windows. It was a competitive market. I wondered if the brain-drain of the recession was biting now the jobs were returning. The young of England have left for the cities and now there's no one left in the provinces to sell us custard tarts.

I took my lunch to the end of Deal pier, as it seemed to offer the best view of the town. The rain had arrived, little more than a mist wafting around and making everything wet. The pier was stark. A local had told me it was the most recent pier built in England, celebrating its 60th birthday this summer. It was of its time, brutalist and concrete, as if a town had been eroded into the sea leaving only the bus station still standing. The main span had a few sea anglers atrophied awaiting an unlikely moment of action. I asked if they felt the weather might improve.

'No', answered one, without looking up.

By the entrance to the pier was a chalkboard with 'Fish of the month' as its title. Underneath was written 'July – no winner'.

The end of the pier had a cafe. It was shut and untenanted, apparently awaiting a new gas main. I walked all round it and looked back at the land. Deal was low-rise and whitewashed, seemingly endless stretched along England's shore. The tallest building besides the church bore the timeball, one of a series historically installed along the channel to aid navigation. These days it rises and falls every hour for the benefit of the curious. It's oddly silent, when you're next to it, lacking the fanfare or bells that such a performance seems to demand, making it a private, voyeuristic performance for the knowing few.

Walking around the edges of town, I found odd rambling streets that opened into sudden empty squares, white-walled and deserted of people and stories, as if the focus of town had not always been a settled matter. Most back streets had a funny little pub, closed and bolted, not open till 7. A 'Senior Service' cigarette vending machine hung derelict outside a long closed shop, weathering like a Gormley statue into a state of decayed unrecognition.

The sea anglers proved to be wrong and it dried up again. I returned to my original pitch for another go. My eye was suddenly drawn left, where a giant white gull was coming fast down the street like a fighter plane, on a collision course towards the back of a woman, crashing her hard and dislodging a flapjack. The bird used the split second of shocked inertia to gather the prize, before the previous owner swung her handbag whilst shouting something like 'You feathery fuck', but too late, and the gull was on a second story gutter, looking down in mocking triumph, beak full of food. The woman looked around the street in shock and embarrassment, but nobody made eye contact or broke stride. There was nothing she could do but carry on down the road, humiliated and without flapjack. Another unreported crime that left no physical trace.

A parent and small child came past. The child was perhaps four years old. He stopped by me, looked up, looked down at the coins, and with the sincere smile of innocence, carefully placed his small plastic umbrella in my case.

'No darling, you can't give him your umbrella,' said the parent, reaching down for it, before freezing, suddenly aware that the umbrella was now technically mine. 'Do you mind?' she asked. 'Of course, help yourself,' I replied, and my brief period of umbrella ownership was over.

The rain threatened a return, so I made my way to an Italian coffee shop, well dug in to the end of the street, generations old. I had a teacake and counted my day up: £106 in four and a half hours. A great result that paid my accommodation, food, and travel with some left over. I ordered a second teacake in celebration of my best single day return in the whole adventure.

Hastings

I ARRIVED in Hastings on a damp, sodium coloured evening, the orange of a setting sun on wet pebbles and worn pavements. I picked up a pizza from Pizzarelli, a new takeaway and restaurant in the base of Marine Court in St Leonard's. Marine Court is a truly huge seaside tower-block that overhangs the English Channel like a projecting chin, balanced awkwardly on the fulcrum between the ice cream parlours and cheap gift shops of yesteryear and the modernity of sophisticated eateries and £5 IPAs in cans. To the east, I could see the pier sticking out into the sea, angular and odd, fizzling out at the end. Staring into the corrugated bottleglass green of the channel, I rang my dad and discussed the week's rugby league action. There's nothing quite like considering Halifax's prospects at Widnes on Sunday to remind you how far from home you are. Hastings was already done for the day, the hum dropping away on the tide.

The new day was wet but drying, and a sense of summery renewal sat softly in the streets. I walked in from on high. Hastings is cliffs, all steep roads and funiculars, penny arcades and Italian coffee. I went for a wee in Marks and Spencers before purchasing breakfast from the 1066 cafe in the new town. The bacon was thick and sweet, the coffee strong. With my sustenance I sat in the sun outside 'DELBOYS – Toys – Sweets – Gifts – And Much More!' and enjoyed the sun. There was already a busker at work, despite the early hour.

At least that's how it first seemed. He had a guitar, a Metallica T-shirt, and was strumming with a persuasive drive that so nearly sold it. The only problem was the lack of any notes. He had the strings damped off and refused to bring any into play. The man had rhythm and a certain panache. He rocked out, stuck his right leg forward, and owned the solo that wasn't. I watched for a while in case this was the centrepiece of some vast performance piece that deconstructed the art of guitar playing before reconstituting it into a towering wall of sound, but it didn't happen. He simply couldn't play, and rather than go to the trouble of learning had perfected the other mannerisms a musician might employ in performance. It had its merits. The good thing about having no music to your act is that you don't need to stop between numbers. I wandered off.

Hastings is a town divided between old and new, separated by cliffs and joined by a thin coastal strip. The towns sit in the recesses in the landscape, where the space opens up. I made my way to the old town and sought out somewhere to play. In the winding road from new to old, amid antique dealers and coffee houses, I found my spot in what is known as 'Butler's Gap'.

It was a good morning. The clean air and sunshine coming after the rain seemed to have put a smile on people's faces and I made money fairly steadily. A small girl was walking a large dog on a lead. The dog stopped a few paces before me, suddenly afraid of my music, and began backing up, going straight between a surprised man's legs, followed quickly after by the small girl. The poor fellow didn't know what to do, and hurried off in embarrassment. I was so overcome by laughter at the situation that I had to stop playing for a moment.

Across the street, at first floor level, a ginger cat came to an open window. It had one of those faces frozen in permanent shocked dislike, and it stared intently at me with it for a good half hour. The proprietor of one of the antique shops came out for a cigarette and to say hello. He didn't really like buskers he told me, but didn't want me to move on, as 'You'd only be replaced by someone much worse. At least you can play!'

Well, this is exactly the sort of endorsement I thrive on, and I played my way merrily through to lunchtime.

I was staying with friends, May and Naomi, a mile or so inland in the St Leonards part of town. When I got back to their house, they were preparing to go shopping. Naomi is a Quaker, and her local group had decided to make a collective contribution towards helping people with period poverty in Hastings.

'There are girls missing school because their families won't buy them sanitary products. There's so many problems with substance abuse in Hastings, and poverty generally, and nobody really helps with period poverty because it's not talked about.'

The Quakers had provided £50 to be spent on sanitary products for the local food bank. I topped this up with a bag of 50ps from my morning's collection. I'm grateful to her for the account of what happened next. Having bought as much as she could with the money, she delivered the supply to the food bank, which is run by an amiable and evangelical sort of fellow, who upon receiving the offering, was surprised to find himself with a tear forming in his eye, and was spontaneously moved to declaim the remarkable line; 'It's beautiful! You've given these tampons to JESUS.'

That evening I played for a house concert. Arriving at the house, the host offered to treat me to a pizza from Pizzarelli, as it was 'the best in town'. Good to know that my instinct had been so accurate in this matter. The concert was fun. I mixed up tunes with a few readings from my travels so far. It went well, and one of the punters invited me for breakfast at the East Hastings Sea Angler's Club at 9am. Never one to turn down a free meal, I showed up promptly the following morning, where I found my new friend with his cycling-and-fry-up-club enjoying a seriously significant feed after a few token miles on their bikes. They were a bunch of lads either side of retirement, and a glance round the other tables showed similar groups. This was clearly where the men went for a big breakfast on Saturday mornings. The walls were adorned with plaster models of record-breaking fish, set into commemorative plaques.

I tuned in to the local gossip. The pier was a major talking point. Rebuilt after fire, it had been rescued by a community group run on donations and public money, which then suddenly folded. The administrators gave another community group (Friends of Hastings Pier) a price of £500,000 to buy it, before quickly selling it to Sheik Abid Gulzar at a point where FOHP had raised £461,000. There is a strong feeling that a lot of public and community money has been spent simply for a private businessman to profit from it, and most people I met were cross about it. It certainly looked a bit weird through the Sea Anglers' club window, like a child's unfinished Lego creation, neither here nor there architecturally, with odd blocky units part way down and leading to not much. I busked again, staking out the same spot as the day before. The street felt different today, dustier, older, with a raucous weekend crowd down for the day. It was busy, but I made less money. This doesn't bother me really, I've learnt to enjoy the street and play for my own entertainment. I soon picked up an older fellow striding towards me, full of that purpose that people have when they've got a conversation lined up for you. He was dressed in a tweed jacket and smart shoes.

'Ee, I've got an old fiddle at home. Maybe you'd want to buy it? It's been there decades.'

I said I'd have a look at the very least and he set off to get it. Immediately after this, another fellow turned up and introduced himself as an artist whose studio was up on the cliff overlooking the road. He'd been listening to me all morning and wanted to thank me. I looked up. It was a long way back to where he was pointing and I was amazed that the sound had carried so well. I was well chuffed and played on. The older fellow returned with this fiddle. It had a beautiful back and scroll but a heavily damaged front. Somebody had loved it once, but it had been broken and suffered the indignity of a bad repair. Normally I'd say 'no thanks', but I had a moment of sentimentality and bought it for £80, leaving me £6 down on busking in the town.

Hastings has a healthy endowment of amusement arcades.

They're of a kind, architecturally, with the colourful awnings made of square corrugations bending up. Rideable dinosaurs flank the ends, unloved fluffy toys sit forever unclaimed beneath bastard cheating cranes, and 10ps clatter down at a constant return rate of about 70 per cent. There is no regional variation in these places at all, and dropped into one at random, you'd not know if you were in Rhyl, Scarborough, or Hastings. Things frying in cheap oil is the nasal soundtrack. Do other countries have them, or are they uniquely British? I'll admit I quite like them, and the reams of prize tickets you collect that never add up to quite enough to win a finger puppet or gobstopper. They don't seem to have changed with time either, working to exactly the same formula they always have. When it rains, a captive market will play the machines, and that's good enough. I don't think I've ever won a thing.

I'd been told to visit 'The Source', a vast underground skate and BMX park on the front. It was apparently down some stairs in a small booth on the otherwise unbuilt seaward side of the shore road. I went down the stairs, and emerged into an abandoned courtyard below the road at about sea level. Another anonymous door led off this and I went down further flights of stairs, into the earth itself. I passed through a shop containing skate fashion and equipment, arrayed all around a cavern, through another set of doors and onto a balcony. Beneath me was the skatepark itself. The fully surrounding balcony allows you to watch the action in the largest skatepark outside London in the UK. There was a lesson ongoing with an attentive class of small children, which was great to see, but meant the level of riding was somewhat limited.

It is a remarkable and beautiful space though, set deep in the earth between Hastings and the sea, filling the cavity left by an old municipal swimming pool, a triumphant reimagining of dereliction. Everyone I'd met was proud of it, even if they really weren't into skateparks at all. It filled the void of civic pride left by the pier. The ramps made an alien landscape, a dance floor twisted and metamorphosed into curving shapes. I briefly wondered what the acoustics were like, before putting the thought out of my mind. It was time to leave again.

I caught the funicular railway up the West Cliff. They would only sell me a return ticket but I was leaving town. I'll keep it for the day I go back. I had been fascinated by Hastings. A complex town of many different communities, layered above and below the cliffs in strata.

Brighton

COMING down the street from somewhere out of sight was the sound of an electric guitar, so I followed it, like a child in a Bisto advert drawn by the scent of a freshly baked pie carelessly left to air on a windowsill. There, tucked up under an awning was a young woman in mismatched woollen clothing, odd socks and no shoes, knocking out bluesy guitar solos to a loop pedal. She was focussed on the music, and I bought a coffee and sat on my fiddle case to enjoy it. It probably wasn't the best busking spot, and challenging, moody blues guitar probably isn't the most effective material, assuming money is actually the goal. But she was good, and something quite different. I gave her a couple of quid and she was delighted.

'Aw bless you.'

It turned out this was her first ever busk, and me her first ever contributor. She said she was called 'Liv' and I wished her the very best, wanting to give her encouragement and hoping my enthusiasm for her music wasn't coming over as creepy. It was nice to hear someone genuinely expressing themselves without too much worry about what the audience thought. Most buskers have an act cynically honed to charm coins from pockets. I find it myself, half the time I'm thinking about what might go down well rather than just playing for my own amusement, and consequently the act becomes hyper-responsive to the street, shifting endlessly to imagined subtle changes in the prevailing mood. A few coins means the tune is a winner, rather than that the right couple of people just happened to be coming down the street. Liv belonged in a darkened music club where a silent and knowing audience could hang on to every note. Nobody else seemed to be paying her much attention. Musical talent, it seems, is not really the key to busking.

Brighton is made up out of bits of town, all stuck together. Whenever you think you've finished with the city centre, you come round a corner and there's another hub with a character all of its own. In the lanes I found a shop specialising in selling rubber ducks and bought one on impulse. Between the duck, the parking charge, coffee, and Liv, I now needed £25 to get back to zero. I wandered again in search of a good spot.

I busked on the main street outside Ann Summers, by a sign that said 'Sexy new lines added', deciding to adopt this as my musical mission statement for the day. A man sat near me on a bench for a short while, appraising my music, before dropping me a pound coin.

'Thank you.' I said, as I always do.

'Well, you're terrible, but it's probably not your fault.'

A young couple took the bench, and proceeded to enjoy a punnet of strawberries in the semi-erotic manner of all young lovers with shareable foodstuffs. They looked like good strawberries too, and I wondered if they might save me one. I attempted to improvise some music for lustful strawberries but the fiddle does not really have the right timbre for this task and I couldn't win one for myself.

Brighton is home to the largest LGBT community in the UK, a tradition dating back at least two hundred years. The pride parade is the largest in the country, but the most obvious thing was how wonderfully normal it all seemed. As a straight man, it's hard to be sure, but my impression was that Brighton is well on the way to becoming a place where one's sexuality matters a little less than elsewhere, rather than a little more. Flamboyance saved for a good night out, rather than a constant and necessary protest against intolerance. Hands were held, and all sexualities seemed pleasingly mundane. I hope this is the truth of it.

The main characteristic of Brighton though is its sheer all-round intensity. It's dense and full of life. Every street has huge numbers of people on foot. The buildings are close together. It's a much larger city condensed into a smaller one, colourful and compressed, as if a middle aged beer drinker had suddenly chosen to wear their teenage wardrobe for a party. Very much like London, your personal space is squeezed to a minimum, but unlike the big city everyone is chatty and relaxed.

A homeless man sat down the road from me produced a drum and joined in with my tunes. It was slightly frustrating, but I took the view that his case was harder than mine, and I handed him some of my coins when I packed down a little later. He offered me a joint in return, which I politely declined.

Down at the sea front, everyone was giving it a go. There were several buskers, including Liv who'd made a few more coins since I'd last seen her, a classical violinist soloing along to a backing track, and a caricaturist in the mandatory beret. Outside the Royal Pavilion, surely one of England's strangest and most out of place buildings, an Ethiopian man was singing along to a giant shaky egg that danced from hand to hand with an infectious groove. His songs were all improvised out of lightly disguised metaphors for going to bed with the various women who passed him by. His voice was stunningly melodious, and he'd fill the gaps with the filthiest laugh I've ever heard. It was absolutely alarmingly compelling. He asked a couple of passing Asian ladies if they were Chinese, and being Korean, they were immensely offended by this, an offence he could not understand.

Eventually, running out of ladies to sing at, he fixed on me, still dancing his egg with that unstoppable rhythm,

'Hey! Where are you from my man?'

'Manchester!'

'Manchester! Manchester! Wonderful! I love Scotland, so many fish. So many fish.'

And pleased to have been given such a fertile theme to work with, he sang me a song about Highland Manchester's wonderful fish. This was definitely worth a few coins.

A few streets above this scene, another busker was working the street, a young woman playing her fiddle. She wasn't really very good, knowing perhaps half a dozen tunes, whose tempo wavered and tuning was questionable. It was very much an approximation of the tradition we nominally shared. She was nice looking and wore a pretty dress, not details I'd normally record as being important were it not that her case was overflowing with coins. This really then was the truth of street performance, a superficial pursuit. I was cross for a bit, feeling cynical and self-pitying. I'm a decent player, hardly the best fiddler out there, but I know I can play a bit, and there I'd been, playing my heart away for a few pounds an hour, and here was a young woman who couldn't really play racking up heaps because she was better looking, better presented, and frankly, more female than me. I tried to pretend that I was cross for Liv instead, who'd dressed for herself, not an audience, and who was playing quality music that inspired her for just a few coins. But in truth it was jealousy and ugly entitlement on my part.

'Those should be my coins', I thought to myself as numerous passing men lightened the load on their wallets, finding myself quite unable to enjoy someone else having a good day.

But such an attitude probably says more about me than anyone else. I already know that street performance is largely superficial, and I play up to it in my own way, adopting the mantle of the scruffy anonymous drifter as I go round, not that it's much of a step from who I normally am. I could dress up in a flamboyant way, play tunes people have actually heard before, and I'd certainly make more money. But it would spoil my constructed sense of self as I did it. Anonymity has served me well and I wouldn't swap what I've learned as this character for some more coins. In truth I was just annoyed to see someone doing better than me on my own instrument, and once I realised this, I was embarrassed with myself. I'd have been fine if she'd played something else. If there was anything to feel peeved about, I decided, it should be the blokes who so readily hand a coin over to a pretty face regardless of the music. I wondered if I did that. I probably did, without recognising it in myself.

'Do you want the spot?' she asked, noticing my fiddle, a generous gesture further highlighting the delicate masculine fragility of my grumpiness.

'No, it's fine.' I replied.

Whatever else busking round England has been, the contemplation time it has afforded me has been invaluable, allowing me to think my way round things that I'd either have responded to on an emotional level, or simply just taken for granted. Filling a place in the street for hours on end has the effect of slowly making you a dispassionate bystander, not just to what goes on around you but also to your own feelings.

After another fifteen minutes, she judged herself to have made enough coins, and poured them all into a bag with a resounding crescendo. Maybe £50 for an hour's work, a figure I have not even got half way to on my best days. I gave the same spot a go, and played with all my soul: £3 in half an hour. But as I reminded myself, for me, the busking has always been secondary to the story. I looked up as I played. Across the street on the first floor, the large window had a sign that read 'Massage Training Centre' and a lady was dancing and waving merrily at me from there. Having caught my eye, she gave me a big thumbs up and continued to dance on the spot. I imagined she must be in massage training, dancing all up and down some poor bloke's back to my music. He'd never be the same again. A passer by stopped me, asked about the music and took a card, interested in the project.

This is the point of what I do, really. On those rare moments when you catch someone's interest through the quality of what you do, they really take note, get to know you, and perhaps follow your work from here. In truth, my main impediment to making any money in Brighton was that it was festival time and there were street performers everywhere. A piano here, two guitars there, fire jugglers over there, street artists of all sorts. I had no way of standing out. A homeless man stopped me as I walked along in thought.

'Scuse me mate, do you have any change?'

'Sorry, no.'

And it was true. I imagined myself at the pearly gates being interrogated by St Peter.

'Why didn't you give the beggar some change?'

'Because I bought a small rubber duck for £7.99, sir.'

And St Peter would reply 'You idiot' before pulling the lever that opened the trapdoor, and not giving me a second thought.

A snapped skateboard was stacked in two halves outside Sports Direct. The day was coming to a close. I made my way back to my car. Another homeless man had created vibrant works of art with chalk on the floor around his drab pile of belongings. A far more worthy attempt at entertainment than my own had been today. I'd look for him tomorrow when I had some coins to spare.

I headed to my accommodation in Worthing, where a couple of musicians I'd met at a festival the previous summer and who were following my blog had offered to sort me out with bed and breakfast if I ever came their way. The coastline was busy, every inch of the shore put to some purpose, crazy golf, ship repairs, docks, a fort, dozens of old boats dragged up above the tideline and converted into quirky houses. This part of the South coast is amongst the most intense landscapes in England. Shoreham contains a fort built in 1857 to defend against Napoleon III. There's a cafe next door called 'Food for Fort' and I wasn't sure how I felt about it. Worthing appeared quiet and sleepy, but a quick wander through at night and a pint in a small pub isn't enough to draw many conclusions. Perhaps another day. For now, it was back to Brighton in the morning.

Brighton Palace Pier is the last pier standing now. Its near neighbour, the skeletal and collapsing West Pier, now looks much like that clichéd final sinking hand extending from cinematic quicksand. Brighton itself is bohemian and modern, a contemporary cultural sphere the remaining pier steadfastly refuses to embrace. It was a saturated morning with thick sheets of rain blowing off the hungry sea, where engorged grey clouds grew fatly from an indistinguishable horizon and hurtled overhead. Abused loudspeakers full of water tried to play 'It's not Unusual' at me as I walked down the boards with my head down against the weather. Each hut along the pier contained a single glum worker in a thick jacket bringing frying oil up to temperature or loading candy floss machines. A gang of weather-beaten men replaced rotten slats in a taped off section.

Piers are pretty strange, when you think about it. 'Let's build an expensive-to-maintain, uninsurable and precarious structure out to the middle of the sea that people can fall through and off, and then cover it with terrible things.' They get battered by winter storms and catch fire in the summer. They are invariably packed with low quality refreshments and dismal amusements, the larger examples also boasting funfairs. They haven't really altered in my lifetime, when all around them the world has moved on immeasurably. Yet they survive and even thrive when the world that created them is long forgotten.

The gents smelled terrible, mixing all the usual nasal signs of hygienic overload with a striking extra note of rotten fish. The roller coaster at the far end of the pier played 'Take a Chance on Me' by ABBA, but a sign said 'Closed owing to adverse weather conditions'. The man who took the money sat wrapped in his hoodie with head in hands, a self-imposed stasis, programmed to wake only in the event of better weather.

Inside the dome was an amusement arcade, the same as every other amusement arcade, with electric racehorses, the ubiquitous penny machines with their endlessly sliding tiers of coins, and cheap toy animals forever ungrabbed by cheating cranes. I had a few 2ps from the day before, and chose to invest one in an Irish themed penny machine covered in Leprechauns. It was playing the same ten jarring bars of cod-Irish music disjointedly over and over. My lucky coin jammed in the mechanism before even making it to the pushers, bringing an entirely new level of disappointment to proceedings. I was one of the first in for the day, preceded only by the lady at the refreshments hatch, selling instant coffee, KitKats, and Tango. She stared out at her workplace blankly, already wishing the day done. The rain pelted the roof like white noise and the flashing mechanical leprechauns endlessly sang their manic song.

Unwilling to lose many more coins to electric oblivion I returned to the walkways. The sea was heaving and slurping against the cast iron legs of the pier like so many molten zombies furiously trying to grab a hold of the soft human flesh walking above.

I loved this pier. I loved that there was nothing new or original about it. Nothing you haven't seen at a dozen other seaside towns. You'd go to it and perhaps tell relatives; 'We went to the pier' but nothing more, because no further description would be needed. In a thousand years, tourists will arrive in space ships, park their hover-boards and go and waste a few coins on the penny machines before taking a ride round the haunted hotel and eating candy floss and cheap sausages. Piers exist, people still come to them in great numbers, so there are no market pressures to change a thing. It's hard to imagine one put to a different and more highbrow use.

It is the mediocrity that I love, and I mean that in the best possible way. Life is mediocre for the most part. Nearly everything we do, every day is just run of the mill, and if you can't love that you will struggle to be happy. There are exceptional moments in life, but they are rare and you can't just wait for them to come along in order to be satisfied. It was much like me, I decided, this pier. I'm not the best fiddle player, but I'm good enough. It doesn't make a lot of difference how good you are after a certain level. It's whether you're on time, friendly, and professional. There are many better players than me, but it's not improving at the fiddle that would make the difference. Most people wouldn't be able to tell, any more than I could tell you which one of two professional gardeners was best. Same with busking. Quite simply, can you put a smile on someone's face? Pretensions to the exceptional aren't really helpful and only serve to spoil your own experience, as I'd learnt yesterday. Better to be truthful to yourself and enjoy the ride.

This pier was honest. I could almost have written my description before I got onto it, but I loved every minute. It was comfortable and a safe space. In a world of confusing change, it's good to know that my 2p will always be welcome on the Brighton Palace Pier. Perhaps if it were exceptional it would fail. People don't come to the pier to be challenged. They come for predictable comforts. Maybe we as artists need to remember this, and celebrate the vast suburbs of the human experience. Mediocrity walking amongst mediocrity, I was at home and happy.

I stood on the slats back near where the pier made landfall again, and watched through rain coated glasses as the waves furiously broke their foam on the shingle, like a giant horn of plenty tipped over by the boot of a careless Viking colossus and forever spilling its boozy contents towards Brighton, until a break in the weather threatened to spoil my reverie. Patches of blue sky began to assemble in the distance and head towards the coast. The rain lessened, and the other pier became apparent in the lifting gloom.

West Pier closed in 1975, finally falling victim to arson and storm damage in the early years of this century. All that's left now is the skeletal frame of a theatre half-collapsed, surrounded by red navigation buoys marking the extent of the former pier like a chalk outline round a murder victim. It's wholly out of character with the rest of Brighton, forlorn, peaceful, resigned and declining. Mute.

Where once a theatre entertained thousands, the final rotting strands of metal mark a spot that is collapsing into nature. Where theatres on the land once stood there will be something else, maybe a blue plaque. Here there will be nothing but sea. It's not coming back. A ruined pier is a peculiar kind of melancholic. Unreachable and beyond help.

I walked up and down the shore, trying to line up the best image I could of the wreckage so that I had a photo to refer people to when they asked me the question; 'How do you see yourself in fifteen years?' There was no info board on the land. The traveller is invited to stare at the carcass and draw their own conclusions.

On the land where the pier entrance would have been, one can go up rather than out. The i360 tower is an observation tower with an ascending pod. It's the tallest building for miles around and carries paying tourists 530ft above the ground, promising views of the area – on better days than this, anyway. It doesn't have a toilet, I was told, and those caught short must go in an aluminium bucket behind a curtain. Buskers can't afford such frivolities, preferring in my case to save their money for nice food and steam train rides. I was happy enough with the view at street level.

The rain had finally stopped and I rushed for a busk before

all the other buskers came out from hibernation. My first hour went well but quickly dropped off as the hordes of performers filled the streets. I tried a second pitch on a pedestrianised street, but an implausible clothes shop called 'Mootoo' suddenly gave birth to a sweating man who furiously exclaimed that it was so loud he couldn't speak to his customers. I looked inside. There were no customers. This upset him even more and he foamingly demanded I went away. 'I rather liked it', said a passing lady. This was too much and he stormed back inside, screaming. Even his mannequins looked angry as I packed up.

It was no great loss. Busking just wasn't going to work for me here. There were too many others at it, too much competition and I couldn't stand out, not a middle aged man with a fiddle, who despite my efforts to smarten up overnight had not managed to advance his attire beyond 'Geography teacher' in the glamour and sophistication stakes. Best to wander again. I headed inland towards the railway station, down narrow streets filled with quirky shops. Beyond the end of all this was St Barts, easily my favourite building in Brighton. A truly colossal church, built of Victorian red brick as if a celestial engine shed had been lowered down from above, it towers over the area just as the cotton mills tower over the little towns of Lancashire. It felt industrial, lurking on ragged streets away from the bustle of town.

I found a pint of Harvey's Sussex mild in a back street boozer called The Mitre. It was my kind of pub. The carpets were ragged and ancient to the point of colourlessness. The upholstery bald and torn. There was horse racing on the telly and a friendly black dog grown fat and sociable on pork scratchings and crisps. The locals were professional drinkers, there for a decent afternoon session. The landlord regarded me with scepticism as I came in, clearly believing that I was a trendy who was most likely lost and would soon leave in bewilderment and for years after regale his friends with stories of how he took a wrong turn and somehow fell forty years backwards in time.

Customers slipped out for cigarettes, usually accompanied by the dog. This was old-fashioned Brighton, hiding in plain sight, just two streets away from the shops that sold crystals and fudge. My pint of mild was poured.

'That'll be £3.'

I paid in coins, already knowing I'd have another.

The Capital

I TRAVELLED up to Bruce Grove to drop my bag off. I was staying with my friend Oscar, who writes horoscopes for the *Daily Mail* among other publications, a job that makes my life seem fairly normal. He made coffee and I asked if he had any advice. He began dismantling a recalcitrant fitted cupboard with an electric screwdriver and considered my request.

'Jupiter, the planet of adventure and opportunity has just returned to Sagittarius for the first time in twelve years. This bodes well for long journeys and quests. Jupiter is the planet of luck and growth, but also of excess, too much.'

This was pleasingly vague, good advice in any situation, and I took it to mean 'have a laugh, don't get too pissed'. I set out again with just my fiddle on my back, determined to get stuck into this quest, and hoping I'd recognise any missteps into excess before the authorities did. My train took me back in, to Liverpool Street. The wind blew, carrying drizzle and bits of paper, and it was clear I couldn't busk today. I was still glad to have my fiddle with me though. With it, I'm a musician, without it just some guy with a notepad with nowhere to go. The world talks to you in a different and more open voice when you carry an instrument. I skirted the edge of the City of London, the square mile of traded value that powers the national ship like an unseen screw, deep beneath the hull, control room locked and anonymous to the passengers. I walked by vast premises whose entire ground floors were glass sided, blank and granite faced, featureless so as to give nothing away, the world traded in bytes just fleetingly within. The pubs were achingly generic as I headed across the south edge of Islington into Camden, all sense of history here gone, each street renovated or built over again and again with feverish regularity.

A man came down the street shouting loudly. The modern trend towards mobile tech and hands free communication means that when someone heads towards you hollering and gesticulating wildly, it is no longer possible to tell if they're a nutter or merely on a phone call.

I wrote this thought down in my notepad, and felt a sudden wave of depressing self-awareness. Here I was, just another struggling and aspiring artist in London. What a cliché. So much more fun to be that in Dudley or Ashington. In a world of brain-drains from the provinces, I'm the slug that prefers to come up the plug hole instead.

A man in hi-vis in front of me checked his watch, stopped, pulled out a prayer mat, used an app to identify the direction of Mecca and got on with prayer. It occurred to me that there must logically be a single point on earth where every direction is equally far to Mecca, and consequently no need to orient oneself. This didn't seem a revelation worth sharing, so I carried on.

In Exmouth market, a saxophonist and an accordionist argued bitterly over a busking pitch in a language I couldn't identify. London contains little in itself unusual, but the sheer quantity of what it does contain and the speed at which things happen make it a fast-forward kaleidoscope for all the senses. I do not fit here. My shoulders tense up, my hands rest on my pockets, fearful of robbery, my eyes flit from left to right. It is overwhelming, and I understood why the Londoner pulls their personal space back inside their own head, a thousand bodies pressed up close on the tube but not somehow overlapping. The eyes are open, but they do not see, other than to guide the journey. To live London day by day, in full sensual experience is too much, and untrained and overstimulated I needed to stop, a country boy submitting and repentant before the sensory circus.

Below St Paul's Cathedral, that great greying mass of stone, which in the dusk and drizzle seemed like a vast beached whale, dead and hopeless, and around which the evening tide of mankind was falling, the millennium bridge crosses to the South bank of the Thames. Between the two, in the wide open walkway a figure was begging to man and God. She was on her front, resting on her knees and lying forward across her few possessions, covered in foreign clothing, the shape of her projecting backside giving the clue as to her likely gender. She was face down, motionless, and holding a cardboard cup up in a single outstretched hand. Probably Syrian? Come from God knows where on a journey I could not imagine, for reasons I could never fully understand, to die here of poverty, surrounded by one of the greatest concentrations of wealth ever known. Perhaps she was already dead and set in this terrible form. I'd watched for several minutes and she hadn't moved in her posture of complete supplication. Rush hour approaching, the suited and power-dressed came by and went past this appalling traffic island, her ragged despair made only more heartbreaking by the clean good order she was set within. A perfectly swept space, every flag equally set, granite and marble, Portland stone. The finest contemporary artist could not have designed such flawless wretchedness. But in the emotional whirlwind of London, you do not, cannot engage unless you have chosen to do so before you set out.

In one small town I know, the first rough sleeper was met with astonishment. Clothes were provided, food, councillors were rung, accommodation was found. More rough sleepers came, the astonishment faded, and they became street furniture. Shock is hard to sustain. Compassion an easier constant, but in a time of hurt, rationed for our own sanities. The first rule of charity is don't make yourself a charity case, physically or mentally. I sat on my fiddle case, a suitable distance back and watched.

A moment of clarity came. In putting aside other things to do what I'm doing, I'd chosen to make it my job to sit here in the rain and watch, to try to understand. Watching, trying to understand, then hating the situations you find is an expensive use of emotions and thought. I can only afford to sit here being judgemental and angry because I've chosen, perhaps selfishly, to abandon other work. The tapestry of people moving past were finishing another difficult day in a demanding job, and London leaves you little capacity for unknown others. Senses are blunted and a universe of problems is far too much to demand individual attentions.

One kind man found some change, and she moved a little, a thank you of sorts. I'd seen enough. I shook out my remaining change, the scraps left from my previous trip, and dropped them off too. She said something I took as thanks, but we had no language to share. Her story would therefore go unwritten, although it was undoubtedly better than mine, and me the second poorest person in the street. I thought of the criticism I might receive for perceiving her so. 'She's playing a part.' 'She's fooled you.' 'You soft bugger.' I looked closely. Her fingernails were stained. Her skin, even on those slender bones was wrinkled and old, devastated by time, salt, and distance. Her possessions, few and wrapped in wasted scraps of plastic. This is unfakeable, the difference between the 'stressed' jeans one sees in shops and the filth wreckage of clothes worn into bitter poverty.

The hopelessness of her cause was incomprehensible. The wealth that surrounded us in such contemptuous grandeur was not worldly. It could not be ripped off the walls, emptied from the vaults and redistributed, only destroyed. Offices here were bare to the point of Spartanism. The wealth that flows through the City of London, almost limitless, inconceivable to mortals like me, unprintable in cash, would evaporate like a cruel trickster's punch line the moment the revolutionaries entered the room. For wealth here is digital, in futures, derivatives, stocks, its engines the particular intelligences and educations of the custodians, its corpus the electrons flowing through machines. It has no physical manifestation, there are no vaults of gold and jewels. Ephemeral, digital wealth is quite unredistributable in this context. Nobody is ever going to walk past a beggar and drop 0.1 per cent of Samsung's shares into their chewed and failing Subway coffee cup.

Physical currency is a leveller. Maybe you have it, maybe you don't, but we all share the same one, with hopes of getting some in the future, a continuum on which we can still all be found. In a digital world, this is no longer the case. In money as confidence, digital transactions, electrical memory, we have created an underclass who not only have no money, but who cannot ever hope to have any. They cannot touch that which does not manifest as a physical token, for to hold modern money, you must first own the digital interlocutor. The cashless society won't just knacker my chances of making a living busking, it will literally kill the poor. Drop below the threshold of digital citizen and you can never come back. All you need to have to use a coin is a hand to hold it in. Digital wealth requires so much more. This wretched soul had picked the wrong place to ask for coins, few here used them. The beggars and buskers, the desperate and unwilling will concentrate themselves in the poorest towns where physical currency lasts longest. It will get crowded and ugly.

If we cock this country up, there will be no physical treasury to pawn to smooth the transition. The wealth will drain from this square mile more surely and swiftly than if the fixtures and fittings of a great country home had been removed and taken away on the bailiff's wagon. The City of London is a confidence trick played by us all on each other. The whole lot could leave down a drainpipe like Super Mario and appear in another zone altogether in seconds, leaving us grasping at smoke.

On the tube it was packed tight. Bodies sullen braced against the ebb and flow of travel, heads unmoving, eyes unfocused. I looked all round, still apparently incapable of acting like a Londoner. One beautiful young woman broke ranks and flashed a smile at me and I allowed myself the briefest of fantasies, imagining a classified advert in tomorrow's Evening Standard: 'Looking for the fat, ginger, bald, badly dressed, prematurely aged man on the Victoria line with the worry lines and likely gout, I was the tall black woman in the red coat...'

I met an old friend, Jess, for dinner, and we caught our lives up. She delighted in reminding me of a time, years ago when I received in my busking collection a detailed and exquisite hand-drawn map showing me the way to the job centre. She had just started in pupillage at a major law firm and was relishing every minute of it, having returned from a year in America working on the defence of capital cases. A painfully sharp character with a good heart, I was glad to see her doing so well. London is such a tough place to be and it gave me a positivity to carry into the next day. We dined at an excellent pizza place run by an Italian family and it was queuing out the door on a Wednesday. Here was the best of London exemplified in opportunity, both for my friend and the proprietors of the restaurant, just as I'd seen the worst earlier. It is not superior or inferior, just richer and denser in every way. Greater opportunities, deeper holes to fall into. Intensity of all things.

Stoke Newington and Hackney

'WHERE should I busk?' I asked Oscar over a coffee and bagel the next morning.

'Maybe give Stoke Newington a go? It's pretty middle class and away from the licensed districts. You might do well there.'

Between Hackney and Tottenham, Stoke Newington is a

thickening of one of those endless main roads that lead into London from every corner of England. I passed the Orthodox Jewish butchers, four young men worked inside, black net trilbies over perfect sprung curls. As the road moved on the shops became more Eastern European, each cafe with a small elderly woman in a head dress sitting on a low stool in a booth by the window furiously pounding endless flatbreads into great mounds. I wasn't ready to play yet, so I walked on and the road got poorer and even more diverse. After a mile or so I made it to Dalston Kingsland and the Ridley Road Market.

Here in the working class reality of North London, all the corners of the world collide. Sometimes I feel like I stand out, like in the street in Smethwick, a white face and ginger beard in a Sikh town, but here there were a huge variety of different ethnicities, mine just one of many. It was impossible for anyone to stand out, no matter where they'd come from. The smell of the cooking of a hundred cultures, each with their own subtle spices and flavours, mixed in the air to create the culinary and aromatic equivalent of when all the shades of paint are mixed together to create the universal definitive brown. It was a metaphor for London itself. The breadth and depth of culture and experience here is too overwhelming to take in as a whole, but must be broken down and experienced bit by bit.

Within twenty yards, I could buy goat meat, Mediterranean fish, hair care products, soap, an incredible variety of clothes, fruit and veg, from Caribbean folks, Cockneys, Muslims and probably at least one person who could plausibly claim to be all three. Half way along was the 'Harmer Ridley Road Shopping Centre', the most desolate shopping arcade I have ever seen. The tiny handful of remaining functional units mostly sold Reggae music or clothing repairs. A sign on the walls said 'Respect your neighbours. Please be quiet. (No shouting).' At the end of the market proper, a sort of shanty market had grown, business set up in welded together shipping containers, all run by black women, the street lighting on wooden pylons made out of bits of packing crates. One was a haircare business called 'Linda the Magnificent'. In the next container, a lady sewed wedding dresses under a fluorescent tube.

It's one thing to have equality in the law, but most of this market exists because equality is about more than just the legal side. Perhaps you need ethnic specific hair care products, tights that suit your skin colour, food that fits your diet, all things you won't find much of in a supermarket. The British high street is still seriously white when it comes to the products it sells. Shopping remains ghettoised for many, and it's hard to see it changing much when so many small communities all need representing. The sheer variety of different things on sale wouldn't fit in even the largest supermarket.

My presence was making people uncomfortable. Men watched me from a container that had 'NO URINATE' scrawled on it in paint. A lady from the general supplies container came out and stared me. The atmosphere began to feel tense. I didn't belong here and I knew I didn't have the words to explain my presence.

Back in the main market I noted down details. A single mannequin leg in a puddle. A giant heap of trotters. The spongy yellowness of tripe. Butchery was anatomical, rough hewn pieces of animal divided into mounds of similar parts, in contrast to the neat and disembodied cuts the white English prefer. Trotters, heads, haunches, organs, all just a few stitches and a bolt of lightning away from a serious problem for Hackney council.

As I bimbled around aimlessly, a dawning realisation came upon me. I was stage shy. Two days in London and I hadn't actually busked yet. The overwhelming totality of London, the sensory overload had left me shy and mute. My fiddle was upon my back, case unopened, frustrated and humming with untapped energy. I walked back to Stoke Newington and steeled myself. It would hardly be 'Busking England' if I just stood and looked at stuff. Besides, I was skint.

Iceland was next to a building sheathed in scaffolding which created a natural busker's hollow on the busy main road. After an obligatory wee in the Wetherspoons across the way, I finally took my fiddle out and started to play. A man on the pedestrian crossing, having decided to run across on a red man, dropped his phone, and had a split second choice between phone and life. He opted to rescue his phone, causing a cacophony of squealing breaks and horns, and he escaped without injury, a survival that would have given Darwin cause for a major redraft.

Despite my fears, coins began to accumulate. Middle aged black women were particularly generous, often walking past before turning with a smile and a coin for me. This is always the most rewarding, when you win over someone who wasn't thinking about making a contribution, but who on hearing your music is compelled to find something. Things were going well, and I warmed my fiddle up to full volume. A man approached me with the sort of pseudo-confident walk that always spells trouble. He had a rainproof hi-vis jacket and a tabard that said, generically 'Security'.

'You need to stop.'

'Why?'

'You can't do that here.'

'Why not?'

'It's against the law.'

I'd done my research on this before I set off. Some areas of London, such as Covent Garden and Camden Town are regulated and licensed. This bit was not. A website done in conjunction with the Mayor of London's office set the rules out clearly. I knew I was in the clear.

'It's not. Some areas of London are regulated, but this isn't.'

He gestured at my open case.

'That's begging. You're in breach of the Vagrancy Act.'

This was rubbish. Case law in the 1980s found that the Vagrancy Act did not forbid busking, so long as you don't actively ask for money. If he'd just said he didn't like it and it was annoying him, I'd have moved. But I hate bullshitters, and I particularly hate that breed of minor authoritarian who seem get off on the exercise of petty power. I stood my ground and told him that he'd have to come back with a police officer if he wanted me gone.

'You're causing a disturbance for the employees', he gestured into Iceland. This was also bullshit. He'd come from the other end of the road, not in there, and with an unamplified fiddle and double glazing, I doubted they'd heard a note. Oh how I hated him now, generic minor authority figure, natural controlling nature given false legitimacy by his 'Security' tabard. Who was he anyway? Who was he even securing? He was just another street performer like me, I decided, and I was here first.

'How many people have specifically complained?'

He couldn't answer this and just glared for a bit. I continued.

'I'm doing nothing wrong. There's a website on this, sponsored by the Mayor of London. Read it.'

I'd called his bluff. He left in a huff of vague threats and empty frustrations. Being 6ft 3in and fairly mean-looking has some benefits. I was not exhilarated by this successful rebuttal, but upset and I found myself shaky and distracted. I hate confrontation, and will only do it if I have to. My next few tunes were rubbish and I made nothing. I got a grip of myself and saved the slot. A Deliveroo driver went out of his way to tell me that he'd heard me play whilst stuck in traffic and had enjoyed it. After two hours and ten minutes I had £43 to show. It felt like a good effort in the circumstances.

That night I played a house concert in Hackney. I'd been booked by a couple who'd seen my previous house concert in Hastings. I made my way over in the early evening and walked around to get to know it. The area suddenly seemed familiar. I knew these streets. I'd been here years before to meet up with a young woman. I'd drunk too much, been ill, and not been in any fit state to manage the trip to Brighton we'd planned the next day. Indeed my personal shame at 'never having visited Brighton' had remained for years a symbol of the excess Oscar had warned me about. The whole reminiscence put me in a strange and melancholic mood.

My hosts could not have been kinder. They sorted me out with dinner, a glass of wine, and set the living room up for the concert ahead. In rows across the back wall was the largest and most interesting record collection I have ever seen. They put on a mood-setter, a doom laden and atmospheric CD soundtrack to a 1968 film about Joan of Arc, played on a single pump organ in fifty-eight unbroken arrhythmic and intense minutes.

Guests arrived and were each dulled into emotional submission by the harrowing emissions of the pump organ. The other housemate, a novelist, had clearly lived there long enough to become immune to this and was soon telling me excitedly about his previous night out, in a squat full of psycho-geographers who called themselves 'The Invisible League' and played 'Urban Poker', where a discarded playing card, found anywhere in the world, must be picked up and duly catalogued, noting the time and place, the number and suit, and the ethnography of the collection point. These cards are then taken to meets, and discussed in earnest detail. Sometimes years can pass between a pick up, but the focus never wavers.

Months later I picked up a king of diamonds at the second lock of the Rochdale nine, on the canal as it heads through central Manchester, beneath the buildings, just up from the gay village, and where signage specifically forbids sexual encounters amongst the dripping foundation pillars of Victorian architecture.

It's a long way from Manchester to Hackney. I was amongst a very different social circle now, and felt a little adrift, far from home, meat pies, Bovril, and rugby league. I'd rather have been the audience than the act tonight, would have loved to be able to sit at the back with a bottle of wine in the low lighting and watch someone else do all the work. But at 8pm a smiling and earnest audience was before me. There were pots of crunchy quinoa roof tiles and bottles of organic Rioja to enjoy. I played my show, tunes from the corners of England I've come to know, stories I've written up. The economic devastation of the Midlands, a wet day in Redcar. My jokes didn't get laughs and I worried I wasn't going down well and relied on professionalism to get me to half time. But it was going well. My audience were a serious crowd, hanging on to the stories, and they asked more questions as the night drew on, genuinely intrigued.

I dropped all pretensions of performance, stopped trying to tell jokes, and just spoke and played from the heart. Here in the last quarter of my concert, they were truly with me. I should have got here much sooner, but it's a lesson learnt. Read your audience and adapt!

After the concert we all talked the weighty talk of the politically frustrated classes. After a few glasses of wine I somehow ended up saying something awful like: 'True tradition lies on the fulcrum between past and future' altogether too loudly during a sudden lull in other conversation, and embarrassed, was forced to follow it with: 'Well that's the wankiest thing I've ever said', which produced my best laugh of the night.

Oscar had come along to the concert too, and seeing my social and intellectual floundering sensibly gently extracted me from further humiliation soon after, taking me home via the 24-hour bagel shop. I was done in, worn out from an intense day.

London seemed far less condensed on Saturday as I went back to Euston for my train home. Perhaps I'd hardened up, perhaps the city was sleeping. A busker occupied one of the official spots in the underground station, and I dropped him a quid.

'I'm thinking of applying for a spot like this. Is it worth it?'

'Yeah, they only audition a few times a year, but it's great, you go for it.'

Return to London

A FEW weeks later, I headed into London again without much of a clear plan. A last minute gig had come up that would already take me into the South and I decided to stay on and wing it for a few days.

Stockport station was damp and over-crowded as I left for the big city. The fragmented remains of a tropical storm had caused delays on the route, and my train was one of the few that hadn't been cancelled. I was a day late setting off myself, owing to an upset stomach. The announcement that I would be 'delayed by wind' summed my week up altogether too well.

There were not enough seats for all the extra passengers, so I sat myself down on my fiddle case in the vestibule. I've always had a re-enforced case for exactly this reason.

BING BONG

The tannoy went off.

'As you can see we are now doing 50mph due to the emergency speed restriction. This is it all the way in now. If you get bored, you can play I-spy out of the window. It's going slow enough. Alternatively, you can join me in the shop which is located in coach C, buy a few beers and we can get tanked up.'

Our train manager was clearly already resigned to a depressing journey. We picked up further passengers at Macclesfield and the overcrowding became such that he had to take emergency action. At the press of a button, the train became declassified, seat reservations evaporated from the mini-screens and first class was dissolved entirely. We were now all equals in a classless society. A river of migrant commuters set off for what had been the first class end, passing my improvised seat, anxious to make the most of their revolutionary potential and take control of the free newspapers. At Stoke, we picked up even more comrades and the corridors became too crowded for much further upwards mobility.

Our socialist revolution quickly passed through the stages. By Lichfield, the first class buffet service had been abandoned, undersupplied and without incentive to serve those who might not have paid. By Rugby, passengers were darkly complaining that it wasn't fair that some had made it to first class when others were stuck down here. 'I had a look in there and I couldn't tell between those who were actual first class and those who had moved in!' Animal Train continued slowly south. The standard class buffet car ran out of enthusiasm and closed, no prospect of a restocking at Milton Keynes, where previously eager passengers saw our progress towards utopia and chose to stay on the platform and wait for something better rather than join us.

Finally, nearly two hours late, we pulled into Euston and the revolution had fizzled out into apathy, class distinctions reasserting as suddenly and surely as the during the appearance of the naval officer at the end of *Lord of the Flies*, compounded by an announcement explaining how bona-fide first class travellers could claim reimbursement for having to share their journey with the plebs who'd eaten all their freebies. Our experiment with a fairer society had failed and only really succeeded in causing both buffet cars to abandon service, making us all worse off. Maybe we hadn't tried hard enough, didn't believe in the revolution fervently enough. Perhaps we should have compelled them to continue buffet service for the greater good of all and the glory of the people.

I escaped the platform and engaged in the first activity that any Northerner does upon alighting in London, and gathered round the tube map with all the other northerners to make lighthearted comments about how big it is. There are so many possibilities, so many sub-divisions, many I'd never heard of at all, each the size of one of the small market towns I'd been slowly making my way round over the previous months. Somebody must know them all, some polymath, but would they know the communities that lived there? What they felt like?

I had appealed on social media for somewhere to stay and was offered a space in North London by a Canadian lady called Kaeridwyn who despite only having met me twice before was nevertheless happy to turn over her keys and entire house to me whilst she went away for a couple of nights.

'Please treat it like home. Burn my incense, eat my avocados,' she said as she handed me the keys.

Such was the generosity of the offer that it would have felt rude to mention that my northern upbringing hadn't really taught me what to do with either incense or avocados. I think I know what avocados look like but I'm not sure I'd recognise incense if I saw it. If it looks anything similar, she might find herself returning home to a heap of smouldering avocados.

I'd had an incredibly long day before, driving hundreds of miles and performing two gigs, and so was content to wander without a plan. I set off from Clapton and headed for the City of London. A large Audi was illegally parked on a crossing. I looked inside and saw that the passenger seat and footwell were filled with half-finished packs of Haribo. Last time I'd walked through the square mile of the City of London, seven or so years ago, I'd been stopped by a Japanese news crew shooting vox pops for their article on the UK economy, somehow mistaking me for a banker or politician. I'd given colourful answers, and have always wondered if they went out on air.

I saw the shining green domes and gold ornamentation of the Bank of England, and immediately thought of the mosques in our northern towns raised too in worship to their god. Next door, the Bank of China took up a large if less ornate building, keeping watch, a location chosen to gently remind us of our relative places in the world in the 21st century. It was Sunday, and the city was quiet, with just a few people walking the streets.

The Bank of England building is a fortress in evening dress, no windows at street level, just walls that exude thickness and permanence. The grand old buildings of London from which we're governed, clustered as tightly as bodies on a rush hour tube train, must encourage a particular kind of conservatism, living and working in architecture that reminds one of who we once were. In contrast to say the Bundestag in Berlin, a modern building set in space whose physical presence makes one think of who we could be.

At London Bridge an open topped cruise ship chugged slowly through, beneath me, speakers pumping out 'Spice up your Life' to the smattering of worried looking tourists trapped on the top deck.

On the South Bank, thousands of people were making a day of it in the sunshine. Outside the Tate Modern, a man with a net and a bucket of soapy water was making bubbles for the children to chase. He wasn't collecting money, so someone must be paying his wage. He wore the sallow, neutral face of a man who was paid by the hour, not by the bubble. I wanted to join in and chase the bubbles down the bank of the river, but sadly, society considers this deviant behaviour for a bald, childless man in his mid-thirties, so I contented myself with a seat on a nearby bench and just popping the odd straggler that floated my way. A child chasing a particularly large bubble tripped forward onto her face, the bump causing her chewing gum to eject out onto the path before her. She lay there on her front for a second, deciding whether to pick it up and continue chewing.

'Don't you bloody dare', shouted her mother.

I walked slowly through the bottlenecks of Westminster Bridge, caused by the blocks put in place after the recent terror attack. A van had mounted the kerb to run people like us over, just because we happened to be there, and because we were in the shadow of this symbol of statehood, the Palace of Westminster, currently reflecting the national mood by being largely covered in scaffolding awaiting an overhaul that could last decades and whose cost and benefits are unknowable and disputed.

Despite the overdue addition of Millicent Fawcett, the statues in Parliament square remain a disappointment, as statues so often are. No matter the pose, dramatic or dignified, whether exaggerated in flowing, windswept grandeur above us or cast as humble and human amongst us, each recipient is somewhat reduced in gravitas by pigeon shit and traffic cones, the two universal levellers of status. Busts are no better, and just imply that the budget wasn't there to do it properly. In the unlikely event of someone ever wishing to immortalise me in this way, I hope they cast something non-committal, like an elbow or a lower leg. Round the corner, George V had a pigeon in place at the summit, enjoying the view, crowning the Feudal pyramid all by himself and cooing gently to his subjects.

Down Whitehall and past the Cenotaph, a row of red phone boxes was buzzing with groups of tourists taking turns at photographing each other inside and alongside them. The red phone box is one of those national symbols that resonate far more with the foreigner than the English themselves. I wondered if they still worked. The first two no longer had a phone in them, but the third did, and I waited for my turn. There was a minimum call charge of 60p, and I rang my parents, who were out. Exiting the booth, there were many eyes on me as I did my walk of shame, having become a Bateman cartoon, 'The man who made a call from a phone box', and I felt the red facedness of having committed a terrible social faux-pas in full view.

By St James's Park, Frederick, the Duke of York was atop a huge column. 'He's got it right', I thought to myself, staring up at his distant crotch. If you must turn into a statue when you die, better to be on a column tall enough that nobody can tell if you're covered in shit or not.

Back in Clapton, I went out for dinner, choosing a pizza place on the main street. My grandma has recently acquired a tablet, and has taken to reading my blog, noting the regularity that I dine on pizza. 'Do you eat nothing else?' is her main comment, and I thought of her as I ordered tonight's, having been seated at the bar to avoid wasting valuable table space on a dubious looking lone diner, and perhaps isolate me from the door to ensure payment. She grew up in Hull during the Second World War, and I owed her a busking trip there at some point before I finished. I wondered what the pizza would be like in Hull.

This one was excellent, and the service good. The restaurant was run by a group of young people doing what many young people have to do to succeed: taking a chance on themselves. They were moving fast, that slightly too fast set of movements where you force your limbs to go a bit quicker than is natural in order to get everything done. I remembered it myself from mad nights working behind the bar as a student in Loughborough.

I walked down through North London to Bethnal Green. It took me an hour but there's always plenty to see. Bethnal Green has London's only winery, where drinkers sit amidst fermentation barrels. I popped my head in, but I fancied beer, not wine and went instead to a back street boozer where I was given a complimentary pot of donkey sausage with my pint.

South London

THE next day I set out for South London proper. I got to Greenwich so early that the street food stalls hadn't finished their first cook of the day and I had to wait for my breakfast. I tried busking on the last bit of road that leads up to the Cutty

Sark, the vast and elegant clipper built to bring tea back from India, now raised into the air on supports and turned into a museum. It's a spectacular achievement, both the original ship and the new setting. I didn't make much money, but I liked the space and enjoyed watching the families heading in for the Bank Holiday Monday, bright eyed, smiling parents and well scrubbed children in clean clothes. One fellow gave me a coin, and I thought to myself 'He looks just like Steve Knightley from Show of Hands', and thought no more of it.

About 11am, a trad jazz trio set up fairly nearby, and I decided I was no match for their euphonium. My friend Jon had been to university round here, and had suggested I try the Dog and Bell in Deptford for my lunch. It was about a mile away, and I walked out of the cosy centre of Greenwich, into a suburbia of featureless flats built on old docks. On one back road a docklands pub, signage just about readable as 'The Thames', stood boarded and colonised by plants, somehow undemolished. There was little else to hint at the old docklands character.

The Dog and Bell was indeed an excellent pub, whose proprietor took polite, professional interest in my travels. He told me that occasionally Jools Holland comes in, buys everyone a pint, and then plays the piano. There was then some debate at the bar about when this had last happened, and where the piano had been in those days. I finished my pie and walked up Deptford High Street. A mile from Greenwich, this is another world. Vastly multicultural, very poor, and largely open and trading on a bank holiday. I busked, mostly to see what would happen. A woman careered over to me on her bike. She was blind drunk. After a while of mumbling and fumbling for coins, she got over to me that her mother had died a year ago to the day. I said I was sorry for her loss. She tried asking me some questions but it didn't really make much sense, and my attempts to politely reply just felt empty and insincere.

'You sound like an advert', she finished, dismissively, before giving me £1.02 and wobbling off. There are some tough lives on Deptford High Street, and although plenty of people would give a coin, they were small coins to match the poverty. A plain white van drew up and two whole sheep carcasses were lumped into the butchers by a round fellow in a shabby white apron who carried them over his shoulder like they were sacks of coal.

I made my way back to Greenwich in the hope of earning enough that I could have a decent dinner. It didn't go well. The Jazzers were still at it, and the other spots around town just didn't work for me, being too busy or awkward. The last families were draining from the area, parents now weary and stressed, children stained and tired. Perhaps understandably, nobody was in a generous mood. Around 5:30pm I had made almost no money and was considering a tactical retreat to North London when I got on my phone and noticed that one of my friends was 'Attending the Show of Hands concert at the Cutty Sark this evening.' So it must have been Steve Knightley after all. I put a status on Facebook saying 'I think Steve Knightley just put 50p in my busking case' and decided to have one more go for the day. Cynically, if four hundred Show of Hands fans were heading to the Cutty Sark, I might just stand a chance of making a few quid busking outside.

I picked a spot outside the Gypsy Moth pub and got stuck in. It worked, folkies were in town for the gig, and many had come early for a pint and a meal. Coins began to gather in my case. My friend Emma came by heading to the gig and spotted me. 'Do you want a sandwich?' she asked. I said that would be nice. She came back from the shop five minutes later with a cheese sandwich, a chicken and bacon sandwich, a giant Scotch egg, an iced bun, and some hand wipes.

'Thank you! That's very generous.' I said

'It seemed a bit less patronising than putting money in your case. Let me buy you a pint.'

This was turning into a good night. I cheerily continued my

evening busk with a pint of nice beer and the warm evening sun. A foreigner gave me five euros. Coins piled up. Suddenly, Steve Knightley was back, striding towards me with purpose and an irked expression.

'You cheeky sod, it was at least a quid!' He tossed a pound coin in to make the point. 'Anyway, do you want a ticket to the show?'

Meekly, I said that I did, and he told me he'd put one on the door when he went back. I thanked him and marvelled at my good luck and the powers of social media. At ten to eight, I packed up and headed in. Mr Knightley hadn't been back yet so I blagged it to the door staff.

'So I was just busking over there, and that nice Mr Knightley came over and offered me a free ticket for the show, but he's not back yet. Er, can I come in?'

They looked me up and down, scruffy as I was, and covered in a soft dusting of street grime. It felt like I was perpetrating some terrible scam, but after some consulting, they decided it was too unlikely a story to have been made up and they let me in.

I enjoyed the show, under the keel of the great ship. An unlikely but iconic space. They're a consummate act, choosing and pacing material to perfectly fit the echoey, cathedralesque acoustic. And there's a thrill to watching a show just a few feet under a ship, a novel space to find oneself, and we all placed our trust in the engineers that raised this hull up into the air. It had not been the day I had expected. It had been a better one.

I sat on the tube train eating my sandwiches, iced bun, and Scotch egg and thinking about it all. A day that at 5pm had seemed like a footnote had blossomed into a series of entertaining incidents and a free concert. London is never dull.

The train out of London was relaxed compared to the way down. The quiet coach was peaceful, save the endless bonging of the tannoy: 'We have all kinds of hot drinks, tea, coffee, hot chocolate, sandwiches, beers, snacks. They're all available here in the buffet car in coach C. We take card or cash.' Just as I tucked back into my book, it bonged again. 'I'm afraid that I simply cannot open the tea cupboard. It's jammed solid. Until further notice, we have no tea. Repeat, no tea.'

An urgent murmur grew. No tea? This was a threat to civilisation far great than the collapse of the class system had been on the way down. Ten minutes later, we were saved.

BING BONG

'I have found a superhero and now we have tea... Lots of it.'

We picked up new passengers. A small child told me about the films of his hero 'Arnold Swatcheniser'. A woman with her friends and a crate of alcopops, heading for a big day out held a loud phone conversation in the seat behind me. Eventually in the course of conversation she asked her fellow travellers 'What coach are we in?' and I shouted 'The quiet one!'

Aylesbury

I ARRIVED at Aylesbury, dropping my things off with my friends, Jamie and Sam, who live in a new build on the edge of town in a massive development called Berryfields. From here it was half an hour's walk to the town centre. My stroll to the market square of Aylesbury took me down the Hale Leys shopping arcade. Nearly half the units were shut. In those that remained, glum and golem-like assistants sat deactivated by unrung tills whilst a stream of people poured by without deviation, earphones in, using the arcade as a warm thoroughfare away from the spring winds and showers. The town centre was in better shape with far fewer empty shops, suggesting a possible uncompetitive rent issue with the arcade.

Being early afternoon already, I didn't want to waste any time before having my first busk. There was a promising spot outside a cafe that had closed for the day after the lunch trade. In truth there wasn't much other choice. Aylesbury town centre has few suitable pitches, being an unusual shape. The market square is wide open, and shoppers cross it on the diagonal, taking them away from obvious spots. There's another square, also too open, and a small number of lightly trodden side roads. That leaves the one semi-pedestrianised street, High Street as the only game in town. Here, there was a choice between the cafe and a single empty unit.

The problem for me was that just down from this ideal looking spot, a small, bearded, and gnome-like fellow was sat on a stool with what looked like a bin full of crude violins and bows mounted on a trolley. He seemed like a busker, but he wasn't actually doing anything. Just watching the world go by, occasionally throwing handfuls of crumbs at passing pigeons. Every so often he'd take a fiddle out of the bin, pluck a few open strings, then softly replace it with the others. I don't like to tread on toes, so I took another loop round the town. He was still there, still not seemingly performing. Eventually, on the third loop, he was packing up, so I grabbed the opportunity and set up myself. It was 3pm.

The acoustics were good, and the footfall sufficient and I made £33 in the couple of hours before closing time. One thing I've learned about busking is that no matter how many times I head out for a busk, I never quite know what's going to happen. Something new always surprises me. A small girl was given 50p and sent over to drop it in my case. She ran past me and slotted it proudly into the top of a nearby traffic cone.

I packed up at 5pm, and walked around a bit more. Every available piece of street furniture had an A3 laminated sign on it with a pigeon crossed out in a red circle. 'Polite notice. Do not feed the pigeons. Unfortunately we have an infestation problem.' There were dozens of them, probably one for every pigeon. A hostile environment.

In the pub they told me that the fellow I'd seen was Luigi.

'He's a bit of a legend. Likes his pigeons.' I wanted to find out more, and hoped we'd meet tomorrow. I slept on an airbed on the living room floor after my friends took an early night. They're new parents and 10pm has become a distant memory for them. The air bed went down after about an hour, as they always do, pitching me comically onto the floor as I rolled over, so I migrated to the sofa, a three-seater made of firm, independent positions and slept fitfully in sections.

The next morning I walked into town, feeling somewhat corrugated, hoping to loosen out the muscles. I traversed the rings of the onion, starting in the outer zone of new builds, still sitting on top of the land, houses freshly sown, scattered on machine-ploughed earth, gardens un-established yet, sterile, sometimes astroturf. A paperboy brought a moment of recognisable humanity to the emptiness as he sat reading and otherwise enjoying the contents of the *Sun* newspaper. The town was spreading, along with all the others in the commuter belt of London, like cultures on a petri-dish, growing outwards until they meet, overlap, and consume one another.

A red kite floated up from behind a 1950s council house. On my right, a trading estate flanked the main road, an everytown of Halfords and Harvester, McDonalds and Topps Tiles. I could have been anywhere in England. The houses on my left grew slowly older, turning into pre-war terraces then Victorian town houses. Finally as I approached the middle I hit the new wave of flats. Our town centres are now re-populating after the previous generation's migration to the suburbs. Trendy flats were popping up in spaces no longer needed for commerce, new waves of regeneration pulsing out from the centre.

In the modern Friars Square shopping centre, with its high windowed and airy interior, a child stood in the complementary soft play area, peering vacantly out over the foam walls like a monarch dispassionately watching their kingdom crumble, citizens advancing upon the castle, a mass of flames and pitchforks. The shops were mostly all in use, but the building was like an airport departure lounge without the soul. At least the toilets were free.

I bought a coffee from the New York Deli, and had a busk back on High Street. A man hurried down from the market square towards Marks and Spencers. As he passed, he glanced worriedly at me and made the sign of the cross. After an hour, rain stopped play, and I was forced to wander round in the damp. I passed the Roald Dahl museum, tucked in a secret garden through an archway in the oldest part of the town, towards the church. The shower cleared, and I set up again amidst the puddles. A man walked past in a huge ankle-length trench coat to which a heavy cotton union jack had been sewn, covering the entire back and rendering him square, like a patriotic wardrobe. The front had numerous other patches sewn on. I wanted to ask him about it, but he strode into the Entertainment Exchange full of purpose. It was the most remarkable garment, and clearly a personal effort.

Another shower came down with a suddenness that left my violin heavily spotted with rain. I took it back to the toilets in the shopping centre, and dried it with toilet roll, airing my duster and case under the hand-dryer and ignoring the funny looks from the other users of the facility. It was a bitty sort of morning. My preferred pitch was outside a closed down British Heart Foundation, next door to an independent jewellers. People were drawn to its window, and specifically the bottom corner near me. When the assistant came out for a vape, I asked him what it was that was attracting so many people over.

'It'll be the Rolexes. We're the only place in town that sells them.' I looked. There were three Rolex watches on display, the cheapest of which was more than everything I'd made so far on my adventure put together. I found their appeal hard to understand. We all have the time on our phones now, and such an expensive watch really only serves to show off wealth. But then, I've bought daft things that nobody else would want, so who am I to judge? We should all be allowed a few pretty things in life. I chided myself. As soon as you criticise anything that's not strictly functional, you undermine our basic humanity.

It was lunchtime, and Sam joined me, with her baby, Rafa. We went for a pub lunch. She's a Mexican who married my schoolmate Jamie. I was best man at their wedding in Oaxaca, a duty I performed phonetically in a language I cannot speak, before attempting and failing to chat up a young woman and finally losing a dance-off to a giant robot.

I asked the barman if Aylesbury saw much night life, now the town centre was filled with new flats. A customer burst out laughing. 'Night life? Aylesbury?' The barman had lived here his whole life and loved the place, but conceded that it was quiet and not much ever happened.

'How is Aylesbury for you?' I asked Sam when I returned to the table.

'It is okay.' Daughter of a political dynasty, her grandfather a former top civil servant, and her mother once the culture minister for Veracruz state, Sam is one of the sharpest and most perceptive minds I know, working as a project co-ordinator for an international telecoms company. But she couldn't think of much to tell me about her latest home town. 'I'm not sure what to tell you about it. It is okay. Not much happens here.'

'But there must be something worth seeing?'

So after lunch, Sam took me to see the David Bowie Statue, under the archway at the bottom of the market place. Bronze, it features two Bowies side by side, one dapper, suited and cool, at rest, the other veined and sinuous, caught mid leap, bright eyed and clutching a microphone. Every hour, theoretically on the hour, speakers set into the walls above play a track from his career at random. At exactly 2:02pm, it came on with 'I can't give everything away', the final track of his final album. We stood respectfully and listened to it, slick pop track, wistful extended playout, the final knowing offering from a unique and much missed talent. People trickled past, pushing prams, on phones, smoking and vaping. Bowie sang to us all, equally. It ended, and the archway fell back into silence for the next 54 minutes.

'Y'know, I was never really into Bowie.'

'Me neither.'

Sam went back home with little Rafa, and I headed back to busking. The market square had a pair of enormous lions on plinths, apparently a gift to the town from the Rothschilds in the Victorian era. Whilst they were being made in Paris, concerned town elders hurriedly commissioned mock-up lions to test potential locations for the final pieces, plinthing them all over town before selecting the current location. They're quite something, and I was somewhat alarmed to find myself drawn to their chunky arses, muscular and detailed. 'Robust', one might say. The artist had seemingly spent more time round the back than on the more photographed features. Well, you've got to get your kicks where you can.

I started to set up for an afternoon busk when Luigi made his way down the street. I was conscious of hogging the good spot, and offered to pack down so he could have a go. I was also eager to have a chat and meet the man, and perhaps see what his act was.

'Oh no, you play!' His accent was sing-song Italian, over the top like a bad pasta sauce advert. 'I just play to make-a some money and then I feeda the pigeons, but now they try to stoppa me from feeding them.' He gestured at the abundance of laminated notices. I'd never heard anyone use the words 'Make-a', 'Feeda' and 'Stoppa' in any context other than a clumsy parody, yet here he was, in the flesh. A preposterously unlikely character that I could not dare invent for fear of being thought racist. Years ago, I used to wonder where on earth the great playwright Peter Tinniswood had found inspiration for the remarkable characters he drew. Now I realise he probably went down to any town centre, smoked his pipe and patiently waited until one went past.

'Oh the poor starving birds.' Luigi continued, a voice full of emotion. A series of plump pigeons had congregated around him, well aware of his considerable potential to emit crumbs. 'They are so hungry!' One pigeon grew tired of waiting, mounted another pigeon and gave it a comprehensive humping. Luigi and I both watched the performance together, in silence. It seemed to deflate him.

'But I am not much good. Go, you play today.'

'Are you sure, I really don't mind?'

I wondered if Luigi was all that he seemed. I allowed myself to imagine that perhaps he was a carpet salesman from Luton who'd tired of his dull, uninspiring life and just quietly slipped out the door one afternoon, grown a beard, affected a cod Italian accent and returned to the world as Luigi on the streets of Aylesbury.

'It is okay. I hope you come back soon.'

He was a kind and harmless man. England, perhaps, is a place where eccentric old men can feed the birds in defiance of laminated notices. He slipped off, slowly, cart trailing behind him, small clouds of crumbs landing amongst the birds that saw him as king. I wondered what his act actually was, or if he even had one, or if I'd possibly just seen it.

I played till 4pm. It was enough for tired fingers, and traffic was light. I'd made £63 in four truncated hours. Enough to pay my way, but nothing special. I walked down to the Waterside arts centre, where the largely ignored Aylesbury arm of the Grand Union Canal comes to an end around the back of Waitrose, fittingly terminating without fuss against the setting of a blank brick wall. An Indian family were hurling entire loaves of bread at surprised ducks. 'Is it allowed?', they asked me earnestly as I drew nearer.

'I don't know, but I'd break it up a bit.'

A life-size statue of Ronnie Barker sits quietly on a bench by the theatre, minding his own business, out of the way. Modern statuary is coming off the plinth to live amongst us, relaxed and human, and I'm fine with that.

Aylesbury. I still couldn't really place it. I wandered over to the station, via the 5pm Bowie performance, a *Spiders from Mars* era track I couldn't quite identify. The speakers were a bit muffled, cones damp, the reality of the English weather meeting the idealism of the artist.

The station was a monument to efficiency. Ticket barriers and a single machine. Most travellers were trading off a single season pass, so there was little need to staff even such a busy station with ticket windows. The humble platform ticket being a thing of the past, and my unwillingness to spend the peak £5 fare to the nearest station, I watched the rush hour from the pedestrian bridge at the throat of the station. A woman went past with a cat in a specially designed rucksack, rigid and domed, like a glass diving bell for cats wishing to chart dangerous and hostile environments. A ginger tom stared out with big contemptuous eyes, looking at me as if I were an angler fish or some other nameless horror of the deep. Below, taxis were drawn to the station like crocodiles to a water hole, gathering in groups, silent, engines off, awaiting the herds from across the plains, ready to grab careless ankles and pull them under. Commuter trains from London burst their ripened pods onto the platform, and the weary and suited began the last leg home from offices and meetings. The rain fell again, and I mused on our national refusal to dress for wet weather. Collars were extended, woollen cardigans wrapped too tight, free newspapers draped over balding heads. Strides slightly too quick.

I followed the herd, perhaps like salmon heading upriver, thinning out, splitting up ancestral tributaries, across the ring road, some into the gym, more into the pub, many just going home. Probably not to spawn, not tonight, not Thursday, when the week is heavy on the body and soul and another effort is demanded in the morning.

My journey back was interrupted by a roaming gang of street preachers. Their leader held a tattered bible and was shouting dire warnings at passers-by. Younger than me, his hair was wet with rain, shoes solid but careworn. Coat basic and modest. Beard, and bright, urgent eyes. He looked the part, wearing this contrived hardship as sword and shield. Jesus went to the desert. He went to Aylesbury on a Thursday afternoon, around about tea-time and raged in the street. His assistants handed out pamphlets and said nothing. He directly told a Muslim woman that Allah was a false God and she was going to Hell. This seemed a bit over the top, but where do you begin in situations like this? They genuinely believe people of all sorts are in horrific danger. Conversation between us is usually difficult as there is no common ground to work with. I looked tatty and bedraggled, sat on my fiddle case, perhaps every bit as contrived as him, and they only gave me a pamphlet when they ran out of other people to bother, saving my soul clearly a slightly lower priority. As I was the only person prepared to sit and watch, the leader eventually came over to talk to me. I didn't know what to say, as anything that came to mind just felt like I was taking the piss, and the conversation went nowhere. We just both felt desperately sad for one another for reasons the other could not comprehend.

I headed back to my friends' house via the chippy. Waiting for my order, I smelled of damp coat. It had been a long day.

After another night of limited sleep on the giant ridge-cut crisp sofa, I pushed my aching body out of the door at 7:30am, an unholy time for a professional musician. I wanted to see the departure of the commuter train to London from Aylesbury Vale Parkway. On the final edge of town, where fields and development potential are indistinguishable, a new railway station has germinated. No ticket barrier here, just a vast car-park, as yet largely redundant, and an austere cafe just for selling bitter coffee to the sort of hardened commuter who has evolved a special digestive organ to process it. I made my way to the platform, where the train was ready to leave, and the headphoned crew of economic England hurried along to their seats. The guard encouraged me to board, as he was ready to set off. 'Oh no, I'm just here to see you away.' This was not an answer that made any sense to him, but the light turned green, and with a shrug, he locked the doors and the multiple unit drew off without fuss in the chalky morning.

I walked round Berryfields. New houses, 5,000 in total, a colossal appendage for any town to absorb. It's well supplied by playgrounds and little else. Pylons cut a path through the middle, repelling houses from their procession. I walked on, by a window with carved wooden blocks spelling 'LOVE'. By them, a small dog with haunted eyes stood with two feet against the window, howling at me with unrestrained horror. The estate was so new that the paths that people wear in the grass that ultimately supplant the mandated routes hadn't fully formed yet and it felt like walking round inside a planner's dream. The cumulative effect of our collective eccentricity takes a long while to engrain itself on new areas.

Here is the deepest level of the commuter experience. Berryfields has figured out the one part of town that is no longer necessary: the town centre. Everything can be delivered, a new car, takeaway, presents, furniture. Fancy cooking for yourselves? Ocado will bring the ingredients. Why would you go to a shop? Anything can be delivered. Need a night out? Stay in London and get the later train back. Uber are there for you. Apps have supplanted shops here. The world can be brought to your door or smart locker. Welcome to endless unfocussed suburbia. A string of Audis and 4x4s crawled into town, each with a parent driving and a single well-scrubbed and treasured child occupying the back seat like a high court judge commanding the bench.

Aylesbury

Aylesbury has history, tons of it, but it's buried, forgotten in the glare of London, that massive weight and economic powerhouse on the fabric of the Home Counties, drawing thousands from all over. There are plaques on houses, and statues galore, but the town is there to feed London now, and is jumbled up and diluted. There's not much of a sense of continuity about it, as if a roaming and displaced people discovered a complete and unused city and just moved in, counting their good luck.

Jamie and Sam are taking a punt like so many others. They can make the money they need right here and now, raise a child in safety and comfort, and get out before they get old. Berryfields is an estate to be passed through, an opportunity that if grasped will liberate your later life. They will work their arses off now, retire to Oaxaca and want for little.

'Come on, let's get some coffee.'

Jamie had dropped Rafa off at the nursery, education and childcare being the one industry there is seemingly no app based solution for just yet. We drove to the nearby village of Haddenham and had breakfast in the most spectacularly middle class cafe I have ever seen. Called Norsk, it was packed, mostly with women in expensive country clothing. A camera crew were making a documentary and asked if we minded being background characters. I replied that I was born to the task.

The coffee was sensational, the food excellent. Are these my people? They look a lot like me, sound a lot like me, if a little more Southern, but perhaps our lives split at the age of 21 when I decided to be a musician. I'm middle class without the budget to really pull it off properly. The psychological element of class is fascinating. No matter how poor I get, I'm destined to always be middle class. Whereas someone born working class usually remains so, no matter how well they do in life. Class is how you start, not how you finish. If you improve your lot, it's your children's class that changes, not yours.

We dropped by the charity shop and Jamie picked up four copies of the *Ring* magazine from 1973 for a fiver. I searched for pint pots with handles, but drew a blank. We headed back to town and I had a final morning's play on the high street. A woman approached me with concern.

'Do you need a coffee or something?'

'I'm alright actually, had a couple of coffees already.'

'It's awfully cold.'

I'm increasingly fat, and jiggling around playing the fiddle I had hitherto considered it a warm morning.

'Really, I'm okay, but thank you for your consideration.'

She left, but minutes later she was back with a packet of hot sausage rolls for me from Greggs. Some people really just are lovely and you can't stop them.

I played on.

A beautiful young woman came down the street. Our eyes made contact. I smiled. She smiled back, and carefully but pointedly put her ear phones in.

A young Moldovan lad stopped me with enthusiasm. 'Do you know Paganini?'

'I'm afraid not. I play traditional music. Mostly English.'

'Then I wish to hear your finest piece of English music!'

I played him 'Lumps of plum pudding and pieces of pie'.

'Yes, that was truly a great piece,' he said, emotional as I finished scraping my way through. 'I came here for work. I work in the bus station!'

Then he was gone.

I hoped Luigi might make another appearance, and perhaps I'd finally hear his act, but it was not to be.

I left Aylesbury for a weekend's work in Milton Keynes. On the edge of town, I passed a reptile boarding house.

I'd been in the South for a while. It was time for a contrast.

Bradford

I NEEDED the loo and so followed the signs which took me to Bradford Interchange station. The loo here costs 20p and I wasn't in a mood to argue, but you don't get much for your 20p at Bradford Interchange. The only available stall looked as if the Andrex puppy and a shit-throwing monkey had been locked in together and told that only the winner of a speedcore dance-off would be allowed to walk out alive. I re-appraised the urgency of my need for the facilities and exited. Another man was waiting, saw the devastation and stared daggers at me. A good start. Outside in the concourse there was a public piano. A man was playing 'Chopsticks' on it over and over with grim determination.

I found a better facility in the shopping centre and felt ready to start the day properly. I walked round the city centre to get a feel for it. I'd been to Bradford many times in my life, but never really stopped to explore. My first impression was of a deeply beautiful and condensed city, all yellow sandstone piled into numerous ornate buildings, sloping into the bottom of the valley. The exception, no less beautiful, is the stunning Prudential Assurance building, a masterpiece of terracotta. The town hall is so grand it's almost preposterous, in isolation, surrounded by the sort of vast open spaces that often flank the great buildings of old Europe, implying that Bradford was once a capital city in waiting, ready to step in if London ever needed to close for refurbishment. Across the ring road, the Alhambra theatre oozes promise and the media museum looks down impressively from the slopes. Bradford is an architectural delight.

There was a busker already established by the five-way junction in the pedestrianised streets. His open case had his Instagram handle displayed and he seemed to know what he was doing. Pleasingly for me, his portable amp was correctly set up so that his vocals were clear and legible. Too many buskers end up boomy or muffled. Callum was clear as a bell. To celebrate this, I got a sausage roll and a coffee and settled in for a bit to watch. He was good. He also had staying power, ultimately holding the pitch for around five hours during the day. Impressive. We had a good chat, and he recommended I try down by Specsavers. I thanked him and dropped off a quid.

I took the long route, seeing what else there was. Bradford is all slopes into the bottom of a bowl. Up one big shopping street, an Eastern European woman sat squeezing a hopelessly broken and out of tune accordion, the same simple melody over and over all day. On her knees was a beautiful bright patchwork crocheted blanket I could see as a burst of colour from the other end of the street. I tried chatting but she spoke almost no English. I got that she was a Romanian, but little more. I gave her a quid too, for different reasons. Whatever her story, it couldn't have been an easy one.

Near her, another Eastern European woman sold squeaking, barking toy dogs. These things walked a few steps, made an electronic bark sound, turned and repeated, endlessly. There were other women selling these elsewhere round the city, and you could never quite get away from the squeaking, passing through interference zones between their pitches. Watch for a few minutes and you realise that each woman has a man standing quietly a few steps behind her, on the phone, letting her do the work. Taking the money. One woman's dogs hung down from a portable gantry on strings, twitching, looking like the early stages of a mass execution.

I tried down by Specsavers. Callum was right, it was a good spot, and I made a fiver in no time at all. A lad came by on a bike, maybe 12 or 13 years old. He danced to the music then came over.

'You're sick at that. I want to learn a violin but I don't know where to get one.'

He was personable and engaging.

'Does your school do music?' I asked, wanting to help.

'I don't go to school.'

'Excluded? What did you do?'

'Pulled a knife.'

'Yeah, that'd do it. What's your name, mate?'

'Travis. You?'

'I'm Tom. Maybe there's some sort of programme through the council you could apply to.' I was searching for an answer, but perhaps there wasn't one. He'd done something pretty bad, but who honestly didn't do stupid stuff at that age? Difference between him and me was that he won't get a second chance. Middle class boys get a chance to learn from their mistakes. They get to say that 'it made me a better person.' It becomes inspirational. Working class boys make a mistake and that's that. No more life opportunities. Travis was personable, open, great people skills, and I immediately liked him. I'm not condoning what he did, but if my life had been determined entirely by stuff I'd done at that age, things would have been very different.

'Perhaps you could get lessons', I carried on, lamely.

'Lessons?'

'Yeah, it's hard. Very difficult to learn by yourself.'

'Music shops have violins, don't they?'

'Yes.' What did he have in mind?

'Good. See you, thanks!'

I played again, full of thought. A man strode over to me from the cafe, carrying a penny whistle in one hand and a slopping cup of tea in the other. He was white bearded, wore a tweed jacket, and had a 'Bradford for Peace' badge attached to his flat cap.

'Do you know a monkey's spotted in my beer?' he asked, gruffly. Was this the name of a tune or was he telling me about his day? He sloshed tea around and waited for my answer.

'I don't.'

'I'll play it with you.'

Now I like a good collaboration, but this bloke was too direct, almost aggressive and I didn't like it. I tried a deflection: 'I'm Tom,' and I offered out a hand. It was not met.

'Tom who?'

'Tom Kitching?' I continued meekly.

'Who?' he barked. 'I thought you might be famous.'

'I'm not famous.'

'Well maybe you're not famous but maybe you're a fascist.' His eyes were sparkling now, he'd found a thread and was pulling at it.

'I'm not a fascist either', I tried, but he wasn't convinced. It's not something one normally needs to deny.

'I'm a lifelong socialist, and if I've learned one thing, it's that everyone lies. You fascist.'

And he walked back to the cafe, sitting outside and banging his mug down. I tried to resume my busk with a tune, but he played his whistle over the top from the other side of the street. I stopped. So did he. I started, so did he. Okay. I packed up my fiddle, sat on my case, and wrote the conversation down.

'What are you doing?' He called angrily across the street.

'Adding you to the list.'

I quickly wandered round town again before the situation could go any further, and picked a new spot on a steep street off the main centre, under a hair replacement clinic sign. It wasn't ideal, as the gradient demanded concentration from passers-by and therefore I got less engagement. But it was fine, and I started to enjoy playing and was gathering a little change. Then there was whistling again. He'd found me.

'Do you know Macclesfield Fair?'

'Maybe. Are you fraternising with fascists now?'

He ignored this and played it anyway. It was 'The Wizard of Alderley Edge' by Pete Coe. Behind him, by coincidence, or perhaps not, the words 'It's a mean old scene' (Another Pete Coe song) were graffitied on the wall of a closed down pub. It was a slightly surreal moment and I couldn't work out if he had any idea of the coincidence.

'Where did you get that tune from?'

'Some old album.'

And he walked off up the hill and out of my life.

Now disconcerted, I made my way back to Specsavers in the hope of a little normality. I busked. Some small Sikh children brought me a box with four cookies in it and offered them to me. I said I was ok, but thanks for the thought. As they ran away I heard: 'Whatever shall we do?'

'If he won't eat them, no-one will.'

A Muslim family came by, and their small son was transfixed by the music, so they all stopped. The lad started jumping to grab the end of the instrument, and I had to repeatedly tilt it out of the way. He was clearly a hard to reach child, and his father was absolutely beaming at the interaction. They were generous and showered my case in silver coins, in fact most people were. I racked up a great deal of silver. Bradford is a friendly and generous place, irrespective of backgrounds.

Another lad came by, and started dropping coins near me, as a challenge. How desperate was I? Would I go and pick them up? I didn't, and after a minute he walked on, disappointed. An older lady came by, saw a 20p near my case and picked it up. Playing a perfect stereotype of a Yorkshire woman, she looked up, across at me, weighed up how far away it was from my case, decided it was fair game and pocketed it decisively. I couldn't help but laugh. What a strange day that coin was having.

I fancied a change of setting, so I moved round to where Callum was now packing up. Higher up the street, a man with a beautiful sunburst electric guitar was playing music that sounded like how I remember every Andy Kershaw programme sounding when I was a child and my dad recorded it on tapes for long car journeys. This was set to backing tracks. He had a dog that barked merrily along in bursts, slightly out of time with the track, causing the guitarist to botch his rhythm. It made for good entertainment. He didn't make much money, as most people were scared to approach the dog.

I had a final play in the lengthening sun towards the town hall. A black family all started dancing in the street. Some Asian children joined in, followed by some white children. As their children danced together, parents of all ethnicities shook hands and got to know each other. I thought to myself that if I'd been able to guarantee this sort of result to the arts council before I set off on my project I'd have been arriving here in a solid gold Rolls Royce. But putting cynicism aside, it really was a beautiful, spontaneous moment. I was struck throughout my busking in Bradford by the extent that people of all ages and backgrounds really felt they could just have a dance along. It's an uninhibited sort of place. My tune finished and they dispersed.

'Jesus loves you' called the black lady, beaming, as she left.

I couldn't wait to get back and pick it up again.

I arrived early the next day, too early to play really, so I got a coffee and just watched the world go by. Bradford is poor now, desperately so in places, but they live amongst shabby splendour. The wool trade built this fine city, and the German bombs ruined comparatively little of it in the war. Pop up shops, discount centres, and dozens of old fashioned independent stores reside in soft yellow sandstone masterpieces, every archway ornate and carved. There is decorative stonework on nearly every building.

I grabbed the plum busking pitch at 10am and gave it a good go. It went well. Children danced, the sun shone, coins accumulated. One family had dressed their two infant sons in lovely tiny blue suits. They danced to my tunes together for several minutes, and not even the niqab could hide their mother's smile. It all felt like one happy family of humanity on a perfect spring day.

Bradford

At lunchtime, I counted up my takings. £46, plus quite inexplicably a 4K7 ohms +/- 1 per cent resistor. It had been a fun morning. A lady had recognised me from a performance at the Topic Folk Club, just up the road, handed over a fiver, and sat in at the cafe across the way with her husband for half an hour, occasionally getting up to have a little dance. The acoustics were great, and I felt the instrument really carried. Although I'd made more money elsewhere, Bradford is cheap and that £46 would go a lot further in a city like this. Nearly all of it was silver coins. Not many pounds.

So what to make of Bradford?

It's a truly diverse city. What's harder to get a handle on is how well integrated it is. Is Bradford a series of non-overlapping communities running in parallel or is it more integrated than that? How much does the answer matter? I wandered round wondering how to answer these questions. A pile of new clothes sat in the street, abandoned by a shoplifter, looking like some sort of clothes-eating monster had gorged itself silly in TK Maxx and just barfed them all up. A police car was nearby, officers making notes. Shoplifting was common, I saw three examples in two days. On one of the other main streets, a religious group had set up stall, playing exalting music loudly through a single bin-linered speaker and soliciting for donations and engagements. An older lady in a wheelchair sat in front of them, and a bearded man laid his hand upon her head, with a smile of calm authority. I didn't detect a miracle, but perhaps they are all in the eye of the beholder.

The market in the Kirkgate centre was self-segregating. You could read the posters on the stall and know what colour the clientele would be. The nail bars were all Asian, whilst the cafe that sells jam roly-poly and custard was decidedly Caucasian. But there was plenty of space for everyone, and Bradford in general retains a great deal of independence with much of the city centre given over to the sorts of shops that have long closed elsewhere. It felt like a throwback to the shopping streets of my youth.

How important is integration anyway, if there's space for everyone? A friend of mine living in Ashton-under-Lyne struggles with it. On an individual basis, he has no problem with the Asians who have come to dominate his area, but finds all the pubs and pork butchers shops have shut and the infrastructure of his community is no longer relevant to him. He can no longer have conversations with all his neighbours, as many of them, particularly the women, cannot speak his language, and don't necessarily feel like they are culturally allowed to talk to him anyway. And he gets called racist for saying exactly this. Me responding with my liberal viewpoints is met with weary exasperation. 'But you live in a white community, and this is out of sight for you. You've not had the things you like close down and go away. If you lived here, you'd feel differently.' I have never heard him say a bad word against any individual, but his experience of significant immigration to the community he has lived his whole life in is very negative. Integration is hard. Multiculturalism more successful in some places and communities than others. If different groups of people all want different things, it can be hard for them all to live in the same community, as there will not be enough of each group to sustain all the services that the groups need. Bradford, perhaps, is big enough in the centre that the space feels shared. The suburbs and smaller towns are perhaps less varied.

But people also talk about multiculturalism too much as a one way street, as if it is solely the responsibility of the new group to integrate. Perhaps the indigenous community to which I so obviously and pinkly belonged on this sunny day could have done rather more to hold up our end of the bargain. In a hostile environment, an incoming community will stick together and keep their heads down all the more, binding tighter and heading for the same streets, streets where their neighbours will understand them. Well documented historic council policies of lumping all the immigrants in one otherwise emptying and impoverished area can't have helped either, forcing high levels of self-reliance on these communities. Had we been more welcoming, perhaps this entrenchment would not have occurred. Perhaps rivers of blood are most likely when the white people decide they are likely. Perhaps we are the determining factor.

My feeling is that we, broadly speaking the Anglo-Saxons, could have handled integration so much better ourselves, done more to welcome people and make them feel like they too can call it home. Especially as immigration seems largely inevitable, and will only increase as the climate changes. If multiculturalism has its failings, then many of them should be laid at our door rather than the arriving communities. And we should perhaps also remember that some white people have also been on the wrong end of these same failings, left to deal with something that needed a lot more external support than was fair to ask of them, consequently losing their sense of community along the way. But isn't such an attitude just typical of the artist? 'If we could all get to know each other better, we'd be fine.' Is it really as simple as that? Probably not, but experiences in Oldham after the race riots twenty years ago show that it definitely helps. Given the inevitability of immigration, and the fact that existing immigrant communities are here to stay, finding ways of making it work must be better than railing against it. It falls to us to make the next move, not them. They have enough to deal with.

A short walk along the valley lies the football ground, Valley Parade, one of two enormous sports stadia in the city, the other being the rugby league ground, Odsal, a hole in the ground that once hosted 120,000 for the 1954 cup final replay between Halifax and Warrington, an English crowd record for any sport. Where Odsal is a stadium built in a hole, Valley Parade balances on the landscape like the sort of precarious stack of washing up that might be produced by a student flat. You can see the stands from the city centre, looming over the terraced streets, the effort of producing a flat space on a hillside leading to one stand dug into the hill and the opposite raised up on stilts. It was quiet today, at rest, just a single groundsman tending the perfect turf visible through a gap in the gate. Round by the main entrance, I paid my respects at the memorial to the fifty-six fans killed in the 1985 fire. Most of the dead were children or pensioners, killed doing what they loved, in the heart of their community.

The largest stand is colossal, and towers over the area. Back-to-back terraces run along the sides, and turning away from the ground you face the mosque. Across the valley, the chimneys of woollen mills have been reduced, and for each survivor a dome has sprouted to accompany it. Some magnificent, but also quite hard to spot, simultaneously glorious and modest, locations chosen to both bring honour to their god and not attract too much attention from the other locals. I once heard a resident in Leigh complaining about a 'mosque' in her town, whilst looking at the domed water tower of a cotton mill.

Children played in the street, and I suddenly realised what it was about Bradford that was so unusual to me. It wasn't the diversity or the architecture. It was the number of children. In much of the Western world, families are small, one or two children, for those who choose to have them. Those children that we do have are shepherded from safe space to safe space in cars designed to shield and protect them. They socialise in curated and controlled spaces not routinely open to those of us unblessed with family. In Bradford, families are large and play in the streets. Everywhere you go, there's the sound of children at play in the big wide world, scabbing knees, having adventures. I found it raising my spirits wherever I went. A world without children is a hollow, colourless world, whose emptiness only becomes apparent when the colour floods back.

Behind the away stand at Valley Parade and over a wall was

a patch of waste land. In it I saw Muslim women in full burqas teaching sons how to play cricket and daughters how to teach their future sons. I'd have loved to wander in and get to know them, but I knew this wasn't my space and such an encounter could be problematic. Behind me, the football ground, its location a legacy of another age, and filled every other weekend by the white people returning on an ancestral and secular pilgrimage. Off the same street on a quiet weekday afternoon, the new population of these terraces were playing their preferred sport in altogether less grand surroundings.

I suppose the question I should be asking myself is 'Could I live on this street?', and I really don't have enough information to answer that, let alone explain my answer. I'm sure I'd get on with everyone, that wouldn't be the problem, but the things I need culturally, are they here? Maybe not. Now imagine I lived here and couldn't afford to move anywhere else. You can begin to see why people find it hard.

I was hitting the limitations of my whistle-stop tour of England. Busking is all very well, and does provide many insights, but it is not going to be an automatic window into hard-to-reach communities. Children all respond the same way, but people from backgrounds other than mine will not always feel they can have a conversation with me. Some doors are still closed, for now at least.

So then, Bradford would remain something of a beautiful mystery to me. I don't know how to use my fiddle to get to know communities so far removed from my own. I thought of Travis, blissfully unaware of a life up the spout already for a decision made at 12 years of age. I thought of children of all backgrounds dancing together and hoped that was the truest Bradford. We'd shared some wonderfully human moments, me and this city, and I was already deeply fond of it. I took my fiddle home to think some more.

Leek

LEEK, Queen of the Staffordshire Moorlands, as it says on the sign. Home to what was until quite recently the only pub I'd ever been thrown out of, the Wilkes Head. Not on the railway any more, not really on the canal which peters out a mile away from town. You can get a bus to Stoke, and occasionally to other towns in the hills.

It was market day. You know you're in a rich town when that means antiques and artisanal loaves instead of cheap clothes and unbranded electrical equipment. A lady was selling a pair of antlers on her stall. Later, I saw she had been successful. The bookmakers was missing the 'C' from Coral in their signage, and the word 'oral' hung merrily over the street in giant colourful letters. I made my way downhill and picked a busking spot opposite a motivational pie shop.

My first visitor was a spritely older gentleman who dropped a pound in my case and engaged me in conversation. He held himself tall and straight and was smartly dressed. He said he was a former Morris dancer and musician from Suffolk, but he hadn't found a side round here. I told him about the local sides I know, including a local ladies side who were looking for musicians.

'Oh no, I don't play for ladies. My side was white men! You know. The proper stuff.' He then gave me a short but energetic demonstration of what proper Morris dancing looked like. It was perhaps not the compelling advert for white male supremacy that he was aiming for.

The thing about prejudice is that I'm never ready for it. Given ten minutes warning, I'd be fired up and prepared to take it on, armed with a witty and cutting riposte. But it's often such a surprise, a casual comment in an otherwise mundane conversation that my first thought is 'Did I hear that right?' and by the time I've thought about it and decided I really did hear that, the moment has passed. I think I managed to say something lame about there being nothing wrong with women dancing Morris, and he was gone. I felt a bit ashamed at my lack of challenge on the various other problems with his statement, and it stayed with me all morning.

I kept playing. Having spent most of my time far from home, I was used to being an anonymous figure, just some guy with a sun-bleached hat and a fiddle. Leek however, was a little too close to home. My childhood babysitter came past and waved with a knowing laugh. Another familiar face came down the street. It was my grandma down from Macclesfield for the day. She insisted on taking me for lunch and I accepted without argument.

'It'll be good to see you eat something other than pizza.'

After I returned to my pitch, well stoked up for the afternoon, the encounters kept coming. One gentleman engaged me in animated conversation whilst holding an ice lolly. He kept talking at me about nothing much, and slowly it melted, chunks calving off and dropping to the floor. Eventually, he reached a full stop and looked at his lolly. It had completely gone. 'I'd better get another one of those.' He said to himself and headed off towards the ice-cream van, leaving me with a puddle.

The majority of the music I play is English, but I have a few American, Irish, Scottish, and Scandinavian tunes in my repertoire as well. With perfect timing, and not for the first time, as I was playing an Irish jig, a lady stopped me to ask if I could possibly play her an Irish jig. I said of course and immediately resumed the same tune. She was delighted and dropped off a pound coin. Another lady asked for 'Danny Boy' and spent the entire tune telling total strangers that she'd requested it.

Leek is a town in the service of the retired. I looked down the main street. It was bald heads and bobs of white hair as far as I could see, the blue rinse being somewhat out of fashion these days. The elderly descend on Leek on market days, and walk or roll the main street from the old market place by the church, down the hill to the new one by the war memorial. The market has been cleverly split in two to ensure that punters walk the length of the main street. On the back streets are antique shops stuffed with oddities that you can't imagine anyone buying until you find something that feels like it was waiting for you. I narrowly avoided buying a working demonstration model of a two-stroke engine when I realised just in time that I didn't really actually need one and I was being silly.

Lunchtime in Leek; tea rooms are full, kerbs are lowered, menus are safe in their predictability. Sandwiches are triangled, cucumbers sliced neatly. It is a nice and entirely unchallenging day out, where those older members of society with a little pension left over can peruse the market, have a cream tea, raid the charity shops, and head home untroubled before the rush hour. It is a town without many of the obvious signs of poverty that so many other places have, and a town where nearly every face is white and nearly every accent English.

Two older ladies came to put money in my case. They stopped at the cusp, suddenly worried they might be doing the wrong thing and asked 'Are you English?' The implications of the question troubled me. If I wasn't? Presumably the money would not be forthcoming. But why did it matter? The thought of a foreigner on their street was clearly an issue. Leek suddenly felt like a designated safe space for the already safe. On reflection I should have said something like 'No mate, I'm Sri Lankan' in my best North West accent to see what happened.

Of course, a couple of sour moments aren't representative of everyone, but they troubled me. I'd not encountered naked prejudice like this in places where the ethnic mix was much greater. Perhaps that was the point. Perhaps keeping Leek white and English really mattered to some of the people who came here. Perhaps in such a town, they felt safe to express views they wouldn't express elsewhere.

The town and the customers are symbiotic of course. The shops, the menus, the items for sale, and the people employed to sell them are all a response to demand. It is self-sustaining. The clientele seek a safe, old-fashioned town, selling safe, old-fashioned things. A product not of overt racism, but of the result of a group being drawn to what makes them feel comfortable and market forces doing the rest. How unlike so much of the rest of modern England Leek is.

As the day wore to a close, another old friend turned up. Robbie, a former student of mine, now fully fledged with a career of his own. He had a fiddle on his back. 'I heard you were here. Want some help?'

So we turned into a duo for the last hour of the day. It was a real change of gear, playing harmonies and rhythms instead of straight melodies, and attracted a lot more attention. I tried to divvy the pot up between us, but he wouldn't take any. I decided to take that as repayment for those times he didn't listen to me in lessons when he was a kid. He's now off to do a Masters degree at the Sibelius Music Academy in Finland, so not listening to me must have really paid off in the end.

The next day, I was busking outside a closed down bank in the centre of town. It had steps and a ramp leading up to the door. I didn't use them, staying at street level instead. At lunchtime I went to get some hot Staffordshire oatcakes, the local delicacy, and returned. My spot had a new performer, so I sat to watch him at work whilst I ate my lunch.

He was a young man, maybe late twenties, and he was a preacher. It was fiery stuff. We were all going to Hell unless we accepted Jesus. And Hell was clearly a very literal place, and he spared no detail as to how bad it was. I tucked into my bacon and cheese double. He was sporting a neatly trimmed beard, and wore a set of high quality sandals. 'Always dress for the job you want' I thought quietly to myself. He'd used the steps as a pulpit, and stood a little over the street, imploring us to sort it out and accept Jesus. A little old lady came by and responded. 'You're preaching to the converted here, but for goodness sake, cheer it up a bit!'

'I'm here to deliver the good news!' he replied, before launching into another dire warning of an eternal roasting.

I really wanted to have a conversation with him, but wasn't sure how to do so. I'm not religious myself and with the best will in the world, I couldn't take his warnings seriously. This would not be good ground to engage him on, with such a mismatch of concern. If I'm right, then it doesn't make much difference to him in the long run, we'll end up in the same place irrespective of our views. If he's right, I'm in an eternity of trouble. It's hard to have a serious and respectful conversation when perspectives are so different.

He was using a microphone and a battery amp to increase God's message. I saw an opening.

'Excuse me!' I ventured during a short pause.

'Yes?' He replied with a smile.

'You could really use a pop shield on that microphone.'

'A pop shield?'

'Yes, you know like a black woolly hat for the microphone. It'd remove some of the harshness on the 'Ps' and 'Ts' and take out the blowing sounds.'

'Thanks, that sounds great.'

I was in. He came over, and we chatted for a bit. His name was Jonathon and he'd had a very religious upbringing and saw the Bible as completely literal. Consequently, he felt a responsibility to go out and preach it. He said that he saw Hell to be 'as real as a burning building, for which you'd shout Fire!' to warn people. It was a good point. If you did literally believe in Hell and cared about others then you would spend a lot of time worrying about other people. It must be very stressful and I was glad not to be going round carrying such a burden and responsibility.

He said he had a wife and a child, and they were hoping to give up work altogether soon so they could drive in their camper van to Pakistan, preaching all the way. Until then he was working at an outdoors centre to save up money. He'd preach on his lunchtimes and days off. He was a great admirer of John Wesley, and took inspiration from how it had taken him decades of street preaching to get his movement off the ground.

We wished each other well and he resumed his spot. It was a tough gig. Most people ignored him. Some were openly rude. There was an occasional Hallelujah. After a while he packed up and tried further down the street. I wondered how he measured success. Was he happy? Probably, yes. Funny how one person's cage can be another's liberty.

Further up the street, two heavily tattooed young men were working out where to hang a smart looking flag outside their newly opened barbers shop. I resumed busking. A lady came out of a shop with a scratch card and worked away at it by my pitch. It became apparent that she hadn't won, and she glared at her coin resentfully before dropping it in my collection with a shake of the head. I didn't want the unlucky coin, but couldn't tell which it was. As I packed down, I could hear Jonathon the preacher in the distance, just the plosives and the bass coming off the speaker, the shape of the rhetoric clear, but shorn of the detail.

I left Leek, the retiree's theme park, and headed home.

Cornwall

IT's a long way to Cornwall, especially if you have designs on reaching the far end. I broke the journey by staying with my friend in Totnes in Devon, and still had over two hours' travel the following morning. It gave me a sense of how angry the protagonists of the 1497 Cornish rebellion must have been.

Anything less than an all-consuming rage would have soon mellowed into wondering if the cat had been put out and an overwhelming desire to get on with redecorating the back bedroom long before they'd crossed the Tamar. Cornwall still feels very distant.

The bloody and failed consequences of the rebellion still seem to cast a long shadow. Born of excessive taxation on the tin wealth of the Duchy, one might say nothing has changed. A king's ransom in metals extracted, and still the poorest county in England, behind only West Wales in Northern Europe. Cornwall is a county that resources leave.

My first destination was Truro. A stunted cathedral city, three grand spires and not much else. The silted up harbour stank of old mud. I parked in a council estate on top of the hill and walked in. The gutters were running with water, but it had been dry. These were waterways, not to simply drain the excess but to carry living streams through town. Cut of solid stones, they were ancient and deep and carried the water past the frontages of what was now Santander and the Co-op. Truro was built with grandeur for a golden age that never really materialised. A provincial town that constructed a magnificent cathedral in expectation of success, stuck out on a limb at the end of the country. Truro wasn't on the way to anywhere.

I busked on the pedestrianised street by the cathedral, opposite 'Jabba the Cutt' barbers. It was slow going. A man covered in so many bandages and slings that he could easily pass for a Mr Bump cosplay made his way up the road, with a sad raise of an eyebrow that said 'I'd give you a coin or two if only reaching for it didn't hurt so much'.

An hour later I packed up and counted my meagre takings. Less than a tenner. Cornwall was going to be tough. No point wasting time on a bad pitch, much better to get walking. Another busker was playing classical guitar outside Fatface. He wasn't doing much better than me. I took stock of the streets.

Cornwall

The city centre was a dense nugget of national chains. Around them, a looser belt of coffee shops, vegetarian coffee shops, vegan coffee shops, vegan cafes, vegetarian sandwich shops. There was a clear theme. On one street a vegetarian cafe faced a vegan cafe. Both were empty and the motionless bearded proprietors stared impotently through their windows at one another. In Burger King, ten doors down, the locals queued out of the door, more than forty of them.

Folks in search of an alternative life away from the maddening crush of the big city had moved west, drawn by the warmer climate, the rural nature of the county, and perhaps just that inevitable westward drift that eventually seizes all the migratory animals. Cornwall is a big cul-de-sac, a long peninsula, and they'd drifted till they could drift no further, mounding up in the towns and villages like a plague of hairy ladybirds, perpetually in waiting for new lands to form further out, or the fleet to finally arrive and take them away to the undying lands. The poorer ones had soon needed work, and sticking to what they knew, had opened shops in their image. Truro was full of cafes that the locals had no use for, each selling the finest coffee, and each new opening reducing the custom for the others by however many fellow migratory staff they employed. It didn't look sustainable. Would some shed their surfboards like fallen wings and give it up for the big city again? Truro had two completely parallel communities, utterly immiscible.

Nobody had any money. The wanderers had squandered what little they had on their follies and the natives had nothing to begin with. I tried busking on Lemon Quay. It was even worse. An open space where my fiddle should carry well, instead I felt lost and invisible. Truro was never going to be a busker's town. I crossed the peninsula.

St Ives and Sancreed Beacon

IT was no longer the summer season. The kids were back at school. Perhaps St Ives would be quiet. I walked in from the cliff tops and saw the whole town below me, vital and crisp in that famous light, pulsing and energetic with movement. Countless bodies moved on the harbour front with a randomness of direction that felt anarchical. To describe such a sight as like an anthill may be a cliché, but I could think of nothing else.

On the harbour front, there were signs that read 'Do not feed the gulls, do not teach them'. I bought a sandwich and a sausage roll and sat on a rare free spot on a bench on the sheer wall facing into the harbour. A large herring gull came my way along the pavement and repeatedly squonked at me for attention, cocking its head. Do not teach them. I aimed a lazy kick at it and my foot caught in the strap of my fiddle case, sending the case sliding towards the Atlantic. I had a moment of utter panic before realising that my kick was too limp to send it tumbling over the edge. The gull had easily sidestepped to the right and remained fixated on my sausage roll, untroubled by my moment of panic. There was a lesson in this, probably.

In common with most seaside towns, the main shopping street is one back from the quay. It writhes, tight sided and narrow, and was extremely busy. The only busking spot I could find was set back slightly in the large blue rear doors of a church. Things were a bit better here than I'd managed in Truro and I started to make a little change. I'd been going half an hour when the shop opposite me suddenly produced an irate baker who ordered me to move on, explaining that the by-laws only permitted twenty minutes in each spot. I searched online and found this to be true.

'I've had banjos, saxophones, and ukuleles all bloody day! Please just go away!' she implored, almost in tears.

'Do not feed the buskers. Do not teach them' I thought to myself and slunk off without further argument.

I walked round the edge of town searching for a quiet spot to gather my thoughts. On the rocks, above the falling tide, I counted out what I'd made. £15 in half an hour. A good hourly rate, but a terrible overall amount for an afternoon. It was 5pm and St Ives was shutting down for the day.

Feeling unloved, poor, and far from home, I climbed the hill back to my car. A man was restoring a huge marine diesel in his garage, and had run the exhaust pipe 100ft down the drive in a wiggly aluminium tube to the road where the open end ejected cheery clouds of smoke whilst saying 'Blomp-blomp-blomp-blomp...' to anyone passing by.

The town was emptying in a huddle of buses, all vying for slots in the single lane roads. Crowds waited agitatedly at the loading points, tired parents promising theoretical fish and chips to unplacated and listless children. A town famous for the light, and the consequent artistic world that had grown beneath this natural lamp, St Ives was now top-heavy with armies of the curious. A place so utterly frenetic and overwhelmed that no artist would find a working peace. There wasn't a lot to do but walk through quaint but overcrowded streets and consume. It was all so pointlessly nice. It would be fascinating to come back on a wet Tuesday in March. Maybe Berwick was like this now, the town I'd seen in the pouring rain back at the start, almost deserted, new spring shoots yet to show through the soil. Maybe not. This Cornwall is a magnet, a county whose direction of travel is dictated far more by the incomer and the tourist than by the local, little packages of character and quintessence parcelled up and sold for export like the metals of the past, to dress the mantelpieces of England and beyond, to colour the conversations over winter dinner parties, never to return. In the soft light, the colour was being drained out. Tourists acting as sponges, soaking it up drip by drip. St Ives was what the visitors demanded of it.

I got in my car and drove, heading further down the peninsula. The county becomes narrow and squeezed, each identical ruined engine house marking the spots where a lode of tin once burst out into the open and was chased back underground by generations of miners. The engine houses represent pumping and drainage and allowed the mines to extend under the sea, providing access to new and deeper ore. Each ruin stood above miles of tunnels, three-dimensional cobwebs pushing out under the thick blue water. The county's presence felt so much wider than the land.

The last town in England is St Just, a surprisingly bleak place on a shallow hill with a striking frontier feel to it, like the gallows have only recently and reluctantly been taken down. A small central square with three pubs, a couple of takeaways, and a few shops was the extent of it. I had no choice but to eat on a budget, and chose the pizza takeaway on the basis of their £6 offer.

My busking coins for the day were few and low value. After my pizza and picking up three bottles of beer for a fiver from the St Just Co-op, there was no chance of affording anywhere to stay. I set off through the country lanes of deepest Cornwall in search of a lay-by to park up for the night. By the Sancreed Beacon, a Bronze Age settlement overlooking the cleft between Lizard and Land's End, the two trailing legs of the country, there was a long space off the hollowed out road and I parked up at the back.

I watched the world come to a halt for the day. Staying in one's car in the countryside is calming. There's suddenly nothing to do, no more stimulation, no more conversation. I'd become increasingly jealous of the other travel writers I'd been trying to read as I'd travelled round and how they always seem to have so much time to read other people's writing. Paul Theroux routinely appears to pack an extra suitcase of quality literature to read on his journeys. I suppose if you're already successful, you don't need to be earning money as you go, and the time opens up accordingly. Something to aspire to! With an hour of daylight left and my notes all written up, I suddenly had time for a proper read.

I moved to the passenger seat in the probably mistaken belief this would shield me from a drink-driving charge and cracked open a beer. Paul Theroux was travelling through Malawi in a paddle canoe. I was marooned in Cornwall in a shabby red Volvo with £8 to my name. The light was fading. A car pulled up at the far end of the long lay-by. A young couple got out carrying a blanket, full of intent. In the falling dusk, they clearly didn't see me as they headed excitedly hand in hand towards the wild and ancient unenclosed lands to my left. To quote Blaster Bates, the gentleman definitely did a little pole vault over the fence. They moved out of sight and I continued my book. After a disappointingly short time, they were back and moving on. I gave them a thumbs up and a cheery wave as they passed my car. It was not returned.

The light went completely. Funny how the body responds so strongly to these cues when given a blanket of true darkness. It was 9:30pm and everything said bedtime to me. I bunked down in the back end of my car, and opened the windows a crack. Silence and peace.

I was not fully asleep when a series of noises started. Bassy and coming towards me, like thunder but felt in vibrations. With growing alarm I flicked the internal lights on. There was nothing in sight all round the car through the windows. What the hell? Badgers. Under my car. When you're in search of the answer, half asleep, and the obvious has been ruled out, a ridiculous answer makes sense. I jumped out with my torch and shone it under the car. There were no badgers. Above me though, the answer loomed in long faces. Horses leaning over the hedge from the much higher field, falsely enormous in the dark were taking an interest in my car, and more were galloping towards the hedge, the hooves on soft soil making the vibrations I'd felt when all else was silent. Silhouetted against the night, they were a peaceful resolution of my situation. I gave the ring-leader an apple from my stash. My offering was suitably votive, and I was returned to peace beneath the clear black skies and above the plundered tin lodes. Tomorrow was another day and £8 would surely buy some sort of breakfast.

Penzance and Geevor Tin Mine

I AWOKE in my car with the rising of the sun, feeling like a corpse laid out in an open coffin. It would be rude to start moving and startle any mourners who might have gathered. It had not been my day, the day before. £25 just hadn't been enough, not when you have to fuel your car and buy all your food on the go. Sure, you can always get chips, but after a few days you start hallucinating about peas and carrots and a proper diet. I needed a good day, but after my failures in Truro and St Ives, I was not feeling confident as I made my way to Penzance. There was a coffee shack on the junction between the two main streets. Craving a modicum of human company as well as caffeine, I confided my troubles in the barista, who showed me the local paper which featured an article headlined 'Hell on Earth', an exposé of St Ives' ongoing war with the hated buskers. Another customer said 'I wouldn't worry too much. It is St Ives after all. Hell didn't have far to travel.'

I wasn't feeling confident as I opened my case to see if Penzance was a better bet. My fiddle had responded to a cold night in the car by slackening off its strings, causing me to wail 'Et tu, Brute?' as I attempted to bring it slowly back to pitch.

It was still early. My body clock, having been forcibly adjusted by enforced adherence to daylight hours had seen me up and about by 7am. I'd already walked the streets of Penzance. The main shopping thoroughfare is Market Jew Street, allegedly named for the prominent Jewish community that lived here until about 1850. This contained the normal town centre shops, the chains, and sloped up from the harbour and railway station to a grand if somewhat austere grey stone market building and small square. Heading off at right angles was Causewayhead, another long shopping street given over almost entirely to local and independent shops. I'd found breakfast in a cafe here, and was looking forward to seeing the street come to life.

I started playing at about 9:30am, too early really because the town wasn't fully functioning yet and footfall was low, but I was keen to play if only for myself. The acoustic was nice, and the sun was warm. Grumpy from losing tension, the fiddle was taking time to really ring, but slowly it warmed up too, and I settled in for a good session.

After a while I was aware of being watched. People rarely watch a busker for long. They may enjoy it in passing, but don't often stop for a period to really take it in. The anonymity serves to take the pressure off the performance. This lady was definitely an audience though, leaning against a wall across the street. She smiled warmly at me and caught off guard, I fluffed a couple of notes.

A homeless man came past and put a flower in my case. It's perhaps a counter-intuitive thing, but homeless people are almost always generous with what they have. I often get a handful of coppers from them. I've come to realise just how important an act this is for people in this situation. Homelessness robs you of so much more than just your home. You lose so many of the autonomies that define the human experience. Most of us consume art of some form on a daily basis, be that TV, computer games, books, music, etc. A few coins or a flower in my collection are a statement of cultural autonomy and an assertion of one's basic humanity. They are a powerful and moving defiance of circumstance and I always try to return them later, with interest.

About 11:30am, another busker showed up. His name was Frank, and I was ready for a rest, so I gladly handed the spot over to him. He was a gentle soul, and had travelled through Spain and Portugal with his guitar the year before. He told me approximately how long he intended to busk for so I could regain the spot when he finished. I decided to take an early lunch.

The coffee shack was the de-facto centre point of Penzance. It had developed its own breed of barflies who instead of getting gradually more drunk like the pub variety, were getting progressively more wired and exuberant as the day wore on. One was a smallish fellow with a magnificent white beard, glasses, and a giant white ankle length coat, embroidered with hundreds of colourful flowers. He started making requests and paying for them a coin at a time, dancing little jigs as I played. I packed up my second busking session at 2pm. Even though the going was good, I had another destination in mind for the day.

If St Ives yesterday had represented the now of tourist Cornwall, then Geevor represents the then of mining past. Just outside Pendeen, it was the final tin mine to close, in 1990. A closure so abrupt and immediate some miners had already gone on shift out under the Atlantic before they could be told. It's an astonishing place. Rather than artefacts assembled in retrospect, Geevor is as it was the day the tools were put down. Nothing has been moved.

Nowhere is this more poignant than 'The Dry', the miners' changing room, where the lockers are as they were after the final shift, festooned with dirty pants, muddy overalls, packets of woodbines, hot chocolate mugs, the room still smelling of coal-tar soap and Jeyes fluid. Graffiti is chalked onto walls, some of it obscene. The only change from 1990 is where a miner has since died, and a small photo and plaque has been placed on the top shelf of their locker. A powerful visual representation of real human stories turning into the cold clay of impersonal history.

We're much better at learning from the living. Each shrine is a voice and an experience we can't hear again. The opportunity for a personal connection to another time and space gone. I've been here before, knew what to expect, and still found myself deeply emotional in such a powerful space.

The loss of the personal connection, the direct first-hand account, is a problem we struggle with as a species. No matter how diligent the recording work, how well presented the information, it simply doesn't carry the same impact and believability of being told things directly, being looked in the eye by someone who saw it, who suffered it. It is so much harder to disregard information told to you directly by someone in the same room, when the wider senses are lit by the touch and the smell of the moment. There is a validation to being told something in person that plays to our egos in a way that simply discovering the information, cold, colourless, and laid out for anyone can't achieve. We have been chosen to hear this. It must be important.

Look at how the yearly poppy appeal appears on the verge of morphing into a nationalistic fetish symbol now that so few of the survivors of mechanised slaughter are still around to remind us directly of its meaning, to hold our hands, look us in the eyes and tell us what it felt like.

We are evolved to listen to those around us, to take directly communicated warnings more seriously, and attach extra importance to information relayed to us in person. This filter limits the collective horizon of our knowledge to that of the oldest active generation. Anything that falls over that event horizon loses that connection and fails to be seen as relevant by the majority. This is what leads people to build their houses on active volcanoes or in flood plains or huge geological faults, both literally and metaphorically. Stories that fall outside living memory become historical irrelevancies, of interest to history nuts and weirdos. It couldn't happen here. It couldn't happen now. In the absence of the living story, new and different narratives can take over, more compelling only because they're told by the living.

If we want to avoid making the mistakes of the past again, we need to collectively finding a way of making tales that have fallen off the event horizon as relevant and compelling as the stories that the living can tell us. Each locker that becomes a shrine is one step towards the loss of this story as a living and relevant lesson and towards it becoming just a collection of objects.

However, there are still plenty of miners left in Geevor for now. Mining is one of those careers that totally saturates the life of many of the people who do it. Retraining is hard, and psychologically you'll always be a miner doing something else. In common with most ex mining communities, at Geevor you couldn't find alternative work if you wanted to. Some had left for work abroad. Probably for less money, and whilst starting their life again somewhere unfamiliar, but at least they were mining. Others were left with the choice of both re-training into something they didn't believe they were and leaving town, or staying around, forever an unemployed miner. One employee told me it killed the town overnight, wiped the pubs and shops out.

Most of the staff of the museum are ex-miners, although that's only a small percentage of the previous employment figures. They're not all old men either. The youngest is 48 and was just three months into his apprenticeship when the work stopped.

One of the employees spotted the fiddle case on my back.

'What sort of music do you play?'

'English traditional stuff, mostly.'

'I'm Marc. I play a bit myself, on the melodeon. Do you fancy a few tunes when we shut up for the night?'

I said I would, and so when the museum closed up for the day we played music together in the winding house, a large concrete and tin building that held the electric motor that raised and lowered the cage to the working levels. The acoustics were good and we knew enough of the same tunes. It felt like a fitting end to the day, looking out across a landscape scraped bare by industry, tumbling down through chimneys and engine houses to the jewelled sea.

I slowly meandered my car round the very tip of Cornwall. Land's End looked naff. A tourist trap on the basis that there's nowhere else you can go once you get there. Lamorna Cove was beautiful, but full of signs telling me it was private and I'd need to pay lots of money to enjoy it. In Mousehole, home of Dolly Pentreath who was reputed to be the last native Cornish speaker (died 1777), it was not possible to park, owing to the tourists and lack of space. This land belongs to the tourist, the passer-by. The locals are the tenant farmers of the towns, the groundskeepers, the caretakers. It's theirs but not theirs.

I wound up back in Penzance and counted my money. I'd made £85 during the day, and after my museum entry price, lunch, coffee, and a stained glass engine house effigy from the gift shop, I could either have a good meal or somewhere to stay. It was not a difficult choice and I returned to my personal lay-by full of food and content with the world. The sky was black and the Milky Way a nuanced and detailed canvas unspoilt by street lights. I spent a restful night untroubled by courting couples or imaginary badgers.

Next morning, I returned to my now familiar coffee shack. There was an old fellow in the busking spot, looking quite unlike anyone I'd seen before. He was quietly playing some sort of unusual whistle, and was haunched down and folded up like a dehydrated Andean mummy, all bones and angles. The barista explained: 'He's the original busker here. Been here all his life. Used to be a fisherman, then when he got too old for that he took up busking with a piano accordion, then when he got too old for that he took up that whistle instead. When he was young, he was famous for his exploits. They say he once caught eighty conger eels on a hundred hook line, and could fish for congers with his feet too. He once made a sail out of seagulls' wings and sailed a boat all round the bottom of Cornwall with it.'

He was ancient, with the long ears that belong to the truly old. He wore sandals with rough woollen socks, darned beyond further repair and now broken and gaping. His feet were leathered and smooth like sea brick. Only his hat was new, a woolly beanie in bright colours that added to his oddly Andean vibe. I gave him some coins and sat by him for a while and chatted. His words were weathered to the vowels, the rough edges of consonants worn away by time and tide, his speaking soft and untethered. He said he made his own instruments out of what he found in skips. This one was a galvanised pipe he'd modified, drilling holes in what he felt were the right places. Sometimes he got the holes wrong and would tape them up and try again. The mouthpiece was more folded metal, set in a lump of hewn cork, all combined with electrical tape. His foot tapped slowly, out of time with the music.

I didn't ask him about the sail of seagull wings. Sometimes it's better to stick with the possibility it might be true than live in a world where it definitely didn't happen.

After a while, I left him to it and travelled to the top of Causewayhead with a sandwich. On a bench was a full mug of tea in a cup that was printed 'Lady of the Manor'. I sat at the other end of the bench in the hope that someone would come along and provide me with another interesting conversation. Nobody came. I reach over and touched the mug. It was stone cold.

Marc, the melodeon player from Geevor mine suddenly appeared and asked if I fancied a duet, so we set ourselves up by the big building on the market place. It went very well, and we managed £25 in next to no time. Marc was happy with this, because it was his day off and he was meeting friends in the pub and that was his round sorted. I continued solo for a while. A dog delivered a steaming pile of critical appraisal next to my collection, and whilst the embarrassed owner did clear it up, the spot had lost something of its magic and I moved on.

I finished the day in a busking slot half way up Causewayhead, opposite the cinema. Frank had been there for a few songs, along with another guy who played saxophone to backing tracks.

'Henley, that's where you want to go mate, at Christmas. They're fucking loaded. A tenner to them is like a quid to someone here.'

I was part of the busker's union now and we shared a few stories, the three of us sat on the step of an abandoned shopping unit. Some buskers play the same few slots again and again, others never stop travelling. I'd been doing it for long enough to share plenty of tales of my own now. It was a nice moment, and I realised I was falling in love with Penzance.

It's a great town, Penzance. Not very wealthy. It has substance abuse problems, but frankly so does everywhere I've been. People tell me about it in every town like it's their personal shame rather than an escalating nationwide problem. What Penzance has that I liked so much is a sense of togetherness. Where Truro felt divided between two immiscible communities, and St Ives like a strange theme park with all the tat stalls and none of the attractions, here all sorts of oddballs had assembled to create a space that felt calm and welcoming. There was a feeling of everyone really wanting to make it work, and not wanting to spoil it for others.

Cornwall is a county where the relics of industry are so old that the countryside would feel incomplete and naked without them. The engine houses crumbling back into the ground they were raised from come from a time far before living memory, and are as aloof and mysterious as standing stones. Dual carriageways have opened the county up, and remote fishing villages have become limbs of the home counties and London, the locals locked in a strange indentured service to their own community. The poorer towns have seen a different incomer. Where the tourists don't bother, the hippies and drifters open their cafés and seek a simpler life. In the Geevor museum is a gallery of Cornish engine houses around the world, their distinctive shape and architecture transported to every continent by Cornish miners in search of work. Cornwall is a county that things have always left. People, resources, ideas, skills, gift shop tat, frustrations, surfboards.

I busked for a final session on Causewayhead, opposite the cinema. It was getting towards closing up time, and there were few people about. The afternoon was mild and gentle, and I played for myself, revelling in the acoustic, losing myself in the music. The violin had fully recovered from the trauma of the day before and sang out, strings rattling as they hit each other, overtopping with joyful energy. I played with a rare freedom and delight, hitting heights I didn't know I had. The only audience was a young woman selling confectionary from a hatch in the cinema frontage. She stared blankly across the road at nothing, chin resting resigned on hands waiting for her shift to finish. I didn't want mine to end. Perhaps I could drift down here and make a go of it? Maybe open a decent coffee shop...

Interlude: My Fiddle

I HAVE more than one fiddle, of course. I learnt on a German trade fiddle, deep brown and light with age. It's a funny sort of shape with square shoulders and the bridge has to be in the wrong place to deliver the right string length. Everything is just slightly off about it, but it sounds lovely and soft, especially on the lowest string. It is fragile with age. My family bought it for me when I was about 11 on the strength of a tip off. An old and retired player had grown too frail to play and wanted the instrument to move on to a youngster and wasn't bothered about the price if it went to the right home. I was the lucky beneficiary of this, although I didn't appreciate how lucky until many years later when I gained the knowledge to actually appraise it. I still play it, but only for a few weeks each year, as it tends to fall apart after a while. In this project I only took it out once, to Carlisle. It wouldn't have coped with the heavy usage the project demanded, but I was keen that it should be involved at least once.

My main fiddle was made by Colin Cross, a celebrated maker based these days in Deal, but once of Buxton and a regular face at the George session that proved so influential on me. I commissioned it, after long discussions on tone and ringiness. I played him my favourite players, took him to concerts, and he thought about it and came back with the instrument I play now.

'See how you get on with it, for a few weeks. If it's not right, it'll sell anyway and I'll try again.' I rang him about three hours later to say he wasn't getting it back.

It's a big ringing fiddle, with tons of projection and voice, but it can go right down to near silence as well, a feature that took me a while to understand, having always been a full-on sort of player in the past. I'm very lucky to have it. My maternal grandmother left me a legacy that allowed me to commission it. She was always a great supporter of my playing, hearing only beautiful music, even when I was just scraping away, all over the place. I am sure she'd love the instrument.

The final part of the puzzle is the bow, often overlooked as part of the instrument but, in truth, perhaps the more important piece. It's the dynamic, living part of the combination, home to all the touch and sensitivity that mark out the really good players. Without a good bow, you won't be able to grow as a player. Students are easily persuaded to buy better fiddles, but persuading them to splash out on a bow is much harder.

Why does the bow matter so much? It's not just a hairy stick.

It runs across the string, rosined up for friction, a constant transfer of energy between vibrating string and stick. The stick is the key, a leaf spring that stores and releases energy by command. A good bow is a perfect balanced spring, even in tension throughout, and it feels to the player like the hair is in the string rather than on it. A good bow softens the player, loosens the muscles and does the work for you.

Mine was made by John Stagg of Bristol. It arrived in my life just before I set off to busk my first town. I played fifty quality bows, all over the country, finding it a hard choice until I picked this one up. I immediately knew it was the right one, a powerful domineering stick, that just like the fiddle could go right down to almost nothing too. I'm a big lad, and I play in a big physical way. My equipment suits my frame, but challenges me to be more subtle and delicate. Both my fiddle and my bow represent space into which I continue to grow. I am enormously lucky to have both of them, and they bring me great pleasure.

It is not always a question of what makes a good bow or a good fiddle, but about what makes a good combination. The right fiddle for the player, the right bow for the fiddle. The right player for the bow. My combination are beautiful objects in their own right, but they work so well together, bringing out depth in each other that leaves me feeling the minor third party, my job simply to have brought them together. They might have been made for each other, although perhaps if attempted it would not have worked so perfectly as it did.

Retford

A STRANGE natural sodium sort of light fell lengthways across the land from a low sun as I drove early into Nottinghamshire. I parked up in Retford by a large and long abandoned council estate pub, working class grandeur being torn down piecemeal by sycamore saplings, ribboning into the tarmac of the car park and easing their sinews into the masonry.

Papa's chippy wasn't open yet, but it already smelled of mushy peas warming up. A tattooed publican was straightening his poppy flags, seasonal hanging-baskets of remembrance. Retford was getting ready for market day.

I got straight to work, setting up for a busk on the main street against a blank shuttered door by the end of the Cashino, its name a tawdry portmanteau for our times. I hadn't been playing ten minutes when a man stopped me. 'Excuse me, are you local?'

'I'm afraid not, I've come over from Manchester way.'

'You see, I run an amateur dramatics group and we're working on a production of 'Ladies in Lavender'. Have you heard of it?'

'No...' Where was he going with this?

'Well, it was made into a film starring Judi Dench, and it's about these two sisters who live in a remote fishing community in Cornwall.'

'Okay...' He continued:

'And one day they find a young man washed up on the beach, and they nurse him to health, and it turns out he's a Polish violinist.'

'Ah.'

'But we can't find anyone capable of playing a shipwrecked Polish violinist round here and I just wondered...'

Usually I like to go with the flow of events and take on whatever opportunities the street throws at me, but a month's unpaid work as a washed up violinist was somehow a little too close to home.

'It's a bit far from Manchester, I'm afraid.'

'Oh well. Let me know if you change your mind. You can find us in the little theatre round the corner.'

His hopes crushed, he headed away. A few moments later I was stopped again. 'Excuse me, are you local?'

'I'm from Manchester way.'

'Ah, you see my wife plays violin, but not like you.'

Mistaking this for a compliment I said 'Well, thanks.'

'No,' he said wistfully. 'She plays difficult, complex pieces.'

'Ah.' He thought about it a bit.

'I wish she'd stop making it so damned hard for herself and play something easy once in a while.'

And he headed off, can of Dulux matt emulsion in each hand and a neatly trimmed white handlebar moustache maintaining watch over proceedings. There's definitely a type of gentleman of a certain age who stops you to tell you something they know about music without asking you anything about yourself, as if knowing that they like Mahler is somehow useful information to you. It's an entitlement I suppose. These conversations always end when they run out of facts about music they know, and without any sort of useful point having been arrived at. A silence descends with me unable to contribute, not having been involved in their monologue so far, and they walk off without leaving a coin, their wisdom surely reward enough. Thank goodness I'm not a woman doing this I sometimes think. I imagine if I were, I'd get twice as much money and four times as many idiots to deal with. There's certainly a blessed anonymity in being an increasingly middle aged bloke with old clothes and a bald head.

I played on and the conversations kept coming. My next visitor was a tall Chinese lady with a preposterously fluffy white dog. She latched onto me from a distance and cut through the street towards my spot, dog trotting alongside.

'Hello, oh I am really enjoying the music. This is my dog, Snowy Pearl Chow Chow, he's on Instagram! He has hundreds of followers. I love your violin, why are you in Retford? You should go somewhere better! Dead end here, I have a camper van.' She spoke in fast chopping sentences with a strong Chinese accent.

'I'm just here busking for a couple of days. Where are you from?' I replied.

'Ah you can see I'm not a local, yes. I'm actually from Hereford, but I know what you are thinking, she does not sound like she is from Hereford! This is because I grew up in Leeds! Haha! You should go to Hong Kong, do you have a degree? You could go on a worker visa, oh they love the violin there, you could play it at night and teach English in the day! Oh it would be so good. My Chow Chow, he's such a good dog. You can follow him on Instagram. Are you on Instagram? You could follow each other on Instagram!'

She was a phenomenon, a breathless whirlwind of words and barely connected sentences. Six foot tall in flats and looked me in the eye with a sincere confidence. Had I created her as a fictional character, I'd quite rightly stand accused of copying a stereotype, yet here she was, going full pelt at me like this, needing no encouragement at all. And then she was gone, Snowy Pearl Chow Chow obediently in tow, on to the next person. It suddenly dawned on me that this was a performance rather than a person. I whipped out my notepad and scribbled down as much of the conversation as I could. Like me, she was working the street as well, playing the stereotype, her morning's work to get some more Instagram followers for her dog. I resumed mine.

An older lady came slowly along, and dropped 60p into my case, before pausing, taking a good look at what was already in there, and remarking regretfully 'Oh. You're doing quite well.'

A little later, a man stopped right in front of my pitch, oblivious to me, and held a long phone conversation with someone of whom he demanded 'Are you peeling onions? ARE YOU PEELING ONIONS?' in an increasingly agitated manner. After a couple of minutes of this, he suddenly hung up and hurried off, leaving me hanging. Were they peeling onions? We may never know.

It had been an action-packed morning, and I was ready for lunch. I picked up a hot pie and a sandwich from the cavernous 'A.W. Bacon and Sons, est 1938', a veritable department store of bakery and butchery, and wandered the town.

It was the week before Remembrance Sunday. There were a lot of poppies about, and not just pinned to the lapels of the passing shoppers. Every other shop had a remembrance themed window display. I documented a few of my favourites. The Air Ambulance charity shop offered a poppy covered bookcase full of paperback spy thrillers. Mind UK's poppy display housed the complete *Dad's Army* scripts. Not to be outdone, the Edinburgh Woollen Mill had a fashionable display of camouflage pattern designer trousers amongst their poppies. A decorative metalworker had created large poppies with centres made of melted and deformed vinyl records. I looked closer, and the records he'd chosen to sacrifice were German Hammond-Organ albums. Good though the subversion of this art was, my winner for the day was an independent charity shop whose magnificent poppy window featured *The Young Hitler I Knew* in hardback as their centrepiece.

Faced with this bewildering series of juxtapositions, I took my pie and sandwich and sat by the inert and ossified Sebastopol cannon, which is rated eleven of eighteen things to do in Retford on *TripAdvisor*, to think it over. This Russian cannon, claimed by the British in the Crimean war in 1855 and plinthed two years later, was retrieved to Retford of all places and set up as a monument to the fallen of that particular foreign adventure. Almost melted down for the Second World War effort, it was saved by local dignitaries for whom the Crimean war still held enough personal meaning to make the symbolism worth preserving. Now it feels impossibly lost to history, a random cannon from Russia, meaningless and incongruous, though symbolically it meant much the same to the citizens of Retford in the Victorian era as our war memorials do to us today.

Retford

The difficulty with the poppy, it seems to me, is what a nakedly powerful symbol it is, so simple and susceptible to being filled with new meaning. Symbols can sometimes overpower their first given meaning. That straightforward design, the splash of colour so immediately visually distinctive against our dull British Autumnal apparel makes for a symbol so clearly full of power, even if you were unfamiliar with the detail.

In Cornwall, at the Geevor Mine musuem, I'd spent a long time thinking about how the message so often dies with the story teller. The history books, the archives, the secondary sources don't carry the same sense of personal impact. With the rapid decline in the number of Second World War veterans left among us, the direct connection to the poppy is being lost, and for many is now a patently powerful symbol without an immediate personal connection.

Thus untethered from its foundation, the poppy becomes a symbol ripe for new purpose, an increasingly empty vessel awaiting new content. This vacuum is being filled by all sorts of ideas. Some are awful. The widely shared images of people marching with swastika tattoos on their necks and a poppy on their chest, and the people waving a poppy flag whilst giving a Nazi salute are particularly shocking examples. Most are much more mundane. The window displays I saw were not fascist or wildly offensive. They were simply confused, almost child-like. The poppy reduced to being a vague icon of past war and present country.

We are as a people unsure of ourselves. It comes, perhaps, of having been the hegemonic power. There is nothing really to rebel against. Our culture and language dominant, World Wars won, subjugated by nobody. There is no greater power in our lives, no true dominant external force against which to assert our identity.

In these difficult times, in a country that still hasn't overcome the banking crisis over a decade ago, where a decade of austerity has taken each public service down to the bone, it seems only natural to wonder if we're at the mercy of greater forces and wonder if we could just assert our national identity a little more, we might regain some sort of control of things.

Within this vacuum, the poppy has suddenly become an available symbol to a population that need to assert something, even if they're not quite sure exactly what. As the last WW2 veterans slowly slip out of the public discussion, the Second World War, like the First, starts to become distant and impersonal history in much the same way that the Sebastopol cannon attracts merely a ripple of confused interest, despite the deep symbolism it once bore. Words like 'Glory' and 'Remembrance', reread in a now secular world, lose their very specific Christian neutrality and take on more dramatic, nationalistic overtones. Glory not as the comforting religious surety that the wasted innocent would be received into heaven, but a Godless and personal triumph in a war of righteousness. Something to be nationalistically proud of, not crumbs of comfort in a hopeless, complex mess.

This too-rarely challenged sense of pride where once there was only sorrow appeals to an agitated and hurting English population seeking to make sense of a divided society, where the gap between rich and poor grows ever bigger, where the high street is fading away, the only growth area the homeless and hopeless. We wonder if only we could assert our Englishness some more, this could be overcome. The English flag itself is a somewhat debauched and tawdry symbol, immediately associated with football hooliganism. Too cheap for this greater calling. In the poppy there is a sense of higher purpose and understated nobility that makes it a symbol suitable for those who couldn't bring themselves to wave the flag. A symbol that appears to offer togetherness in the strained union of the UK and a sense of identity in a shared past. It's a very English form of patriotism. Simplistic, understated.

People need symbolism and the poppy fulfils that need, and whilst there are some awful images of misappropriation of the poppy available to find, most uses of it just look a wellspring of uncertain identity allied to a vacant and potent symbol.

Symbolism by itself, though, is a shortcut that bypasses the complex necessities of identity, a shortcut where the symbol becomes the totem of identity itself, rather than a natural expression of an identity richly and broadly arrived at. The poppy here gets us no nearer to an expression of Englishness other than to expose an unmet sense of yearning and need. The misappropriation of the poppy a symptom of a wider failure to understand ourselves, an unhelpful attempt to simplify the complex and layered identities of our country into a single expression, nationalistic and exclusionary.

That evening, I chewed the thought over with my friend Edwin in the Lord Nelson pub in Sutton on Trent. I told him about the window displays I'd encountered in Retford, and how they seemed to jar with the messages I'd been brought up to understand the poppy stood for, and my own consequent reluctance to wear one. He'd been taught in Berkhamstead school, which with its close links to the military had seen many pupils go straight from school to slaughter.

'Remembrance is a constant, low level thing. It's there every day in the memorials on the Chapel Wall, the garden of Remembrance, and the stories attached to some of the names, like, 'he was a bit of a shit' or 'he was shy but a brilliant mathematician'. It's a stark reminder when the same names on the awards plaques, cups, team captains, and in the school history books are the same ones as those on the lists of the fallen. Remembrance is about the hope for nobody having to do this, unwillingly or voluntarily, ever again. It shouldn't be a divisive symbol, but there's people on many sides trying to make it one: Trying to make it so you're either for it or against it whatever the current 'it' of the day happens to be; but to me it feels like it should be inclusive, not divisive. By making you feel uncomfortable in not wearing one, yet another way of making it a symbol of division, those seeking to divide people have then found yet another way to do so. It's meant to be your choice. My school felt very strongly that one should not be caught up in the populist upwelling of emotions.'

I couldn't help but agree, and felt I should get myself a poppy the next day. My reasons for wearing it would be mine and mine alone, and nobody else need read too much into it. I still feared the direction the poppy might travel in, but perhaps my refusal to wear it might only speed that distasteful process up. I saw no glory in it, only sorrows. A lull fell over the conversation. The chatter of the pub washed over us. I took a sup of my pint. 'Nice drop this, what is it?'

'It's called Bomber Command.'

'Ah.'

Next day I was back in Retford. Yesterday had been market day, although the stalls had only really filled about half the square. There'd been cheap electronics, cheap clothes, a bit of fruit and veg. Nothing too remarkable, other than the stall selling 'Zombie Apocalypse training', where two strapping young individuals in camouflage clothing holding air rifles had stood meaningfully in front of a screaming pockmarked blue mannequin head, offering the chance to prepare for the coming end times. It seemed entirely reasonable in the circumstances.

Today was different. It was the bric-a-brac market, where the heady world of market trading was thrown open to the amateur and enthusiast as well as the professional. It was infinitely more interesting. Nothing for sale was at all useful or had any genuine value, but there were oddities galore. One stall presented the splendid juxtaposition of second hand model railway equipment and new underpants. They must know their market. Another, brass sextants and a life size model walrus. My favourite was a stall completely buried in crocheted animals, all the work of one lady who was selling them very cheaply. Clearly an obsession where the main requirement of the stall was to clear the living room down a bit and make room for new balls of wool. I asked her if I could photograph the scene, and she said I could if she got out of the picture first. I did so, bought a crocheted bee for 50p and headed towards the busking spot.

It was already in use. A man wrapped in so many coats I couldn't tell how big he was had set up a small guitar and vocal amp and was singing away. He had a charity bucket for collection. I got a coffee and settled in to watch for a bit. The music was gentle and pleasant. I tuned into the lyrics.

'I didn't mean to hurt you, but I'm just a jealous guy...'

It didn't seem to matter, and coins were going into the bucket. I stepped over for a chat. His name was Paul and he busked for Cancer Research. He was a retired teacher, and this was his final busk of the year, as the cold was getting to be too much. He was really interested in what I was up to, and we had a good conversation, made awkward by the fact he'd left his clip-on vocal mike turned up, causing his half of the chat to be broadcast loudly to the street.

He was nearly done, having been there an hour and a half already. I was soon set up and got a good session of my own in. It would soon be time to drive the eight miles to Worksop and see what life was like there.

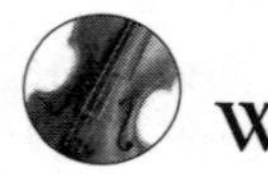

Worksop

WORKSOP is Victorian red brick and peeling paint, a once handsome and forthright town ground down to bitter poverty by the action of a vast economic ice sheet, brutally gravelled and piling up in terminal moraines. Pinched like an hourglass, the town narrows to cross the Chesterfield canal on a single lane bridge, the black oily ribbon running anonymously through the town like an alien artery, unknowable and bleak. On the tall windowless rear wall of Yates's Wine Lodge by the town lock, above the scummy and rodent infested chill waters, a sign is hung with tragic optimism: 'No Bathing'.

On streets slick with dull water, traders hunched their shoulders under inadequate canvas triangles and turned themselves inwards to phone screens and Bensons. The bright burning lights of the pawn shops and gambling emporia diffracted the gloom from the streets and filled my eyes with their false electric rainbows. Above the shops, window frames rotted outside tenancies untaken. Worksop was on its arse.

I'd been here before, five years ago, on what can only really be described as a poorly conceived romantic break, where the highlight was probably narrowly failing to win the meat raffle. It hadn't been a rich town then, but how it had gone downhill, ripped struggling out to sea on a falling tide.

Amazingly, the hotel I'd stayed in on that ill-fated trip, the Station Hotel, was still in business, but was now retreating and withdrawn to the central-most section, Victorian outbuildings with plywood where the windows once were, abandoned sections of bar barricaded off by a wall of tall stools, lights removed from sockets. Other pubs and shops, it was hard to say if they were open or not. Many were, but it wasn't obvious. Staying afloat had meant not spending a penny more than you had to, and paint was flaking away, lights had failed, signage was weathered unreadable. The town was opaque and hard to read.

Shops didn't sell much in the way of new goods. There were pawn shops, second-hand, exchange, a whole raft of genuinely local businesses alongside the bottom end of the national names. So much of the residual economy here was not in the sale of new goods, but the incremental redistribution of what they already had. Most of the rest was in escapism and false hope. I found a disused awning out of the rain and loaded the fiddle up for a good scrape.

Worksop

The Wikipedia page for Worksop notes several times that 'Unemployment is lower than the national average' without giving a source or a date. Well, maybe it's true, but it has the feel of an incongruous line inserted into the page by a different author with a clear political agenda. Certainly, nobody had told the lads outside the pub next to my spot, out in the rain to enjoy a cigarette. They flowed gently across the road to BetFred and back, at ninety degrees to the shopping traffic, a steady stream each way. The lads coming back to the pub would often divert up to my spot and find a coin or two. Gamblers are always generous.

The flow up and down the main street was steady enough, but every other person or so was limping, or using a wheelchair, or hobbling about on crutches. Worksop was the sort of place where people were too ill to afford to get better, and where the current state of the economy and the nature of the work that they'd lost gave you plenty to be ill of. And yet the money piled up in my case. On a wet quiet day in a horribly poor former mining town, I made £25 in an hour. It was humbling.

Down the street was 'Fair n Square', the ultimate low-budget 21st century supermarket, rambling uneven floor space across several joined units filled with piles of almost out of date crisps and chocolates and a handful of toiletries, all at about 20 per cent market prices and without shelving. I got four cans of Pringles, a Lucozade, and a grab-bag of Monster Munch for £1.80. There were plenty of customers and it's great that this stuff is being sold instead of wasted, but I doubt they had a branch in Alderley Edge or Witney. Back on the street, a salesman stopped me.

'Excuse me sir, who is your gas supplier?'

'I don't have a house.'

And I faded from his view like a ghost, his eyes lost focus and he looked straight through me. I had become invisible to him, no longer of potential value.

The butcher was shutting up shop for the day. He had a jolly life-size butcher effigy on the street outside his shop, and he stood by it in the gloom for a moment, gazing out in total grumpy contrast. I took a sneaky photo.

Next day I set up early in the main street again and got stuck in. It was busy, with plenty of footfall. Just like Dudley, most shoppers were searching for a few specific items at the lowest price instead of buying luxuries or stuff on impulse. The market stalls were bare essentials and budget items. I'd crossed the canal, waving at a boat in the town lock, heading down. It was covered in a pretty even mixture of remembrance poppies and Christmas decorations. 'Ho, ho, ho, Merry Poppymas' I said quietly to myself as I headed past.

My morning was eventful, if not unpleasant. I had a large number of interruptions which rather prevented many coins building up, but anecdotes are my other currency on these trips, so I didn't mind. Sometimes you see someone coming down the street and you just know they're going to have something to say. When I saw the thin white fellow in his 60s with the green dreadlocks, Rastafarian's hat, and crutches, I knew instinctively he was coming my way. He smelled of alcohol and had a lot to tell me.

'You'd love the reggae stuff, y'know. Have you heard of the Afro-Celts? I've got all their records in my camper van.'

He then let off a massive loose fart that drew the attention of the nearby market stall holders before continuing.

'You should come round when you've finished playing, I've got loads of music. We can listen to it all. I've got loads of Dub.'

Was it a proposition? He saw my hesitation.

'Oh it won't smell, rear end trouble that's the problem.'

An old fellow then turned up and tried to tell me something about violins, and the two of them spoke over each other and at cross purposes for a while whilst I just stood there. The old fellow's wife then dragged him away, and defeated, my new dreadlocked friend decided he too should move on.

'I'd better go. Drive home. Let me know if you change your mind.'

Half an hour later he was still at the traffic lights fifty yards away, talking to shoppers who were trapped waiting for an altogether different green man.

The cadet force was out in numbers today, selling poppies up and down the main street. Little clusters of teenagers in camouflage uniforms every fifty yards. I honoured my decision from Retford and purchased mine with a handful of busking coins. What did the poppy mean to these kids, a century on from the Armistice? It must be hard to contextualise it in an era where the last voices of that war have fallen silent. Does it really feel any different to them than talking about the Battle of Hastings or Agincourt? Living history on the verge of becoming mythology.

As I was considering this, a Tyrannosaurus Rex came round the corner and began making its way down the street towards me. It was about 9ft tall, and seemed entirely plausible until I spotted that its legs were wearing camouflage trousers. It had a couple of handlers, and was posing for pictures with people instead of eating them. I waited my turn and got my photo taken too. There wasn't much point in busking whilst it was around being the centre of attention so I packed up. And not a moment too soon, as the skies opened and soaked the streets again.

I took shelter in the grumpy butchers and got chatting. My original photo, uploaded to the internet, had caused a friend to get in touch to recommend his tomato sausages. Such is the power of social media. I was pleased to find out that he wasn't grumpy at all and he cheerfully sold me half a dozen of the famous sausages. I told him I'd taken a picture that made him look grumpy and he replied that he usually was. We agreed to set up another more positive shot, to even the score.

I took my lunch pie and ate it under the canvas of an unused market stall out of the rain. Better weather was blowing in fast from the West, and soon a huge rainbow appeared, fountaining out of the middle of the main street, framed perfectly by the buildings. A mother and daughter went past and I heard the following exchange;

'Rainbows! There's bound to be unicorns at the end!'

'We can look for them after I go into Superdrug.'

The rain stopped as quickly as it had started and I found a spot away from the residual drips, opposite the book stall. I asked the lady running it if she minded me playing, and she cheerily replied 'Not at all.' This friendliness was worth reciprocating. I had a rummage in the boxes and found the autobiography of snooker player Steve Davis, title: *Interesting*.

'How much?'

'£4.'

'Right, I'll busk for it until I have enough.'

This proved to be an amusing idea for us both, so I set up and started to play. The first pound coin came quickly, and I started shouting out the running total after each tune. After fifteen minutes, I found myself marooned on £3.19. It wouldn't budge at all. Just at the point where I thought I might have to renegotiate the terms of the book withdrawal agreement, one tune suddenly produced £8 of contributions in three minutes. I shouted triumphantly that I'd raised enough, and she brought me the book over. I asked her about running her market stall. She said she had to raise £60 to cover the cost of putting it on each day. Every book had a profit margin of about 40p.

'Problem is that people who don't work have an issue with people who do. They're condescending towards us.' She nodded at the smoker's zone outside the pub. 'Like there's something wrong with trying to work and make a living. One bloke told me he didn't like your playing and I said 'at least he's trying to do something!''

This is exactly the sort of faint praise I thrive on.

Business was declining.

Worksop

'People are lazy, just clicking or on phones. They'll lose all these shops and stalls soon because they can't be bothered to use them. They just drink in pubs, smoke, take drugs, and knock people who try.'

It was a bleak assessment of Worksop. She thought about it a bit and saw the other side of the coin.

'But I love it on a good day. Talking to the old folks, keeping them company. Feels like you're doing a kind of service.'

As I've mentioned, in my travels round the world, I'd encountered two kinds of extreme poverty. In China, in the back streets of Pingdingshan, where every back street had a dozen workshops in a single basic trade it was 'Work as hard as you possibly can and you might just have enough to survive till tomorrow' and in Eritrea, in the barely developed countryside and under an utterly corrupt government it had been 'There's no point trying because no amount of hard work will make your life better'.

Worksop looked a lot more like it was heading towards the second one to me, to the extent that people openly couldn't see the point of trying and quite reasonably spent their days in idle escapism and 40p per book in a declining market looked like a tough gig. Not much here to encourage someone new into the world of work. How would it make their lives better than not working? The current governmental response of slowly eroding unemployment benefits until not having a job kills you seems to perhaps be coming at the problem from the wrong end. Before I could start up playing again, some kids arrived on their bikes.

'Hey mister, are you any good?'

'I'm alright... tell you what, I'll play you a tune and you can decide.'

I launched into some reels, and they responded by dancing around the street.

'Whoah, you're really good', 'Awesome!', and finally 'You're nearly good enough to be a professional!'

They found a shower of change to drop in my case and cycled off. The pattern of generosity was repeated again and again. Gangs of youths, boys showing off to girls by dancing past me, taking the piss, then stopping and returning with coins. One teenage girl found a pound coin, gave it to a boy in the group and ordered he bring it to me. Blushing, he did. People on crutches with serious health problems found change. Unemployed folks, elderly. All generous. I made better money here than nearly anywhere else, and had more conversations per hour.

A woman stopped me and asked if I knew anything Baroque. I didn't, but found something close enough. She said she studied classical flute in Paris and busked at the top of the steps at Montmartre.

'They probably wouldn't allow that now', she reminisced.

'No, they probably wouldn't.' I agreed, remembering being manhandled by some ecclesiastical brute for wearing the wrong sort of Slayer T-shirt by the church there a few years before.

Worksop was a much more open place. Everybody had a story or a friendly word. Everyone, no matter what their circumstances, could find a coin. Worksop deserved better than it had got. Yet another desperately crap town through no fault of the people who live there.

Quite what the answer is I don't know, not now it's got to this point. Rationing the support the state gives the needy might force some back into work, but others will become ill, disillusioned, or lost to society through the escapism of drugs. Many will never go back to work, and for the want of a bit more support up to now will forever be a burden on society. Ripping so much out of the benefits system seems like a false economy when you see the wreckage it leaves behind. A generation lost to useful work for lack of the right support, now destined to cost society, one way or the other, for the rest of their lives. A stitch in time could have saved so many more here, especially when the fabric in question is society. The decisions of recent years have created problems that will not be solved for a generation at best. I like to refer to it as the 'Social Debt', the corollary of the National Debt, where one partner in the social contract, the government, is badly in arrears, with all the knock on effects that being in any other sort of debt would create. The lack of trust, the refusal to do further work for, the taking drastic and reckless action in the hope of forcing a change – populism.

Heavily reducing the system of support is basically telling the unemployed that it's their fault and their fault alone they haven't got jobs, and is an abdication of responsibility when it comes to holding up the government's end of the social contract. Worksop is a mess, not because its citizens collectively chose not to go to work, but because economic forces far beyond its control shaped it so. Yet the prevailing policies of the day imply that each economic misfortune is a personal failing by the recipient. It holds unemployed individuals personally responsible for global economic trends. A suggestion darkly comic when spelled out so plainly. As if the unemployed lads of Liverpool had personally invented containerised shipping one night and consequently had only themselves to blame for the lack of docker's jobs.

The world may not owe anyone a living, but any reasonable system should owe its citizens the right to try and make one of their own, and support anyone who tries to do so, as well as those who genuinely can't. All stick and no carrot might thrash a few into self-sufficiency, but too much stick will break many of the others, just as all carrot would breed dependency.

Ultimately, such a breakdown benefits nobody at all. A generation who lose faith in government to hold up its end of the bargain feel they owe nothing back, and have no skin in the game of preserving the good bits. The Social Debt will be recalled, by whatever means are available, and given the chance to vote, they'll vote for change on principle, irrespective of the nature of that change. They have nothing to lose. By excluding such a large group from the social contract, a nation sows the seeds of destruction of the things it holds dear.

Fixing it should transcend party politics. Whether your viewpoint be based around the moral position of letting a generation go to waste in underemployment doing bullshit jobs, or quite simply the ultimate financial cost to everyone else of sustaining a generation prevented from providing for themselves, it benefits nobody at all to make these mistakes, left, right, rich, poor. Short-term gain for a few will be at the expense of huge long-term problems and political instability for all.

In virtually every town I've visited, people have quietly told me that it has a serious substance abuse problem and it's getting worse. After all my travelling, it was pretty clear that it's not any one town but the whole country, only nobody has drawn the dots together yet. It's survival of the privileged out there, those who are lucky enough to have a strong family or good friends with resources to spare to fall back on will survive, for now.

Worksop was a beautiful place in ragged clothes. I'd had nothing but positive engagement and generosity from the town. I thought of the kids on their bikes, unbroken souls yet, and feared for their futures. If they failed to get meaningful work as young adults, a tough ask in a town as destitute as this, the system would treat this as purely their personal failure, instead of working hand in hand – individual and state together – to accept the joint programme of rights and responsibilities that underpins any social contract. Anyone who's prepared to work for it should be generously supported in doing so. (As should those who simply cannot.) Not only does the current arbitrary system penalise those who fail through no fault of their own, it also stores up long-term problems in the form of Social Debt that will ultimately cost far more to repay than the initial support would have done.

I left Worksop in a bittersweet cloud. It would take some getting over. Back home, the tomato sausages were excellent.

Loughborough

I DROVE to Loughborough. The traffic was horrible. I followed a newish Mini at close quarters down a crawling road. Every time it braked, its two rear lights lit up to form the two halves of a Union Jack picked out in red and black. As my radio news relayed the latest failures to come to terms with our international status, this seemed as good a visual metaphor for our current situation as any. The simplest emblem of national identity, a distillation of our national flag, that base visual representation of nationhood, but glowing from a car built by a company owned in Germany, manufactured according to the 'just in time' principle where parts from many countries flow across multiple national boundaries without tariffs or delay on their way to the final production line. As an object, this mini was a marvel of international cooperation. As a symbol, the Union Jack brake lights were another empty assertion of misplaced national confidence. The flag lit up whenever the car wasn't going anywhere, which seemed entirely appropriate.

Loughborough had been my home fifteen years ago, when I was at university. I met my friend Pippa for a few drinks and a catch up. Quite predictably, the evening became a tedious series of my reminiscences. 'This was where the burger van was that I ordered a hotdog from after my first night at the Pack Horse folk club'; 'That's the Poundland where my mate Big Dave, whilst tanked up, veered off course and fell straight through a plate-glass window'; 'That's my old house where I kept my collection of traffic cones in the cellar. I wonder if they're still there?' Pippa was patient and let me unload all these memories.

It was cathartic. I needed to get it out of my system so I'd be able to see Loughborough for what it is, rather than my patchy and selective memory of what it was. You don't really notice the changes when you live somewhere, but when you're away for years they slowly add up into something big that surprises you when you come back. Return to somewhere after a decade or more and the place takes on the uncanny air of being both terribly familiar and somehow wrong.

'I knew him when he had hair', said a voice from behind me. I clearly wasn't the only one reminiscing on how things had been in the dim and distant past. We were in a pub on the edge of the town centre and I turned round to recognise Ian, my old boss from when I'd worked behind the bar in another pub in town during my student days. He was at the pool table, and it was only natural to lay down a challenge.

Readers will have noted how any pool challenge I enter into is invariably lost. Tonight was to be different. I was invincible, clearing table after table, defeating all comers. Spooked by my mysterious and unsolicited new powers, I tried to leave, but they insisted that I couldn't until I was defeated. It turned into a lock-in. Eventually I ran out of challengers and was allowed to exit the building through the back door. It was late.

'I've got to see something', I said, leading Pippa to where there had been a dreadful night club called 'Echoes'. I wondered if it was still there. It had featured in a memorable cultural exchange in my first year. Being an awkward and deeply uncool individual, two women on my corridor in my halls of residence had taken pity on me and suggested an exchange of nights out. I can't remember their actual names, as they were always known to us all as 'Pingy and Dingy', and comprised a formidable double act. I seem to recall one of them studied pornographic pottery, or 'pornottery' as she called it. I don't think I'm making this up. Anyway, the deal was I would take them and some of their friends to an 'old man's pub' and then they would take me clubbing. I'd kicked off the evening with an introduction to real ale in my local, the Swan in the Rushes, where my appearance with several attractive and confidently dressed young women was a significant surprise to the other regulars and had caused my stock there to rise for a few weeks. Pingy and Dingy then concluded the evening with a trip to Echoes, home of highly caffeinated alcopops, sticky floors, and strobe lights. To my astonishment, Echoes was still there, closed today, but promising a 1980s UV disco on Friday.

There was one ritual left to fulfil before I could put my own personal past Loughborough to bed and start engaging with current Loughborough. I entered the independent takeaway 'Pizzeria' on the road heading back to the university. No Friday night was complete during my time in Loughborough without a visit here. My friends would probably have said that no Monday, Tuesday, Wednesday, Thursday, Saturday, or Sunday night was complete for me either. I told Pippa that they'd probably remember me. She was a little sceptical of this. It was twelve years since I'd left town and I've got a lot older and balder. I walked through the door. The serving man looked at me, froze, said 'Whoah' and ran into the back. I heard some animated conversation along the lines of 'He has returned!' and the whole staff came out to shake my hand. I tried to order, but they were already making my favourite, pepperoni and pineapple, and quickly sent it into the oven.

Loughborough had been home. I regarded it fondly, but in truth it had been a chaotic time in my life, a string of short and sometimes disastrous relationships, too much drinking, and eventually leaving under something of a cloud. Quite how I got a degree (Politics and Social Policy 2:1) is something of a mystery. But I'd stayed in touch with my department, and three years ago was invited to give a lecture on my old course concerning folk music and nationalism, a moment of particular pride in my life. My former lecturers always greet me with 'You're looking well!' when I turn up, not so much a compliment as an involuntary outburst of genuine surprise.

I can't entirely remember if I was happy here or not. The fun stuff comes back to mind very quickly, the stresses and problems and my own personal failings less so. I like Loughborough a great deal, but separating one's own personal creation myth from reality is much harder. Hopefully I'd exorcised the past with this night and would be free to see the town with clear eyes in the morning.

The next day, I wandered into town at about 9:30am. It was market day and a steady drizzle was falling. Busking wasn't possible in the rain, so I just wandered about for a while. Loughborough market is a big one, filling the main street in several rows for hundreds of yards. A couple of Sikhs sold offensive T-shirts on their stall, including 'I work harder than an ugly stripper', 'Same twat, different shirt', and 'If you're offended, I'll help you pack', which was emblazoned above a big Union Jack. I wondered if the sort of person who might want to own such a shirt would be likely to buy it from a turbaned Sikh.

A shop had cards for sale in the window that said cheery things like '18! Welcome to adulthood, the day that fun dies'. The ubiquitous Cashino had a sign that said 'Staff wanted, come and join the winning team'. Despite this candid admission that it's the house that makes the money, gamblers were still heading in, full of purpose and optimism. On a back street, the famous BRUSH Engineering Social club had closed forever. Perhaps the employees of the enormous factory on the North edge of town no longer wanted to socialise there after work.

The rain let up enough to justify a busk. I set up opposite a group of religious types with their placards and leaflets. Facing a sign that said 'Will suffering end?' I got stuck into playing, aiming to provide them with a fresh perspective on their philosophical conundrum. After an hour, they answered their own question by packing up and moving on. Suffering can end, it turns out, but only if you choose to end it. A suitably humanist interpretation, I felt. One member of the group pointedly dropped a leaflet in my case on the way out; 'Will you consider Jesus?' A score draw, I reckoned.

Loughborough

A lad of maybe 10 years of age tugged on his grandma's coat for a coin for the busker. She smiled, found a pound coin and sent him my way. On his journey across to me, I saw as he carefully and dexterously slipped the coin into a pocket and instead produced a single penny which he dropped in my case. 'You little shit', I thought to myself, and they were gone into the crowds, clearly a well-rehearsed fraud. A bright future ahead for that one.

A smartly dressed and well spoken man began handing out leaflets. He was in tweeds, expensive boots, high quality hat, and was probably approaching 70. I wondered what he was promoting. I chose to imagine it was the '80s UV disco night at Echoes.

I bought a lunch pie and a coffee and headed into Queen's Park for my break. I picked a bench facing the magnificent carillon, an extraordinary bell tower and war memorial with no fewer than forty-seven bells, all cast by John Taylor Bell Foundry on the other side of town. Every Thursday lunchtime the tower performs, and one can eat one's lunch listening to all manner of music made baffling and unfamiliar by being performed on too many bells. It is a solo instrument. Wikipedia notes that 'The combination of carillon and other instruments, while possible, is generally not a happy marriage.'

Loughborough's carillon was built after the First World War as a homage to their popularity in the towns of Belgium, where there are countless examples. It is a fine thing. As the bells rang and small children played hide and seek with their parents, a sudden drama unfolded. A juvenile sparrowhawk brought down one of the numerous market-fattened pigeons with a thump. It ripped away at it, pulling thick clumps of feathers out, but in its inexperience failed to complete the kill. People were watching, some with phones out, some explaining to surprised children what was happening. You don't get many life and death struggles on CBeebies. Facing the paparazzi, the sparrowhawk became distracted and allowed the pigeon to wriggle free. The pigeon flew for its life and the sparrowhawk set after it, but was immediately mobbed by a dozen crows and had to abandon the chase. The drama was over, with just a pile of feathers on the grass as evidence.

I busked on Market Street for the afternoon, by an empty unit and opposite a Turkish restaurant. As the day drew on, a shop next door began piling rubbish bags up against the empty shop front. They kept coming, until a huge mound had been created. The assistant looked at me and said 'Sorry'. I replied that it was fine as it was a suitably metaphorical happening.

At about 4:15, I called it a day and counted up. I'd made £69 in about four hours and fifteen minutes of playing. A reasonable return, but I was cold and achy and ready for a break.

I met another friend, Sarah, for a pint that evening. We arranged to meet in front of McDonalds at 7:30pm, which seemed to me most splendidly teenage thing to do. I was early. When she arrived, she'd had the same thoughts. 'This takes me back! It's been many years since I arranged to meet a young man outside McDonalds!'

We toured a few of the newer bars, places that hadn't been open when I'd been at University, the Wheeltapper, the Cask Bah, the latter of which was a rockers pub with traditional real ales repackaged as Lemmy's Legend and Hendrix Experience instead of Bitter and Mild. Young drinkers in black T-shirts were drinking it in vast quantities. I was coincidentally dressed for the occasion, and within minutes the soundtrack of the pub was 'Clutch', a band I'd told the landlord I liked whilst he poured our round.

Sarah works on a badly deprived council estate in Leicester. 'We've probably not had a busker for forty years. You'll have to come along and try it.'

The next day was not a market day. Teams of burly men dismantled dozens of empty stalls, and the streets grew broader and quieter. A filthy cold wind whipped up Market Street and drew the warmth from my fiddle strings. I busked opposite a large pawn shop managed by a man with a striking resemblance to Paul Bearer, the corpulent late wrestling manager. Coins were slow, hands were frozen in jeans pockets, heads were down. It was a dry day, but the wind was forceful enough to reach into gutters and puddles and whip stagnant droplets along the road. I grew cold, yet persevered. If I made £25, I'd have broken even on the trip, and I'd promised myself I could spend any excess in George Hill's wine merchants. Pigeons came and went. I looked for one with a prominent bald patch, but yesterday's survivor was not out and about.

Old friends appeared, my ex-housemate Fiona, various people from the university. Over four cold and windy hours I raised a meagre £45, before consigning the fiddle back to its case when my fingers became too chilled and sore to continue. This at least gave me a reasonable budget to work with in the wine shop.

I headed up Market Street, towards the town hall. There was a *Big Issue* seller. She'd smiled warmly at me as she'd headed to Greggs for lunch earlier. I went to buy a copy, the Xmas special at £3. I asked her where she was from.

'I am from Mongolia.'

'Which bit, Outer Mongolia or the Chinese inner bit?'

'China!'

'Which city?'

'Oh you would not know it.'

'Try me.'

After some back and forth, we established she was from Lindong, part of Bairin Left Banner, Inner Mongolia, China. I'd visited this city twice, the second time in 2005, aged 22, to make contact with a family my father had been in touch with and deliver presents on his behalf. Having been the guest of honour for a meal, I was then driven around town in a bubble car owned by Wei Bing, the son of the household, listening to Chinese rap, to a cyber cafe where in an effort to share my Western culture, I'd loaded a viral animation called 'Magical Trevor'. Without apparently paying me much attention, every other youth in the room had the same animation on their screen within the next few minutes. It was a memorable cultural exchange.

Why was she here? Her English was good and clear, but she didn't have the biggest vocabulary yet. I established that she'd had a child that her family hadn't approved of, and having run out of other options had come by land across two continents to Market Street in Loughborough. Her son was five next week, and she was saving up for a present for him. She was currently living in a caravan, and selling the Big Issue was her first serious good break in a while.

My trip to Lindong was a comfortable soft class sleeper car on what had been the last steam hauled express train in the world, in its final weeks or service. Her trip here had been a colossal effort by the cheapest transport through the 2,000 mile dusty emptiness of Northern China, across the baked brown and empty countries north of the Himalayas, across the Urals, through Europe, language after language, country after country. Yet she was full of an extraordinary good humanity. She'd seen I'd had a hard day at the busking with not many coins, we'd shared the street, and she double checked that I could really afford a copy, a question that nearly broke my heart. To have such warmth for your fellow human after all she'd been through was astonishing.

'May I know your name?'

'I am Madi.'

She wrote it down in four large and clear letters in my notepad. Another fleeting glimpse at a story far greater than anything I can tell from my own life. Those with the best stories are generally those least able to tell them. If you have a good education, a settled existence, and the right connections, it is also highly unlikely you've been through Hell to give your son a chance in life. Madi had a story worth telling. I wonder if it or any like it will ever easily be told, or would hearing it hurt our sense of self too much? Can we cope with knowing our *Big Issue* seller has overcome near impossible odds to be there? Or is it easier to imagine they sort of bimbled up here one day and need our charity because they are lesser and incapable? I thought about the challenge of getting to Lindong over land on a budget of spare coins, goodwill, and luck and without a British passport or credit card in my pocket and didn't fancy it at all. We live in a society where remarkable, capable people sometimes live in the streets and wait patiently with a bright, warm smile for their chance to contribute.

I wondered if she felt any nostalgia for the world she'd left behind. Would she be able to return one day and take a big goofy tour round all the places she used to hang out in, or is that door completely closed now? Would she even want to? Was it all going to have been worth the effort for her? But I'd taken enough of her time up already. I took my diminished pocket of coins down the road with my *Big Issue* Xmas special. A homeless woman called to me: 'Ere. Do you actually read that? Does anyone?'

She was referring to my *Big Issue*, poking out of my hoodie pocket. She was reading a crime novel and spoke with a strong Essex accent.

'I was planning to. What are you reading?'

We compared notes on novelists for a bit. Her copy had lost its covers but thankfully hadn't shed as far as losing the end of the text yet. I wondered if this meant the homeless had their own informal lending library. I gave her another handful of my coins, leaving with that shame I always feel when I walk away from someone in such a horrific situation. Should I even buy a bottle of wine when there's people destitute like this? I walked into George Hills. I had enough coins left for an 'entry level' bottle.

Whilst in Loughborough I'd chucked some money in what I hoped was the right direction and this bottle represented the totality of my profit for the three days. I hoped that was fair enough in the grand scheme of things.

I went back to my car. The street lamp next to it had a sign that reassuringly read 'Police Warning. Car arson is a crime'. Thankfully, this had deterred the casual arsonists and my vehicle was still there. Time to go home, out of my past and back to my present day.

Carlisle

CARLISLE came late to the national party, joining England as recently as 1092, having previously been part of Scotland and therefore omitted from the compilation of the Domesday Book. Having transferred allegiance, Carlisle quickly reverted to its original Romano-British purpose of keeping the troublesome Scots out. Industrialisation saw the decline of Carlisle's military importance, although in 1698 the early English travel writer Celia Fiennes remarked that it was still 'Rife with alcohol and prostitutes' as befitted a proper garrison town. I wondered how things might have moved on.

Having parked outside the almost limitless disk-zone, I walked in to Carlisle via Botchergate, one of England's most notorious drinking streets. Pubs, bars, and takeaways made up the entire trade of the road, a shabby vibrancy about the place, quiet and at rest now, preparing for the weekend ahead - a spectacle a friend had insisted I visit and experience for myself. It was cold Friday morning in December, and all was at peace with just a few discarded glue bottles and empty cash bags littering the street and giving clues as to what lay ahead.

Further towards the city centre, the road opens up into a large square. There was a lot of noise coming from it, made by a busker with a powerful amplifier singing in the dreary Ed Sheeran mould. He was audible from hundreds of yards away, and with his central position had ruined the majority of the city centre for anyone else who fancied a busk. Normally I like to say hello to fellow buskers and drop off a few coins, but this was selfish and entitled behaviour, so I ignored him and wandered around for a while instead, getting to know the city.

Inside the arcade was a bronze statue of Jimmy Dyer. A brass plaque informed me that he was 'A well know itinerant fiddler and ballad singer.' Bearded and in a shabby coat and top hat, fiddle tucked under his arm, pipe at rest on a battered briefcase, he was out of time and place in the synthetic fluorescent brightness. I searched for more information online. There was not a lot, other than that he was something of a fixture around the turn of the 20th century, a couple of photos showing a very ragged man with no discernible technique and who was apparently 'infamous for his unconventional lifestyle.' I liked him already. In my Will Haven hoodie, dog-chewed baseball cap, and worn out fleece with paint stains and a melted zip that no longer fastens, I felt happy to assume his mantle for the day, and so stepped out into the streets again to find a spot away from the over-amplified wailing.

I picked one of the small medieval streets towards the cathedral that was sheltered from the din, and found a quiet spot opposite a pub. Things started slowly at first, but soon picked up and by lunchtime I'd made a good pile of change, plus a fiver from a gentleman who when I told him about my project really wanted to cover my fiddle case in pro-European stickers. I replied that I wasn't very keen on antagonising people, and that the project wouldn't work so well if I did. He wasn't convinced but I remained unstickered.

At lunchtime, I met with a fellow called Richard who'd been recommended by a friend as someone worth meeting. He works in the planning department and probably knows Carlisle as well as anyone. With a ginger beard, an easy laugh, and an interest in good beer, we seemed somehow to get on very well. As we sat on a low wall outside the cathedral with our sausage sandwiches, I asked him what the big controversies were in the Carlisle planning department at the moment.

'Well, they want to move the swimming pool into a potential flood zone.'

'Makes sense. It won't matter as much if it gets wet.'

'Tell you a story, you know that big chimney? Belongs to Dixon's textile works.'

It was visible from nearly everywhere in Carlisle, a huge brick chimney, very tall and slender, tapering away into the sky.

'Yeah.'

'It was the biggest in the UK at one time, bloody huge. Well a few weeks ago on a Friday afternoon when things were a bit quiet, this little old lady turned up in the department with these hand drawn and coloured plans she'd made to put a revolving restaurant on top of it.'

'Genius. What did you say?'

'Well we didn't want to offend her, so we told her we'd take it into consideration. What else can you do? Right, come with me, I'll show you something else.'

We walked through town, down to the council offices, pretty much the only concrete brutalist block in Carlisle, to where Richard showed me the commemorative plaque, installed in 2015 to commemorate the 2005 floods. It was fitted on the wall at the exact high water mark of the flood.

'You see that line above it, where the wall changes colour? That's where the water got to the day after they installed this plaque. They didn't risk tempting fate again by putting a plaque up for that, just decided not to clean the wall.'

I told Richard that my plan was to visit Botchergate in the evening, to get a sense of it. He laughed and wished me good luck, and I went back to my busking.

The afternoon was a case of slowly diminishing returns. The weather grew colder till breath filled the air in white clouds, fingers turned cold on strings, and coins proved harder to dislodge from pockets. A schoolgirl grew tired of a chirping lad, and suddenly took him down with a slick rolling arm bar manoeuvre, earning cheers of delight from her friends. A man walked past with ostentatious headphones and a white beanie that said 'DOPE' across it in large letters.

After a while I was forced to retreat to the gents toilets in the arcade to warm my frozen busker's fingers up in the powerful Tornado hand dryer. I needed £100 from my two days here to break even, and I'd have to wring every last pound out of busking. £36 on fuel, £30 for my B&B, leaving a notional budget of £34 for food and drink. I'd already had a sausage sandwich and a coffee, and Botchergate would be a serious night's work. I headed back out into the gloom of dusk. A young man was on the street with a hangdrum, a metal saucer the size of a small table that makes different notes depending on where you spank it. It made a beautiful sound, but as I came to realise, only had one trick. I asked him about it. He said he'd gone into the shop looking for a djembe and ended up with this instead, then he'd learnt to busk. I found a space where I made a meagre £9 in the last hour as the darkness fell, and defeated, set off to find out what sort of lodging my £30 had bought me.

To my surprise, and slight disappointment, it was perfectly decent, and well on the way to being en-suite. I tidied myself up, counted my coins (£58 in nearly four hours) and hit the town again. I went for dinner in a bar called 'The Last Zebra'. Having been found a table, I was brought a menu titled 'Drinky Poos', printed in pink on white and utterly unreadable under the similarly pink LED arrays that illuminated the central section of the bar. I speculatively ordered a pint of bitter, a chicken burger and a salad. The thought of eating the salad under the watery pink lights was not appetising. When it arrived, I asked if I could move to a table on the fringes where the light was more yellow and normal. Instead of this, the waiter pulled out a tablet and loaded an app.

'What colour lighting would sir desire?'

I was not ready for this question, and hurriedly cycled through a few colours, searching for one that would suitably illuminate my lettuce, all the while aware of the eyes upon me from other denizens of The Last Zebra, wondering who this twat was who needed green lighting before he could enjoy his pint.

But when did I start writing restaurant reviews? I'm more interested in what these places tell me about a town. The young people running the Last Zebra were doing what hard working young people are doing all over the country. Trying to make a go of something and stand out in a difficult market. The food was great, the beer well kept. Perhaps this is why there are so many quality coffee shops around the country. If you're young and ambitious and not qualified for one of the few well paid industries remaining like engineering, you're left with a choice between shelf-stacking and running your own business. The Last Zebra was great, if you know in advance what colour light you want.

At 9pm on a Friday and Saturday, Botchergate, part of the A6, is shut to all traffic, with gates drawn across and traffic diverted right round the town. It's not worth the risk of leaving it open as people flood from bar to bar in growing states of drunkenness. Friday is payday and Carlisle knows how to celebrate this. I had met up with my friend Lucy, a Carlisle native and my guide for the evening. It seemed appropriate to start the night by being present for the ceremonial closing of the gates. In my mind, this was sure to be a grand performance. I imagined a hooded and robed figure, the Master of the Gates, surrounded by flaming-torch bearers, emerging from the darkness by the laserquest and theatrically closing the gates to the wailing of bagpipes and shamanic chanting of a febrile crowd.

At 9pm we were at the South end of Botchergate, just past the last bar, and not a lot was happening. The moon was full and bright and rising slowly over the kebab house. At ten past we started to doubt ourselves and wondered if perhaps it wasn't happening tonight for some reason. Finally, we saw the glint of a high-vis uniform appeared in the distance, heading down from the station. He was a young police officer and was clearly surprised to see us waiting for him like this. This was not normal, and I detected a small moment of worry as I got my notebook out to ask him all about it. He said they shared the job out from week to week between the officers. He went round the corner to activate the diversion signs, and returned to close the gates themselves. As the second gate clanged shut and he locked it in place, we gave a polite but enthusiastic round of applause and I asked if he wouldn't mind posing by the gate for a moment for a photograph. This he did, his community policing training narrowly overcoming his obvious desire to get away from the nutters, his quiet evening task transformed to a choreographed performance under critical appraisal. Photos taken and interview done, we let him go, and he ran off into the night as fast as professional dignity would let him.

If there's a measure of Botchergate's significance in the panoply of English drinking streets, it's that there's the two cavernous Wetherspoons almost next door to one another. It was into the higher up of the two, the William Rufus, we poured ourselves a little later. It was still early on in the grand scheme of things, and conversation was just about possible under the music. Having tried and failed to explain fractals to me, Lucy rolled a cigarette and headed out of the nearby door to smoke it. I pulled on my hoodie and followed her. The bouncer was onto me in a flash, irate that we'd dared to walk out of this particular door.

'Can't you fucking read what it says?' he bellowed into my face.

I pulled the door back a bit and carefully read the sign back to him, deadpan.

'Push bar to open.'

He did not appreciate this answer at all.

'You can't go out of there, it's a fucking FIRE DOOR.'

'I'm terribly sorry, it wasn't obvious, but now you have explained my error to me, I promise not to make such a mistake in the future.'

The bouncer desperately searched for something to object to in this, failed, slammed the door behind me and gestured through the glass in the direction of the approved but otherwise identical door of re-entry. I rejoined Lucy.

'You got me in the shit, there.'

'Yes, it was pretty funny to watch.'

We tried the other Wetherspoons next door. It had an older clientele, no music, and anti-EU brochures on every table. It was a mess, crowded and dirty. The gents had a trail of shitty footprints leading to an abandoned five amp fuse, a series of clues that even the great literary sleuths like Poirot and Scooby-Doo would have struggled to get to the bottom of. We soon drank up and tried our luck at 'Concrete', a night club. It was dead, so we went back down Botchergate again. It wasn't quite the riot I'd been expecting. There were a lot of bored bouncers, some resigned to their fate, others like the coked-up bruiser in the first Wetherspoons looking for any minor infringement to leap on so to justify their existence.

'It's coming up to Christmas. Fridays are dead, everyone goes out Saturday this time of year.'

Such was my luck. We went into a nightclub called 'Bronx' with a bottle bar and a £5 pool cue deposit and played pool. I made a strong start and cleared all my reds away. Lucy fluffed a shot and dropped her cue in despair. As we were about to abandon the match, we received another of my occasional visitations from the fairy kingdom. A little old fellow with thinning blonde hair and a soft Cumbrian accent was suddenly by her side.

'You must nivva give up, lass, nivva give up.'

He seemed to freeze the time around the table, a bubble of calm. He carefully picked up the abandoned cue, and with permission took up her cause. I had one shot on the black and it wasn't pottable so I moved it into the middle of the table for next time. The little old fellow then carefully and methodically potted yellow after yellow, never hitting it hard, just rolling the balls gently into the pockets. After the black followed them all in, he handed the cue back to Lucy and holding her hand, looked her in the eye and repeated the message;

'Nivva give up. In pool, or in life.'

Lucy turned to me and said;

'I think I love him.'

We looked back, and he had gone.

It was now well past midnight, and with two Coronas for £5 we were wondering what to do next. A bunch of lads came in and headed straight for the boxing machine, where the investment of 50p causes a punch bag to lower from the top allowing punches to be measured for their power. It's remarkable how often the score would just narrowly exceed the previous effort, causing the lads to find a further 50p for another more definitive round. After a while of watching this, Lucy told me that she used to go out with the brother of one of the lads, and shouted them over.

I was amazed at just how open they all were with me. Within a short while I was learning all sorts. One lad was approximately the middle child of eleven. In his words 'She had eleven kids because she was too lazy to want to work.' Other stories were of relatives lost to drug addiction, wasted on the streets. They didn't show much compassion for these characters they described. This wasn't for a lack of humanity, but when there's so many problems to deal with, you have to prioritise those who seem most worth spending your compassion on. Sometimes, people just had to be cut for the sake of others. It was a survival tactic, and it was bleak. I told him how much it made me realise my own upbringing had been incredibly cushy, and I drunkenly said I was sorry it'd been so tough for him.

'Nah, not at all. It makes you who you are doesn't it? I've got four of me own now and I'll look after them.'

It was 1am in the Bronx nightclub and people were just stood around talking candidly about the most personal details of their lives to near strangers. Carlisle is like that. It's rough and tough, but friendly to the point of innocence. Your weekend night out takes on some pretty big significance if your life is fairly bleak the rest of the time.

At 1:45am I finally had to admit that Lucy, a woman half my size, had drunk me under the table, and I went back to my B&B, leaving her in the club with the lads, and fell asleep with my notepad open on the bed.

I set an alarm for 8:45am and barely responded to it, the refusal to miss a breakfast I'd already paid for the only thing dragging me out of bed and into the dining room. I was soon back on the street, walking into Carlisle again. A traffic warden had parked on double yellows whilst he went into the newsagent. A woman handled a pair of mannequin legs in the window of a big shop. The legs had a pair of trousers on, which promptly dropped to the ankles and made her job entertainingly impossible and a few of us gathered round to watch. On the main road, two BetFreds looked across at each other in smug satisfaction. I tried busking in yesterday's most successful spot, but a bleary eyed publican politely asked me if he could have some more sleep after his eighteen hour shift, so I moved on.

I slogged away at it all morning and by 1:15pm had £45 to show. Hardly a fortune for three hour's playing, but I'd just about hit my goal for the two days. It was lunchtime. Saveloys were being loaded into the hot cabinet in the chippy. The arcade security guard had his sunglasses on. The Christmas lights were up, and looked entertainingly Soviet. I bagged my coins up and walked Botchergate one more time. Brewdog were opening a new bar which was currently hidden behind chipboard and scaffolding. A man and his wife were staring at the big blue Brewdog logo. It wasn't familiar to them.

'Whatever is that? I just don't know!'

Botchergate wasn't going to lose its crown any time soon and in a few hours, the gates would swing shut again for another night's revelry.

The Durham Coalfield

THE thing about coal mining is that it does not really bring prosperity even when the times are good. Coal is too plentiful, spilling out of the ground all over the place across the world. You cannot corner the market in coal, and will always be in a price war with a thousand other producers. It is self-regulating to make minimal profits at the best of times, and horrible losses at others, leaving you with a political choice between exploitation of workers or state sponsored mining at a regular and growing loss, or just simply importing from the world market and making that someone else's problem. Coal is a trouble filled, dangerous industry that can kill you now or later, and never pay you much. The money is made by others, further down the production line.

Durham is a vast coalfield, discovered under what had been a largely empty county, the coal then liberated by hundreds of mines dotted across the land. Each attracted workers who built their basic houses loosely around the source of their meagre income, leading to nearly the whole county being a patchwork of small towns and villages, each coalescing around a mine or two, constructed and populated only by those low paid who had no other choice. It is a county at complete and utter disconnect from its county town of Durham, that ancient city was bypassed by the coal industry altogether, other than to play host the annual miners' gala, one of the largest political gatherings in Europe.

I had read that coal mining in County Durham fell into decline from the 1930s. This seems to me to be the wrong way to look at it. It never had a peak in any human sense, being an industry that causes short and difficult lives in either spate or drought. Increased tonnage simply meant more people working dangerously for very little, whilst slumps and unrest in the industry starved and reduced those who'd previously been busy shortening their lives through work. Writing in 1934, J.B. Priestley wrote of a ruined landscape of roads fallen into disuse with only the coal needing to ever come or go, slum housing in ribbons, vast spoil tips slowly burning from within and leaving each pit village isolated in a permanent sulphurous fog. A land and people wrecked by the geologic chance occurrence of coal beneath them and the desire elsewhere to burn it. 'The Cotswolds', he concludes without humour, 'were to be congratulated, it seems, on their lack of coal deposits.' As with Cornwall, the money will never be where the resources are.

Post-war Britain looked at the state of the Durham coalfield with its sub-standard housing and dreadful living conditions and declared, as was the spirit of the age, 'Something must be done!' A 1951 County Council review of the county divided the towns and villages into four categories, A to D, depending on their economic prospects. An A rating assumed a prosperous future and continued investment. Category D meant the end. The town or village had no economic hope whatsoever. All council funding would be withdrawn, no further development would be allowed. No new businesses could open. The remaining inhabitants would be encouraged out into the new towns of the Durham coast, allowing final demolition. One hundred and fourteen habitations were graded D. Durham would be levelled and reconstituted into new towns, village by village. Mine and village were viewed as one. Without the mine, there could be no further justification for the village's continued existence. A new and consolidated county fit for the future would emerge from the ruins.

I drove into Chopwell (now Tyne and Wear) on a grey Thursday the week before Christmas. Originally a Category A, in 1964 the anticipated loss of the mine in 1966 saw it regraded as a Category D. This is not some small place of a few rows of cottages, but a small town of several thousand people destined for demolition. Parking outside the healthcare centre I was surrounded by proof that Category D had failed in its most central task. Chopwell was abundantly still here.

Finding a parking space was not an issue. There were streets with no houses in and amongst the sprawl of miners' cottages, where Category D had got to work but not finished the job, giving the town a sense of gap toothed hollowness, as if a book had been printed with dozens of blank pages obfuscating the story. I walked down the hill to the lower part of town, along roads with names like 'Marx Terrace' and 'Lenin Terrace'. Where conditions are the worst, so does politics become the most radical. Chopwell had taken down the Union Jacks and replaced them with Russian flags during the general strike. Once known as 'Little Moscow' a badge at odds with what is now quiet and sleepy, a town unsure of itself, unvisited, not on the way to anywhere on a back road up in the hills. I came back on a loop to the top of town via the park, and didn't see another person. The open spaces of the cricket and football pitches were blanketed in dewy silence. Cats on the prowl would stop mid-step and watch me on my way before reclaiming the morning as theirs alone. The bowling green had turned to a pillow of moss. The crazy golf was reverting to moorland, holes overtopping with late Pennine rainwater that blackbirds and robins drank from. Back in town, the Phoenix pub was closed now but suggested dimly that it might still be a going concern. Upstairs a dog howled at my passing. Sullen armies of derelict armchairs and sofas watched my progress from driveways that couldn't afford a car. Rows of miners' cottages faced one another across a grass walkway, never turned into a road for lack of need. A woman was hanging out washing but scurried inside as I came up the street, perhaps detecting a little too much purpose in my stride.

The main street had just a handful of surviving businesses. There was a barbers, a Co-op, a cafe, and a takeaway. The Chopwell, a once grand and spacious pub building, was chipboarded shut, cellar drop mossing back into the soil. The bookies had gone bust, and a faded sign advised punters to pick up outstanding winnings from their branch in Seaham. Online, I could find no evidence of this establishment either.

Stunned, Chopwell doesn't know what to do next. There is no business in the town at all, no trading estate. Nobody can buy anything, there are no jobs whatsoever. The Category D review was right, in a sense. This town has no purpose any more, and hasn't for decades. It's just a place where people exist. There's nothing to do and nowhere to go. You can't earn your way out of here. Chopwell is waiting for someone else to make a decision on its future. It has not the resources or focus to do so itself. Category D crippled it but refused to administer the killing blow, perhaps the cruellest act of all.

Over the hill is High Spen, designated Category D right back in 1951. The Church was for sale. Not an auspicious start, I considered. But this place was somehow in better shape. A gentleman walked two Salukis, shining coats and proud heads. Gardens were neat with filled bird feeders. The school was plump with children. The pub looked smart and well kept. Perhaps after Chopwell anywhere would look well, but High Spen was almost prosperous, the few miles nearer to the city making it a sleeper town for Gateshead and Newcastle. Amongst the tidy porches and creosoted fences patrolled by bright-eyed pets, it was remarkable to think that until 1977 this was a village deemed so irredeemably awful by its own elected County Council that only total demolition would solve the problem.

A gateway appeared on my left under some trees. There was a sign attached in laminated plastic, tucked under a loose whorl of ivy.

> 'TOWN AND COUNTRY PLANNING ACT 1990. The SECRETARY OF STATE hereby gives notice that the Order under section 251 of the above Act to authorise the extinguishment of the public rights of way comprising the whole of the footpath network at the former doctors (sic) surgery commencing from Bute Road South and extending to its termination point at the rear lane of Hookergate Lane at High Spen in the Metropolitan Borough of Gateshead, referred to in the Notice published on 02 October 2018 under reference NATTRAN/NES247/3480, will not be made, the application for the order being withdrawn.'

Such is the language of the sore loser in the battle for the common person's rights. Here was a right fought for and won, an ancestral pathway kept open for all, regardless of birth and rank. Such rights should never be taken for granted, and I celebrated this shining victory by persons unknown against the colossus of the uncaring state by seeing where the 'Whole of the footpath network' might take me. Fifty yards later, I had crossed a small patch of land about the size of a house and garden, past a single berth garage and a fruit tree to emerge on a road I could easily have got to by walking two hundred yards around the corner, the far end of my inalienable right of way being marked by another laminated sheet stapled to a post. A cat looked at me suspiciously as I turned round and went back, no doubt wondering what that had all been about.

Down the road, in another one of the endless dribble of hamlets that line the lanes I found a butchers called 'The Chop Shop' which sold hot sandwiches. There was a queue. In front of me were an older couple, so I asked them about the area.

'What's it like living round here?' Perhaps not the most creative first question.

'Well I don't know, you just kind of get used to it', replied the lady.

I asked what difference it had made when the pits had shut, how the area had changed, but they didn't know how to answer. If it had changed, they hadn't really noticed, watching one quiet day turn into another in a glacial world without work. It was all a bit awkward, and I sensed perhaps nobody had ever asked them about their part of the world before, and to do so was a strange thing. Why would I want to know? This place doesn't matter. Gateshead's much more interesting, a young man like me should go there. They'd lived here their whole lives but didn't know about Category D designation. The threatened complete demolition of their entire community had somehow passed them by as an event and the revelation did not interest them. Perhaps this ignorance, wilful or inadvertent was the key to the survival of these places. Of one hundred and twenty-one villages and towns scheduled for demolition, only three were ever totally wiped off the map. The rest perhaps damaged, but resolutely still there in small typeface on the OS map. Reduced but not quite removed, lack of engagement and education opportunities ultimately contributing to their survival, people staying on out of a sense of unremarkable destiny. 'This is where I was born and this is where I'll stay.'

A few miles further on is Marley Hill, a perfect square of red brick houses in several rows. Despite holding onto its mine till late on, it was still a Category D village, with no development occurring for fifty years, other than some temporary prefabs after the war. I parked up at the end of the final terrace. The village sits on top of a hill overlooking the whole of Gateshead and Newcastle. The view is magnificent, and I thought it as good a place as any to eat my lunch.

A woman parked her car about fifty metres away from me. She looked at me, got out and headed over, before tapping on my window.

'Yes?'

She was a little nervous. Her shoes were too smart for the pot-holed gravel and puddles, her makeup too careful, her clothing too considered.

'Are you Neil?'

In that split second, I thought about being Neil. Perhaps his life was better than mine, perhaps this could be a new and exciting future, starting here on a windswept December hill by the ghosts of Durham past, overlooking the grey and glittering Tyne valley with all of its history and tradition. She looked across at the passenger footwell, an ad-hoc installation of crisp packets and Lucozade bottles, and down at my tatty hoody covered in crumbs and the odd blob of mustard. Neil had not made a good first impression. I snapped out of it, remembering a girlfriend at home, kind and remarkably forgiving of my single-minded determination to bankrupt myself travelling round England.

'Sorry, not me.'

'Are you sure?'

I was sure.

I wound my window up and finished my lunch. The Tyne shone in the distance, diffracting slivers of sun that otherwise hadn't made it up to this lonely hill. Another car drew up behind, a blue Audi, sports model. This time it was Neil, and they set off together into the woods beyond the village. In a landscape like this, trees mark where the industry was. Where the earth is too disturbed and full of wreckage to be made arable. Trees are quick, far faster than we imagine them, and a colliery levelled and splintered becomes a wood nestled in the cutaways of the land in just a few decades, home now to the animals and wildness again. Finishing my portion of carrot cake, I got out and walked round Marley Hill, first inspecting Neil's car. The footwell was empty and vacuumed. There was one of those pine tree shaped air fresheners hanging from the rear view mirror. It would never have worked.

I walked down the far terrace, away from the main road that bisects the village. Families were out in their yards. Conversations faltered as I walked past, a lone pedestrian in a backwater. At the bottom of the village, the church, graveyard too full another clue of an industrial past. The top of the village had a large set of allotments, featuring a good selection of scarecrows. One was a highly detailed effigy of Michael Foot.

So this was Durham, Category D style. Villages lost in time, quietened and sullen. County diffuse and inefficient. Communities resilient in the face of well meaning but clumsy attempts to help. The coal was a long time gone, and so now were most of those who remember it.

I drove to Easington Colliery, a pit village so indivisible from its purpose it bears the name of its industry in the title. Easington was a huge pit, employing the adult male population of the village, a village that existed solely to serve this modern, high output mine. Older mines demanded villages but this vast employer demanded what was effectively a full town of labour to drive the cutters into the retreating wall, out under the North Sea. Four shifts worked it round the clock, overlapping to allow for the travel time between coal face and shaft. It had closed in 1993, a mere twenty-five years ago.

The settlement slopes gently down to the shore, but stops a thousand yards short, a seaside village left impotent and fumbling for validation. The gap is a wide open space, bounded on the seaward edge by the railway. The former colliery, now demolished, flattened, landscaped into an uncanny bald conformity that slopes up to the remodelled, reduced, and gentrified peak of the spoil tips, broken only by the concrete caps of the shafts and the old pit cage, as far away from the shaft up the hill as it once went down to the waiting seams. The Who photographed an album cover here once, amidst the Martian rubble of colliery waste, coal washed off, giant angular gravels renewed then each day to create a landscape unlearnable and dehumanised. The smoothed lands leading up to it were yellowed and pockmarked, wan grass on earth so ruined and contaminated it grew in a filthy jaundiced patchwork, ungrazeable.

We don't have spoil tips any more. Where the Durham coalfield was a sequence of stinking, smoking pyramids of waste, where the 'Yorkshire alps' stood as recognisable as Drax, Eggborough and Ferrybridge power stations, they were carted away for roadstone in the age of the motorway. Aberfan's collapsed onto the village in 1966 on one of Britain's most shameful days. A sequence of events that look remarkably like the Grenfell tower disaster in cumulative procedural abdications of responsibility. Different age, same humanity, same failings. Same whitewash.

Easington's had spared the town. Not much else had. From the park I could see the town as a whole, sickly and subdued, in mortal stillness. The land can be put back level and trees and birds will come in time, but the people don't recover so quickly. A town with a diverse economy can alter, fluctuate, respond, renew. Easington lost almost every job overnight, and when the banks left town, so did the shopping. The main street was a horror story. Almost every shop was shut, the slender remainder catered to subsistence or death. Chemists, basic food and household supplies, funerals. It was five days to Christmas and not a single decoration lit up the few scattered windows that still lifted their shutters. Everything was in survival mode. Two fellows stood outside a club, the only indication it was open. Bodies shaped by economic stagnation, powerful accents discussing the football as they smoked. A sincere sign asked customers to tether their horses with consideration for the neighbours.

Halfway up the street is the most striking building in town, now that the pitheads are gone, the Social Welfare Centre, renamed from the Miners' Welfare. The notice board informed me that *Aladdin and his Magic Lamp* was on tonight in the ballroom. I went inside. There was a reception with a bloke behind the desk, on the phone. I sat down, surrounded by the extraordinary memorabilia of a mining town. He finished his call, and agreed to show me round, without me even having to explain why I was there. The lower floor contained a three table snooker room and a reading room.

'We had three regular youth groups here, till the funding ran out earlier this year.' He said with a shake of the head. He didn't seem bothered for his own situation but detested the abandonment of youngsters who through no fault of their own were here and had so little to work with.

I asked him if he had connections with the colliery. Not the first daft question I'd asked today.

'Oh aye. My Father and Grandfather both worked in it. My dad was 16 when he started and my grandfather 13. I joined up too, at 18. I was 35 when it shut, I was one of the youngest. They'd stopped hiring a decade before. The writing was on the wall.'

We passed a photographic display, dozens of men in black and white photos, each with a name and a number. The number related to a number in the schematic diagram of the pit next to the display, showing the place where the body had been recovered from following the 1951 disaster, when a firedamp (flammable gasses emitted by coal seams) explosion ignited coal dust in a continuous blast that ran throughout the level, killing eighty-one instantly and two more in the rescue.

Easington is rare in this regard in that it still has a specific cultural memory. Disasters happened shamefully commonly in this most brutal of industries. Most former pit villages being further removed in time have slipped beyond specific memory, with memorials that mark the catastrophe but don't connect you to the people and their lives. At Easington, it is kept fresh and raw. It is curated and becomes part of each citizen's sense of being. They are us and we are them. On the opposite wall were photos of an Easington Collieryman who won the VC, and another who liberated Belson and arrested the commander. This arrest had been documented by the cartoonist Carl Giles, one of my greatest heroes. His experiences in Belson left him with a constitutional hatred of authority figures that permeated his work thereafter, and led him in my opinion to be the finest documenter of postwar England. Such is the interconnectedness of all things.

Upstairs at the Social Welfare is the grand ballroom. The janitor informed me that it was;

'One of only two fully sprung dance floors in the country.'

I bounced around for a while to show willing. It was an exquisite floor, although *Aladdin and his Magic Lamp* had necessitated several hundred chairs to obstruct the main expanse.

'They've come up from Newcastle to perform it for a couple of nights. Said we should put out three hundred chairs, but they had forty in last night. Should've gone with, what do they call it, with all the tables out too?'

'Cabaret style?'

'Aye, that's the one. It's busiest part of town, this room, they hire it from all over for dances.'

Back at reception I got chatting again. 'Did people leave after the mine shut?'

'No, not really, mostly they were older. They'd stopped hiring, so most were over forty when it shut. Didn't want to move, so the town just stopped where it was. Children move away, but the adults stay.'

I asked what happened to the houses that became vacant.

'The council move people in from elsewhere, people they don't know quite what to do with.'

'So Easington is a bit of a dumping ground for problem families?' It was a clumsy question,

'I wouldn't put it quite like that meself, but it's not easy for anyone in that situation. Nobody chooses to move here, spare houses are boarded or burnt.'

Councils down South had sent some of their social housing tenants here, telling them it was that or homelessness. A tough place to try to start a new life with no connections or resources.

I made a note, an act he noticed.

'Are you doing a project?'

My cover was blown, and the question was as embarrassing as it was telling. Easington is the perverse poster child of post-industrial desolation and as such receives more than its fair share of middle class arty types on 'projects' to interpret the hideous ruination. As the set of hit film *Billy Elliot*, Easington attracts the wreckage tourist, the well meaning idiots. I was ashamed. To return to J.B. Priestley, he wrote of meeting the Durham colliers' wives in 1934, each woman scrapping to stretch every last coin to feed their families: '(they) were neither resentful nor whining, but nevertheless made me feel like a rich fat man. And I object to feeling like a fat rich man.' Painfully aware of his own privilege, he found he could scarcely believe that people so forcibly removed from him in economic and social terms could be just a short drive away from home, under the same system of government and having the same theoretical rights.

Likewise, I felt rotten. I have no money at all, but I have friends and family with enough surplus that I can embark upon such a trip as this with complete confidence; the worst that can happen to me is therefore not very bad. I will not end up in a shop doorway, or trapped in a pit village, unable to earn the money to escape. It is privilege pure and simple, and allows me to pursue this journey without real fear of consequence. No child of Easington could dream of doing so, at least not without risking genuine destitution. A misstep or bad fortune and they'd have no net to catch them. I stood stripped naked by his question and confessed that I was indeed doing a project. He was not upset, just indifferent, this is how it is, and remained happy to advise and chat.

The Easington Social Welfare is the lifeline, the pulse that won't die. It hosts a computer room where they hold 'job club', the simplicity of the name seeming so brutal. Lads play snooker. Dances and shows take place in the ballroom. Easington could be beautiful, rolling down to the sea off the gentle Durham hills. But it is dysfunctional. Youngsters who can leave get out as soon as they can. Empty houses are filled with council tenants from elsewhere with no jobs or prospects of having any. Old miners waste the second half of their lives awaiting the return of an industry that's been erased from the landscape. What for them is a life barely gone is an unimaginably distant past to the bright world of London or even Manchester now. Coal mining belongs to another time and place, one of black and white photographs, moustaches, leather footballs, steam trains, empire.

Coal mining in Durham is now seen only in the rows of cottages, the memorials to those who died, the graveyards that seem too big for the villages, the wrinkles and folds in the land that sprout young and vigorous trees, the network of roads and footprints of lifted rails, the street names, the social clubs hanging on by a fingernail, the headgear set in the bus turning circle, painted mute black. A wealth of circumstantial evidence with no corpse.

I walked up the hill, back to my car. I passed the old school, two colossal brick buildings divided by a courtyard, one for boys and one for girls. They looked for all the world to be two cotton mills, derelict like the North West of my youth. The entrance to one had a sign attached above the old doorway such that it read 'Danger, Keep out. BOYS.' There was no such warning on the girls' school. A local later informed me that it had been slated to be demolished before English heritage had slapped a listing on it, and now it stands in disrepair, much to the annoyance of the town who regard it as an eyesore that needs redeveloping. A modern school round the corner was rated excellent in the most recent inspection.

But how do you help such communities? Perhaps under another system the coal mines might have stayed open a bit longer, but we're moving towards a post-coal economy, and for environmental reasons the sooner that happens the better. At some point you'd inevitably face the same problem, an entire town losing its employment at once. These problems are inevitable in a de-industrialising society and do not sort themselves out. People do not get 'on their bike' to find other employment unless they are either so young they haven't put down roots or face death if they do not. History and current world affairs tells us that nothing short of starvation or massacre compels people over 30 to move in any great numbers, like the Cornish tin miners who emigrated to Australia after the collapse of their industry. Institute any kind of welfare and people will stay. The dole, meagre though it may be, is enough to sustain the communities that people already have, albeit at a subsistence level. No amount of charity will provide more than temporary relief, as only empowered individuals can reshape a community, and empowerment comes through economic autonomy. Jobs. The fact of the matter is that the architect of the Category D village policy was right in one sense. Durham remains home to dozens of villages that don't economically work. A city sized workforce spread over a rural county in bits and pieces. Where cities concentrate resources, efficiencies, opportunities, the coal mining legacy of Durham has left it unfocussed, inefficient, and impractical.

But they were wrong in another more important sense. People are ferociously attached to their communities, and the spirit within them is extraordinarily strong. What can seem like a desperate place to outsiders is home to insiders, invisible connections between people making community. For the poorest, this can be all they have, and it burns bright, the threat of losing it for a vague and uncertain future was enough to rightfully cause the policy to fail. What makes perfect economic sense is also social cleansing and dehumanising. It takes away the community that Durham has fought so hard to maintain.

Nobody should advocate distressing people into making decisions that benefit the wider economy, even ultimately themselves, so what the heck do you do? Even when presented with new towns, better housing, schools, transport, the residents of the D villages stayed put, preferring what they knew, the communities they had built and participated in. Change only started to come when the last of that generation died out and new people moved in with new reasons for being there. Can that sequence be shortened without abusing and breaking people? Can work be found that doesn't require the artificial creation of loss making and inefficient industry in the wrong place? To support industry that the market wouldn't sustain indefinitely is to impoverish others and store problems up for the future, and therefore should always be regarded as reckless and immoral. Can technology help? In the information age, are there jobs that could happen in these places with a comparatively small amount of technological investment and a degree of lateral thinking? Could their supply of labour in an otherwise tight market and cheap prices give them a new competitive edge in a digital world, given the right opportunity? Can the city of the future be less of a physical construct and more a function of connectivity? This is wild and perhaps optimistic speculation. It is, as ever, far easier to analyse the problems than it is to come up with practical solutions and I don't expect I shall get a street named after me in Chopwell any time soon. Perhaps that is why politics has given up on the Durham coalfield. Interventionist, socialist policies were met with resentment and resistance. Letting market forces trash the county was a far bigger crime. The people of Easington held public celebrations when Thatcher died, despite their colliery surviving her premiership. It is hard to blame them. Her government and its successor had abandoned them.

At the very least, the youth of the town deserve a chance to make it in the world, and the loss of the youth groups, small though it may seem in the context of the greater problems, is appallingly symptomatic of lack of interest the nation has in these places. I got in my car to drive home, pausing at the crossing as three children ran across, kicking a tatty football, joyful, unaware yet in their youth of their place in the wider world, of the hopelessness of their town, the poor hand they'd been dealt, having at such a tender age only other poor hands to compare it to. It is all they know, and they seemed the happiest people I'd seen all day. I fear it will take another twenty-five years and the deaths of the last miners before it even starts to turn around, so utterly abandoned is it to its fate.

But the Durham coalfield is more than just a bunch of historical stories winding down. If history tells us anything, it is how seemingly dominant and untouchable industries can collapse overnight in a cloud of hubris in the face of global adjustments. Coal is dead. Cotton is dead. Tin is dead. Our main industry these days is finance. There is a surety of our pre-eminence in this market that is eerily reminiscent of cotton in 1920, when grand buildings and civic works sprung up all over my native North West, great town halls, public buildings, squares, schools, funded by top-hatted magnates, eager to get their name in the history books not just for their economic prowess, but also their character. The London I'd walked through two weeks before felt like a digital Cottonopolis, glass sided civic and commercial masterpieces befitting the titans of the trade. By 1929, the cotton magnates were ruined, the mills closing, the weavers starving. Distant, subtle shifts in global trade and politics had bankrupted a seemingly unstoppable juggernaut of commerce in just a few years. In Durham, coal had ebbed away more gradually, ruining the county town by town rather than all at once. The effect had been the same. It wouldn't take much for global finance trade to shift its flow, and the great buildings of London to fall empty and abandoned like rusting headgear and derelict mills. The myth of Northern differentness hides this possible future, it couldn't happen here because we're the prosperous South and that's the uncivilised North. Economics is blind to these prejudices.

I NEED to pause for a moment here. This book originated as a blog, and blogging as you go means that if you do write something controversial, it's picked up there and then, allowing chance to explore the issue before you've had it signed off and committed to print. My blog post about the Durham coalfield got me in trouble; but it ended up being a stroke of fortune, and I learnt a great deal more for having upset people.

Amongst other things, I was exploring the long term consequences of de-industrialisation in communities with little economic diversity, and County Durham had seemed a good place to look, having lost coal mining in waves of closures over the last eighty years or so. I sought to trace a continuum from villages that had lost the colliery a lifetime ago through to places that had lost their mines much more recently. As an economic study, I don't feel I was too wide of the mark. But that wasn't what upset people, and the nature of the offence caused was illuminating.

People who were Durham coalfield 'expats' tended to agree with my first impressions, and shared the original blog post pretty widely. Within a few hours it had made it back to Easington Colliery and had been shared round the community groups, who were furious. The gist of the anger was twofold. While there wasn't much they directly disagreed with in it, they felt I'd completely failed to highlight the positive things going on in the community, and more importantly than that, they were angry that it wasn't their voice telling the story. Another outsider had come and told them about their problems.

One resident, Heather, whilst cross about it, offered that if I were to come back, she'd show me the other side of the coin and set the record straight. We set up a return visit. This is how it went.

Return to Easington Colliery

I DROVE up the A1 early one morning, full of nerves. It's a scary thing to drive across the country to meet a group of strangers who are all cross with you, but I've tried never to shy away from things like this in life. If you're upset people, you should front up about it, try to learn why. I was mainly worried that we wouldn't get on, we wouldn't agree, and that what I'd then write about it wouldn't make things any better. I wondered what I could do if this was the case, deciding that I'd be best explaining the difference and providing space for a full right of reply.

Afraid of being late, I set off first thing and actually arrived two and a half hours early, giving me time to explore Easington village, the older half of the settlement further up the hill. I parked by the entrance to a new housing estate being built, and wandered for a bit. What had historically been the main street for the village was down to the last few shops, the centre of activity having moved to Easington Colliery half a mile away when it had been built. A foundation block read 'This stone was laid by' with the lower two lines of text obliterated by one hundred and fifty years of dog pee.

The church stands on the highest ground and overlooks the village. The stained glass windows are covered in rough Perspex sheets to protect them from stones. In the graveyard, an angel had lost its head, trumpet hanging by its side, redundant. Across the road is Seaton Holme rectory, now a municipal building, but once home to Bishops, apparently including Nicholas Breakspear who went on to be England's only pope, operating under the name of Adrian IV. A good story, although there appears to be no solid evidence of his presence here. Outside, a colliery tub had been turned into a decorative planter.

I drove through both halves of Easington and down to the park where the colliery itself had stood. On top of the now landscaped spoil tip, the colliery cage has been placed, as far from the car park across land as it once went down to let the miners out under the sea. Striking in the distance, hard to assign perspective, it cuts a melancholy shape up close up, where the starkness of the riveted sheets of steel is set off by a series of ribbons tied to it. From a distance, it is mysterious and powerful, all incongruous shape. Up close it is lost and confused, a singularly functional object shorn of purpose. 'Why am I here?' It asks.

My meeting was due. Heather had arranged for me to meet a local councillor, and a local business owner in the Welfare. I walked in, wondering how this would go. In the small office off the main reception, they were waiting for me, and found a fourth chair. It seemed that they were as nervous as me. They hadn't expected me to accept the offer to visit again, and even when I said I would, were still unsure if I would actually show up. People like me don't normally come back.

'One man came from the *Guardian*. Walked up and down the main street, went back to London and wrote this horrible piece.

Wouldn't reply to any messages! We have his picture on CCTV if he ever comes back', Heather told me.

Yikes. But it wasn't a threat. It was a passionate need to get a voice heard, a voice that they felt was routinely ignored in any appraisal of their village.

I got out my notepad and starting writing down what they were telling me. The business owner was called Ellin and was particularly direct in explaining what had upset her:

'What made me so angry was the lack of meeting people.'

Over the course of an hour I was firmly given the stories I'd missed, the undercurrents, the society. Being naturally genial people, periodically they'd forget they were supposed to be bollocking me and would revert to their natural state of good humoured chat and anecdotes. When the subject moved onto allotments, something County Durham is particularly notable for, the local councillor Steve recounted being given a bunch of prize carrots from his father's allotment to take into school for the harvest festival when he was 8. Being hungry, he'd nibbled the tips off, something that was spotted by the master. Upon being questioned, he'd immediately replied 'It must've been hungry pit ponies', an answer quick enough to ensure that he avoided punishment.

The atmosphere in the room had lifted a great deal. A man with a small and impossibly friendly dog dropped by for a natter and a tail-wag, and the already strong Durham accents became much stronger, almost to the point of impenetrability for me.

We talked about some of the things I'd written about in my first piece. Housing was a hot topic. The majority of the housing in the village was low quality miner's terraces, some of it unoccupied, and much of it in a poor state of repair. In the view of the room, the dense streets should have all been demolished and replaced by more modern housing, incorporating more open spaces. Instead it had largely been sold to a small number of private absentee landlords. One of these landlords had then done a deal with Durham prison to provide accommodation for families of those imprisoned there, and housing for the recently released. This had placed a huge burden on the community.

'I'd say people with problems rather than problem people. Our difficulty is that we haven't also been given the budget to help them integrate', said Heather. Lots of issues to deal with and no resources.

'We're being used a social experiment. I've even had the ministerial aide tell me that to my face', said Steve. 'The next village got housing co-operatives which weren't much better, but we got total sell-off of the housing to absentee landlords who make millions on contracts with the council. We get a huge influx of people straight out of jail from all over and no budget to support them. They don't integrate and it leaves the community divided.'

Only one of the prison incomers had made any real effort to integrate into the community.

'That canoe man, who faked his death, John Darwin was it? He ended up here, and he was a character. Used to come down the welfare, great sense of humour!'

What about the school?

'Everyone always goes on about the school. It's the first thing they see.'

The old school had closed in 1998, and had stood abandoned ever since.

'Biggest pigeon nest in the North', said Steve.

Subsequent efforts to demolish and regenerate the site had failed owing to it also passing into the hands of a property developer and being listed by Historic England, twin inertias that had left it rotting and derelict, a symbol of the village's inability to force the regeneration it needed. It's an eyesore, hugely prominent and an immense frustration to the locals.

'So people who come here see that, they see the housing, and all we get is a bad press. But I know how hard people are working to sustain this place. The community raised £30,000 to save the church. The Methodists run 'Cafe Together' where you can get a £1 meal.'

'We didn't lose the strike. We won. We're still here. We met in the Welfare. We built it with our wages. They took the jobs away but we still have the welfare and the sports grounds.'

'It's an informal network – who needs what, who can provide a skill when needed? We have benefits champions to help others, winter champions to keep the roads clear.'

'Mining's not dead. Children are taught about it. We had that problem with Durham University?' (A couple of years ago, a Durham student society attracted anger for having a Miner's strike themed fancy dress event.) 'Now they're making their own banner. It's a big improvement on disengagement and disrespect.'

The strike was still foremost in the collective minds of the village. It had been the central event in the modern history of Easington colliery, as with so many towns, perhaps even eclipsing the closure of the colliery. It was where the community had bound tightest and burned brightest.

'We went on strike for jobs, not money or victory', said Steve. 'After it ended, we didn't think we were defeated. We asked 'What's our learnings?' So we got elected. Onto councils and unions. We opposed the opencast. When the mine shut, 40 per cent signed up for education the next day. I was kept on at quarter wage for a year when they mothballed the pit.'

I was invited by Ellin to see the business she'd set up beyond the edge of town. A camping venue called 'The Barn' which included some luxurious camping pods, a full campsite, and a wedding or events venue. It was the future, as they saw it. The countryside is beautiful in Durham, and over the ridge from the village, you'd not have known of the row of coal mines that once stretched down the coast towards Hartlepool. The beach has been cleared of colliery waste, and the colliery site was being transformed into a nature reserve. Ellin was a film maker who'd moved up here after falling in love with the area.

'It was all fully booked right through the summer.' She told me, pointing across the camp site.

The land sloped down to the sea, folding into the wooded burn. Heather told me that one evening last summer, the sun setting over the ridge had been so spectacular that the event in the barn had spontaneously stopped, with everyone just heading outside to enjoy the moment in peace. It was a lovely spot.

Perhaps the best insight of the day for me came towards the end, as we walked back up towards the farmhouse from the barn. Heather was telling me that every village had its own clear identity, and were constantly scrapping with each other, with clear dividing lines only visible to the locals. As soon as an outsider came, they'd instantly band together and present a united front.

'So they're your fights to fight?'

'Yes'

And there in a nutshell was the problem with my first piece. Easington Colliery is in a tough place. In some regards the situation here was even worse than I'd first realised, but it's theirs, they take ownership of it, all of it, and it needs to be their voice that tells the world about it. Easington won't be helped by outsiders making ill-informed decisions over their heads. It needs support, lots of it, but that support needs to be designed and coordinated by the residents. Good or bad, it's their story, and as writers are always tempted to do, I'd made it mine. I'd taken away the one thing they still had after others had taken away the work and the funding.

The community spirit was clearly key to taking the place forward. How could they pass that spirit onto the next generation, now there wasn't the industry to bind them together?

'It's hard, trying to help the youths and I worry about it', said Heather. Ellin continued: 'But negative press really doesn't help. I worry about them internalising the outside negative narrative.'

I shook hands with Ellin and Heather. It had been a draining day, probably for all of us. I'd learned a lot. Not least about the power that comes of having a readership. I'd thought of myself as some dude with a fiddle writing a few words in a harmless sort of way. I hadn't appreciated how significant those words can be, and how wounding and frustrating they can feel to the reader. My underestimation of the power of my writing had meant I'd failed to consider the responsibility that comes with it.

I'd also failed to appreciate the powerful connection between people and place. If someone came and wrote something negative about my town, I doubt it would bother me much. My relationship with my town is entirely different. Maybe that's because I left and moved to the city. Maybe it's because I never had to stand and fight for it. Indeed, when I wrote the first piece, the response from people who'd grown up in County Durham and left was entirely different to those who'd stayed. I needed to be much more attuned to how people feel about their place, instead of assuming they'd think like me.

The criticism I'd received was justified. I'd try to do better. I think Heather deserves particular credit for being brave enough to invite me back. She didn't have to do that, and it was a generous olive branch. I'm grateful for it, as well as for the time that Steve and Ellin gave me.

Easington Colliery is not a hopeless case, but is in danger of being turned into one through outside abandonment. The Barn points the way for the sort of place it could be, but it will take a significant change in sentiment and political will. For myself, I see why the first article was such a problem. For change to occur, there needs to be a much wider understanding of what goes on under the surface of such a place. Ignoring that re-enforced the narrative of hopelessness, making it more likely to come true.

'We were always that bit more rebellious here. An academic said we had the strongest women we'd ever met', Heather reminisced at the end of the day.

I couldn't argue with that. In a sense, I'm now glad that the first article received the criticism it did. It opened my eyes to a strength of connection between people and place that I hadn't really understood before.

Cirencester and The Cotswolds

WINTER dragged on. Christmas had come and gone. Cirencester carried a damp air of muted gentility. Rows of piggledy town houses led through narrow curving streets to the centre, windows haphazardly filled with bunting and colourful children's frocks. The road into town boasted more hairdressers than will ever seem entirely reasonable to a baldy like me. Weathered, the yellow Jurassic limestone of the Cotswolds had lost its true edges, giving the town a soft and pillowy feel.

Cirencester is a hub of independent shops, something to be found at both ends of the economic bell curve. In the poorest towns, independents provide the few services people have any money for, where the chains fear to tread. In Cirencester, they are expensive and bespoke. One sold hallmarked sterling silver lids for condiments such as HP sauce, Marmite, and Colman's mustard. Luxuries I didn't know I couldn't afford.

Finding a pitch was not easy. I try not to be a nuisance and so pick empty shops to play in front of. There were few of these. In 2017, there were barely three hundred unemployed people in the whole of the Cotswolds, the lowest rate in England, and business was thriving. One or two shops were sold, awaiting a new tenant, and I found a spot near the church on the big open square. The rain had let up, and I slowly warmed up the fiddle, enjoying the acoustic of the high walls across the road. A huge man, bearded and at least 6ft 5in came striding over to me with a grin, pushing his belly before him like an icebreaker seeking a Northwest passage. He strode right into my personal space, looked me straight in the eye, paused, and said 'Nooice one, son!' before thrusting a fistful of boiled sweets into the pouch of my hoodie.

A woman came over to me and mumbled at me for a bit, before waving her hands at me whilst chanting. It appeared that she was casting a curse. I continued playing, wondering what would happen. It's remarkable how no two busking pitches are quite the same. The curse began to take hold and the money dried up for a while. The square was damp, but little patches of dry started to form on the stone paving. The sky began to glow. After a soaked day, the sun had finally appeared in time for sunset, lighting up the sides of the thick clouds and warming the golden stone of the church. People stopped in the square just to enjoy the few minutes of soft light. An American tourist was so overcome by it she felt it necessary to hand me a £10 note which I gratefully trousered. The curse had clearly not been a long-lasting one. Maybe she was just practicing.

I packed down at 5pm. As I was putting the bow away, a woman gave me a pound coin.

'It's nice here. I lived in South Africa and Zimbabwe for forty years until I moved back to England. Only came here for six months, but I stayed.' She paused before concluding wistfully: 'I suppose this is it now.' After another moment she gestured round the square. 'But it is pretty, isn't it?'

I started again as early as I dared the next morning. The best weather of the week was due and I was determined to cash in while I could. The skies were clear, but a bitter wind barrelled its shoulders along the streets. I wore several layers, topped with a very old and tired Barbour jacket and a woolly hat. I concluded that for a bloke at least, one path to busking success was to set your appearance just right so that you seemed a little down on your luck whilst leaving open the possibility of redemption, a redemption that one could contribute towards with just a few coins. A good deed done.

I busked on, and the day quietly built around me. In front of a sign that said 'Do not feed the pigeons', an old man was liberally feeding a large and multiplying flock of pigeons with numerous fistfuls of crumbs from an oversize shopping bag. I wondered if he really ought to be doing that, but he won my silence by slipping me a fiver as he went past.

The well-heeled came and went about their business, wearing beautiful, expensive and understated clothes. Cirencester was a wool town, and that's still what most people would wear on a day like this, from scarves to tweeds, fleece lined boots. Stylish and pastel coloured, all neatly fitting. It really was a very well dressed place, led by the small groups of plump, pink cheeked young men from the agricultural college. Older men gave me advice on better busking pitches. 'Down the main street near Nationwide, that's where they go. You'd do better there.' Maybe I would, but the acoustics in this square, backed by the church were wonderful and I didn't want to leave them. 'You must have cold hands.' was a recurring theme. Proud grandparents told me of grandchildren learning instruments and doing terribly well at them. 'That's great. Perhaps one day they could be doing as well as me', I thought of replying, but it seemed cruel and I let them be.

At lunchtime I entered the church, mainly to get out of the wind for a bit. I was immediately handed a brochure by a grey haired man with a smile that managed to convey all of 'I know why you're in here, but I'm far too polite to say so, so I shall pretend I believe you're an interested tourist and hand you this brochure, but I'll look at you in a way that makes it clear that I know you're not. And so does God.'

The brochure contained a map conveying the usual sorts of information, such as 'Pulpit – 1450, in a rare and finely-worked wine glass design' and 'Garstang Chapel, Established in 1440 for the tomb of a local merchant.' I was about to stop reading when one more piece of information caught my eye. 'Tower – Erected in 1400 with funds taken from the rebellious Earls of Kent and Salisbury, arrested by the townspeople and executed in the market place.'

It couldn't happen now of course, the heads of tax-avoiding global corporations dragged out into the street, executed, and their assets used to erect a massive vindictive tower, although we can all fantasise. I shook a few coins into the collection box with a tinkle. The welcomer raised an eyebrow over by his desk and I shot him a big smile right back.

I took the collective advice of Cirencester and tried the more commonly used busking pitch. I made a little more there in an hour than I had back in the square, but it was crowded, I felt in the way, and the acoustics were crap. Preferring to play for pleasure than money, I headed back to the main square and saw out the day, £79 in four and a half bitter hours. Staying at my friend Elspeth's house, I got back and hugged the radiator in silence for a while, body cold right through to the middle.

The next morning I drove over the hill to Bibury. The frost was melting away as I parked my salt-stained and unenthusiastic Volvo by the banks of the river Coln, across from the internationally renowned Arlington Row houses, and stepped out onto a pavement already abundant with Koreans and their bulky cameras. Behind us, another row of houses, which would have qualified as picturesque just about anywhere else, were largely ignored, although many garden gates had laminated 'No Entry, Private' signs, with multiple translations into East Asian languages beneath.

Arlington Row is a set of houses that represents the absolute quintessence of the Cotswolds. Set back from the road across a sparkling river, by a frost tipped meadow, this enthusiastically jumbled terrace of not quite matching windows and doors is deemed one of the most important architectural assets in England. It's on the inside cover of the UK passport, features in the 'Mini Europe' display in Brussels, and is preserved by the Royal College of Arts.

The first task of anyone wanting to use it for a period production would be to remove the hundreds of signs that decorate the place. It is a strictly controlled area. On closer inspection, the cottages looked damp and poorly lit. Nice to look at, but not my ideal home.

Elsewhere in the village, the architecture remains sublime, yellow stone houses set in perfect wintry gardens. Good order and simplicity. Driveways are chained off.

The church notice board gave notice of the ailing condition of an unnamed local ex-cabinet minister and urged us to spend less time on our phones. On the grass of the well-tended graveyard, the immaculacy was only heightened by an impact circle of feathers around a little pile of bones and gristle where a bird of prey had taken breakfast. The old hall next door was cocooned in scaffolding, morphing into something new.

Walking up the hill again, past gates, 'Private, keep out' signs, and smartly Barboured dog walkers who couldn't quite tell if I was a tourist or an invited visitor out for a stroll, I wasn't sure what to do with myself. Bibury was the architectural equivalent of a strip club. Cheap to get in, but you can't touch and the drinks are very expensive. And in truth, you know it's not like the real thing. Inside the houses, worried residents, suffocated by the beauty that drew them here in the first place, put up cameras and signs, buy hairy dogs, and in the largest properties hire security guards. Living in such a contrived place is perhaps no more real than visiting it.

A few miles further up the road is Burford. A small place of a little under 2,000 people, Burford is a carefully cultivated Cotswold town, immaculate main street where every bespoke, handmade shop is exquisitely crafted by artisans to extract maximum tourist cash. The council estate is hard to find, tucked away out of sight down a back street. I passed an Olde Worlde sweet shop and a wooden brush manufacturer, where a glance inside revealed a young woman in an apron planing down a block for the next brush, soon to be sold to an American or a Korean as an accurate and representative souvenir of olde England. 'Oh yeah, I've got dozens at home', I explained to an American looking at the window. 'We all do.'

Having done my bit for the economy, I headed into the Sue Ryder shop in search of a new shirt. The lady behind the counter was called Diana and she filled me in on the town's recent history. The vast priory building at the bottom of the hill had recently featured in the divorce settlement of one of Rupert Murdoch's children. I later took a look, and found a giant wooden gate covered in go away signs and cameras, surrounded by a 14ft stone wall. It was cold and stood alone from the town, as if a tragic novel had recently concluded, leaving only a long series of blank pages before the endpapers.

The church has some serious history inside. A good portion of it is given over to the tomb of Sir Lawrence Tanfield (1551-1625) and his second wife Elizabeth. Their tomb came with an interpretation. I read it expecting a gentle summation of the great man's life. Instead I got an excoriating biography, detailing how this Eton educated man had been utterly detested for his harsh practices and cruelty towards his many tenants, his vast corruption as Chief Baron of the Exchequer, and how his cynical enclosures of land had infuriated other landowners, all egged on by his equally hated wife. The tomb was immaculate and beautiful, with life-size and highly detailed painted wooden effigies exuding 'who, me?' innocence. It was clean and well cared for. I got the distinct impression that the town, in a safe Conservative constituency until recently represented by former PM David Cameron, was secretly rather proud of him. Elsewhere, I learned that the town only finally rid itself of their terrible presence when Lady Tanfield's spirit was trapped in a bottle and sunk to the bottom of the river. Something to aim for there, I think. I know just the bottle.

At the other end of the church there was evidence of another sort of politics. In 1649, three hundred and forty deserting soldiers were imprisoned in the church, after mutinying and joining the Leveller movement. One, Anthony Sedley, famously scratched his name into the font whilst awaiting his fate. I went to find the inscription but found that rather unfortunately a great many other people had had the same idea down the years, and the font was covered in scratches and patterns. I took their word for it. This revolt had ended with the ringleaders being shot outside the church, an event commemorated yearly when socialists descend upon the town to remember the executions and talk politics. It's a connection that half the town wishes it didn't have, an intrusion of socialist politics into the otherwise safe and gentrified world of the Cotswolds.

It certainly seems to be the churches where the action takes place round here. Executed Earls, revolting soldiers being murdered, restless malevolent spirits being trapped in bottles.

On Diana's advice, I also visited the gift shop '3 French Hens'. It was a narrow cavern of densely clustered souvenirs. On a quiet day in town, it was still surprisingly busy, with a steady throughput of people who didn't know what they wanted but felt sure this was where they could get it. I got talking to the lady behind the counter, who'd initiated the conversation by pointing at my fiddle case and asking me if the bow was longer than the violin. I have never been asked this before and found I actually didn't know the answer. I opened the case on the counter and we immediately discovered the bow to be significantly longer than the violin.

'Y'know, I've been playing it for twenty-five years and never thought about it before.'

She's moved down from London a few years ago, as she put

it. In the Cotswolds, one goes 'up' to London, despite London being to the South and East.

The soundtrack being played round the shop was strange electronic music with a certain hippy vibe to it. The female vocalist then transitioned from singing to having an orgasm, and clearly a good one too, filling the shop with cries of ecstasy. I looked round. None of the other customers seemed to have noticed, or perhaps they just weren't fazed by it. Maybe this was normal for piped music in Oxfordshire, and the weekly shop at the Co-op was similarly explicit.

Whilst I was awkwardly transfixed by the audio, a customer arrived at the counter with a couple of signs for hanging up back home. They read 'If a meal doesn't have wine with it, it's Breakfast' and 'All of our visitors bring happiness. Some by coming, others by going.'

After the sale was made, the shopkeeper introduced herself as Angela. The music had returned to normal and I was able to concentrate again. She said I should approach the Warwick Hall for a concert, and I bought a small glass pig with googly eyes as a thank you. Another customer arrived at the counter with an 18in tall moulded plastic hare for which she parted with £34. I asked her what she had in mind for it.

'I've got a space in the conservatory that really needs something like this.' She stared into its eyes, smiled, and added 'I think I've found him.'

Outside, a young couple were laughing without inhibition at the window of an estate agents, finding each new price funnier than the last. I sympathised. Burford is the sort of town where I measure house prices in units of careers, i.e. all the money I will ever earn. 'This one is a three career house, and that's a five career house.'

Either way, that figure wouldn't be arrived at any sooner by me standing here complaining, so I decided to have a busk, despite the very quiet nature of the town out of season. Finding another gift shop that was closed for a fortnight, I set up outside and began to play. Heads popped out of the smattering of souvenir shops to see what the noise was, but nobody seemed to mind. After a little over an hour, I'd raised £23, all of it in pound coins. A pound was clearly the lowest denomination of coin in Burford, anything smaller too trivial to bother with. I suddenly remembered receiving tiny tatty legacy bank notes not much larger than postage stamps in rural China in my change and asking the guide what they were. 'Ah, you have ten nothings there', he replied. Meaningful to the villagers but inconceivably small in value to me. Here I was the peasant, adding up the nothings.

It was quiet today, but I could imagine a summer's day, with the coach park full, and hordes of tourists on package trips being corralled round the shops until they'd hit their quota of traditional scrubbing brushes and woollen socks. It's the same the world over, places that exist to sell tourists unnecessary things to give to relatives who don't want them, delivering a percentage of the profits as kickbacks to the tour operators who shepherd them in. We all have a bizarre shelf of odd objects that represent the final stage of this powerful global economic process. Diana told me the locals do all their shopping in Witney. Burford is a pretty place, for sure, but oddly disconnected, and mistrustful of reminders of the wider world. Muttered grumbles about the small council estate and its place on the Socialist travel map speak to a desire to have things just so, without challenge. Tourists are welcome to come and consume the atmosphere and gifts, but ideas, like dirty shoes, must be left at the door.

Why is it all so beautiful? This was the question I struggled with as I pottered from village to village. The water-mill and central stream of Lower Slaughter, the low arch bridges of Bourton-on-the-Water. I sang 'The Stow-on-the-Wold is all mine, all mine, the Stow-on-the-Wold is all mine' to myself as I drove through. Why do I, and so many others instinctively look at these places and consider them beautiful? There are some very nice houses here, for sure, but that's true of many places. Some of the most 'picturesque' probably wouldn't make great homes at all, being pokey and from entirely another era, one with different practical limits on central heating, not to mention the problems imposed by planning regulations. Is there something inherent about a land like this? Sheltered, green, lush and watery, stone the colour of winter sun, that speaks to some ancient and deeply seated need to find a safe and fertile place to make a home? Does it just simply feel right? Perhaps it's also cultural? Is this the England we'd prefer to be proud of? Instead of the pit villages, the manufacturing towns, the trading estates, the call centres that produced the wealth that bought up these pretty places from their ancestral inheritors. Is the England of work, toil, production a dirty secret that mustn't be told? Do we have some innate cultural sense that really the hard work should be being done by someone else, far away and preferably brown, and if it is done here, then perhaps they aren't really, truly English? Letting the side down a bit there, old chap.

The Cotswolds are a place to seek separation from the wider realities of England. There's no unemployment here, and plenty of job opportunities. But the jobs are all in retail, with no hope of providing a realistic income to live here independently. The poor aren't happily employed, they're gone to the city in the hope of reaching the bottom rung. Economics is selective, and drives out those who can't raise the bond to buy their way into the game. For the rest, it's an untroubled horizon, shorn of real poverty, the poor pushed one by one beyond the boundaries of their world. It's an England of period dramas, postcards, good food and durable, high quality clothing. The undulating land and short horizons allow one to believe it's all like this, an unbroken England of happy peasantry and perfect squat cottages, still thirstily parasitic on the shackled body of Empire. It's where cabinet ministers retire to convince themselves it was worth it, where the moneyed buy weekend homes to clear their minds for another onslaught at the world of finance on Monday morning, where foreigners come to taste a slice of an England that probably never quite existed. If it did, it also included mob-executed robber Earls, Levellers, the great industrial canal that finally safely linked East with West, and the lives and deaths of so many poor people who could never have believed that their simple homes would become internationally renowned, the subject of a million camera lenses that would never think of photographing a peasant house in another own land and will never see the similarity.

I finished my musings for the day on top of the enormous Roman amphitheatre back at Cirencester. It was not easy to access. I knew it was opposite Waitrose and across the dual carriageway, but I couldn't work out how to get to it. I tried going round to the right, crossing the road on a footbridge and ended up in some hospital grounds. I climbed a fence and strode through a field, trying to maintain the confident air of someone who's meant to be there. Having scaled another fence, I was in.

And there's no getting away from it. It's huge. It held 8,000 spectators, and was fashioned out of the stone quarry that had provided the material for the town's walls. A measure of Cirencester's immense importance in Roman Britain, this earthwork remains deeply impressive to this day, and would still make a great venue for all sorts of things, were it not stuck awkwardly out of the way between a council estate and the ring road. When the Romans left, the amphitheatre was converted into a fortress, to defend the locals from Saxon Invaders. It must have been a chilling and uncertain time, the collapse of an empire, the loss of lines of communication, and a country suddenly without a power structure, fragmenting into small towns of worried and unconnected people, not able to know what threats lay round the corner. I once heard a scholar say that the people of post-Roman Britain, collapsing away from civilisation, losing the continuity of literacy, had within a few generations found themselves wandering amongst the ruins of the great Roman cities wondering what race of giants had built it, why, and where they might have gone. One of the earliest writings in English, known as 'The Ruin' captures this moment.

It begins, in Dr. Aaron K. Hostetter's translation:

These wall-stones are wondrous —
calamities crumpled them, these city-sites crashed, the work of giants
corrupted. The roofs have rushed to earth, towers in ruins.
Ice at the joints has unroofed the barred-gates, sheared
the scarred storm-walls have disappeared.

I scrambled up and from the top of one embankment I gazed into the amphitheatre and imagined lions, chariots, and gladiators in a great show, thousands roaring on their approval, all beneath a vast billboard proclaiming 'This project was made possible thanks to European money.'

The official way in was at the other end, I now discovered, and I left with slightly more decorum than I arrived with, passing a 50ft obelisk in the dusk, whose interpretation board informed me that it was not known who had built it, when, or why. This seemed like an excellent wheeze, the cult of the random obelisk planters.

On my fourth and final day, I headed into Cirencester a little later, having explored around the countryside a little further, and finding the east portal to the two-mile long Sapperton tunnel, the link between the Severn and the Thames, on the now long derelict and dewatered canal built to connect the two. Finding a cheap breakfast was impossible. Everywhere was fancy, and there wasn't a Greggs to be seen. Having resigned myself to paying too much, I decided to do it properly and entered a very fancy cafe with a centralised open kitchen.

'Ah sir, table for one?'

My dishevelled and scruffy look is not necessarily a disadvantage in Cirencester. There's always a chance I might be extremely rich.

'Yes.'

'Regrettably, we only serve breakfast till 10:30.' I checked. It was 10:40. 'And our Brunch menu is not activated until 11.'

'Okay, no rush.'

'But in the meantime, we have our in-between menu. Here it is.' I had a very expensive sandwich, absolutely outrageously good.

Fortified and light of pocket, I returned to the streets. The rain was permeating everything. I wouldn't be playing today. In the park where the abbey had stood, I followed the lines of the medieval culverts, streams networking through in all directions, an ancient managed landscape, scabbed over in parkland. A flyposted message promised 'Free money and no catch whatsoever' and provided a phone number to ring. One culvert was close to being blocked by a rubberberg formed from hundreds of decaying dog toys. I left Cirencester in the mizzle and started slowly heading my way over to Stroud where I had a gig that night.

Unable to busk and taken by a sudden fancy, I decided to find the other end of the canal tunnel, where the Severn and Thames canal bursts out of the escarpment after 2 miles of dripping and now partially collapsed tunnel, where ancient and exhausted boatmen would finally rest after hours of legging through. It was not easy to find, not being a tourist destination and not showing on Google Maps either. I'd have to find it old-school, reading the land. The canal bed has gone in places, built over, as it rises up many locks from Stroud, and I drove all round trying to follow it, through the tight sided valley, road clinging onto the side, where houses are packed tight in messy clusters above you and below you. Sometimes you get a glimpse into an attic room or a cellar. It was like driving through an old-fashioned children's toy box, all put away for the night in a jumble of shapes.

Eventually when I couldn't find any more roads, I struck out on foot. The rain continued to fall, too thin to make sound, and my fat footprints in the mud disturbed plump woodland birds who left upwards in little flocks, wings batting against winter branches. The abandoned canal sometimes made itself obvious, with vertiginous lock chambers, unprotected holes for the careless or drunken to fall into at night. Gates missing, maybe rotted away altogether leaving a scattering of swelling rusty brackets in shallow pools. Sometimes there was just a linear hollow to follow, willows pushing up through the cofferdam. You couldn't go far wrong, as the valley was tight and the direction clear. After an hour in this perfect post-industrial wilderness with just my thoughts and the sound of tiny water droplets slowly combining on leaves and finding the next little step of their journey out to the Bristol Channel, I popped up by a pub, a road I had somehow managed to miss, and the other tunnel entrance. The pub had a mound of dirty boots by the door, and unwilling to take mine off, I eschewed liquid refreshment and made my way back to my car.

Looking down at the muddy mess my legs had become raised an important point. I was due to play for a wedding reception and had no spare trousers. I glanced at the clock. 3.30pm. Time was against me.

I'd love to tell you about Stroud, but really all I saw was the inside of six charity shops, finally locating a pair of trousers vaguely in my size in Sue Ryder UK, five minutes before closing time. Strangers will have been taken aback by the sight of a large and animated man bursting out of the shop holding a pair of trousers aloft as if a military standard, shouting 'Woo, woo, woo!' and sprinting to his car. I got to my gig exactly on time. The buffet was excellent, and best of all, someone else was paying.

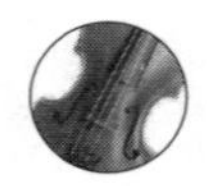

The Stroud and District Skittles League

AT the Tudor Arms, Shepherd's Patch, near Slimbridge, it was time for this evening's fixture in the Stroud and District Skittles League Division A, between the home team, the Patch Rats, and great rivals Chalford AFC. The game of skittles is slightly different in every town, but in the Stroud and district league it features nine slightly bulbous pins and three balls (otherwise known as cheeses). It is the ancient and noble ancestor of the rather more glamorous sport of ten pin bowling that graces every decent out-of-town trading estate.

My friend Debra and I got a pint and settled down in the audience area, outside the alley but adjoining with just a glass panel behind the alley itself as physical division. There was a steady stream of players to and from the bar.

I focused on the action. Before releasing the cheese, each player briefly adopted a pose entirely of their own devising, like a catalogue of illegal moves that have been banned from Indian classical dancing on the twin grounds of taste and safety. Players would contort their bodies low to the ground, maybe with one leg stuck forward whilst cradling the cheese to their bodies, looking up at the skittles, composing themselves, rocking a couple of times, inhaling, snorting, then bursting forward and releasing the projectile at a running speed. A rugby player lining up for a conversion would be proud of such a contrived physical performance. From our position behind the panel, our perspective on this ritual was an unending series of meaty arses reversing up to and gyrating against the glass.

For a seemingly simple game, there were a lot of rules and variations to learn. I started asking questions, about the scoring system, what was going on, who was winning, and got the same reply each time; 'Eh, do you not have skittles where you're from? What do you play in pubs?'

The thought of a pub without an alley was a difficult one to comprehend. The passionate players play five or six times a week, and the Stroud and District League has five gents and two ladies' divisions of fourteen teams. Gloucester has so many teams it is split into four leagues of numerous divisions each. Skittles is life.

What did we play in pubs? I said sometimes darts and pool but mostly we got drinks and chatted to one another. This was met with confusion. Why would you do that when you could be playing skittles?

I asked if women played and was told they had their own leagues, desegregation having been resisted predominantly by women who preferred ladies only nights. Looking round, I could see their point.

Eventually when they were satisfied that we genuinely didn't play much in the way of skittles up in Manchester, and therefore of our consequent inherent inferiority, the players relaxed to my presence and began to open up about what was actually going on. The match consisted of two halves. Each team put five players forward for each half, at the end of which the cumulative score determined the winner. Each half was worth two points in the league, and if you won both halves, you gained an extra two points bonus. There were eight legs in a half, where each team would play all five of their nominated players in turn. Each player got three shots at the skittles per leg. Rarely were they all cleared. The skittles are small, well spaced, and the cheeses light. Knocking them all over in one is known as a 'Flattener' and a rare event. To get three flatteners in your go is so rare that Wikipedia states it was most recently achieved in 1960. They're probably still buying the round that followed. This is a tough game full of disappointment and with little in the way of reward or gratification. No wonder the bar was doing a roaring trade.

Slowly I started to make sense of the scoreboard. As half time approached, it was clear that the Patch Rats were losing and would need a strong second half to take anything out of the evening. Debra, who'd worked in another pub up the road with a strong Skittles team asked if it was 'chips and rolls for the interval?'

The players were scandalised.

'Oh no, not here. We're traditionalists round here. Ham, cheese and bread it'll be.'

I chatted further during half time. One player was a farmer who claimed twelve generations farming in the village, and sadly told me that his wife had put a stop to it, moving them to Sharpness, four miles away.

'I've still kept a bit of land though, on the quiet, with sixty head of cattle and thirty sheep. Might build a shed, just so I've got my roots down.'

He told me the move had come after a child they'd fostered had burnt their house down.

'I don't think we'll be taking on another.'

The second half began, with the Patch Rats needing a win to avoid the whitewash. The landlord took the last turn in the leg, and with a glorious flourish, managed to miss the whole lot three times in a row, a performance that was met with jeering and taunting and the sarcastic ringing of the alley bell that would normally be reserved for a 'Flattener'. Wearing an American football shirt and a 1970s porn star moustache, he visibly shrank in stature and slunk back behind the bar in shame. I wondered uncharitably if perhaps the captain felt unable to demote their landlord to the B team.

Skittles has games within games. Certain combinations of scores prompt a mass outbreak of betting amongst the team known as fines. Eight down means all players flip 2ps and the active player calls heads or tails to win them, nine down is 4p, and a spare (all nine down in two goes) is 10p. Each player must arm themselves with clunking pockets full of shrapnel before setting out and every team has their own ancient and slightly different combinations.

At the far end of the alley, a lone youth jumped and scrambled to replace skittles all night. Known as a 'Sticker' he was on £20 pocket money for the work, and was without doubt the most bored looking person I have ever seen in my life.

The evening continued. Skittles is played at a relentless pace. Despite a brave comeback, the Patch Rats couldn't make up for a poor first few legs and conceded the whitewash to Chalford AFC. Glasses were downed, hips were hoorayed, and the final scores written on the board and in the official scorers books. Patch Rats dropped to fifth in the division.

'Too good for us tonight' was the verdict of the non-playing captain, a gentleman approaching his eightieth year as he stood next to me in the gents after play. I never quite know what to say to strangers who chat in the gents, that most public of private places, so I recalled and delivered the line given to me by an ancient fellow called Reg in the gents at the Swan in the Rushes, Loughborough when I was a student.

'In here,' I said. 'We can hold our own.'

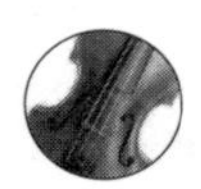

Bolton

I HADN'T planned to come to Bolton at this point. I may well have ended up here, in due course, but it wasn't a town I had made any specific plans for. It was a damp day in February and my house had become a nest of workmen, each vying with the others to see who could do most to prevent me achieving anything productive with my day. The electrician had been winning with periodic power outages until the plumber finally saw off the kitchen and bathroom with a total under-sink clearance and stop valve manoeuvre.

Unable to do anything useful and feeling distinctly in the way, I left early for my evening gig in petulant mood, drove to the nearest town to the venue and got the fiddle out for a few hours. The pay and display was a charity car-park in an otherwise abandoned bare concrete building. Bolton was a grim and stormy setting, and a cruel wind found a funnel in the high sided Victorian grandeur of the main street by Marks and Spencers. I set up here for a play, determined to make the best of such an unpromising situation. Having flounced out of the house, I couldn't renege on a busk, despite the conditions being singularly against it. I was wrapped in my faithful and ancient Barbour jacket and woolly hat and I positioned myself in front of the shop's enormous lingerie poster, testing far beyond breaking point that old maxim that 'sex sells'. Standing before an image of a large and well filled bra, backlit and prominent against the gloom of the street, I pressed my bow into the string to stop it being whipped away in the gale, developing an ugly, crunchy sort of tone and did my best.

A woman prepared a few coins for me, but paused and asked: 'Do you really need it?'

This was a new question so I stopped and thought about the answer. 'Well, music is my sole income. I'm writing a book about England and this is how I'm paying my way round.'

She nodded. This was worthy enough: 'My husband's writing a book too, about the cricketers from Bolton who went on to play test matches for England. It's terribly interesting. Here you go. At least you're doing something.' And dropping her coins in my case she gestured round at the homeless, in every other doorway, constantly searching for spaces away from the sapping wind where they might still have a chance of a coin; choosing between shelter and the possibility of a meal. As before in Braintree where I'd heard this false equivalence between my busking and rough sleepers in need of money, I was upset by this and wanted to respond, but by the time I'd worked through this chain of thoughts and arrived at an answer she was already gone and I was left to play on.

A man had appeared in the doorway to Marks and Spencers

wearing a bright blue fleece, pink cheeked, well fed. He relaxed casually against the wall and looked up and down the street. A minute later, a homeless man came bursting out of the shop and fleece man gave chase, tackling the escapee into a doorway across the street. It was an unfair contest, as the homeless man had a limp, was drawn and weak, all elbows and seized joints. Chocolate eggs spilled from his bag and other homeless people, alert to the raid, grabbed them and scattered. Further store officers arrived from neighbouring shops and concentrated their efforts on the first thief, forcing him roughly into a corner. I wanted to shout angrily to the woman, 'See, they are doing something!', but she was out of sight.

Imagine being so desperate, cold, and hungry that you'd nick chocolate eggs. At least they'd gone for the good ones. 'This is not just an egg raid, this is a Peruvian, 100 per cent cocoa Marks and Spencers egg raid'. It was a strange and unworthy thought, amidst my general anger and frustration at the tragedy of the scene. I'd stopped playing. This didn't seem like the sort of situation that needed a jolly soundtrack from me. They took the thief away. If he was lucky, he'd be arrested and get a warm night in a cell with a meal. If he was unlucky they'd let him go. I picked out the coins the lady had given me and gave them to the first rough sleeper I saw. I didn't ask if they really needed it.

It had been a dramatic afternoon. Although I'd not planned to be in Bolton, I knew as I packed up I'd be back very soon.

I returned a few days later. The sun was glorious and the wind entirely absent. Bolton was transformed. It is a really rather beautiful town, containing some of the finest architecture in the North West of England. The prosperity that the cotton industry once generated has left Bolton a fine legacy of buildings. Home to both Arkwright and Crompton, two of the fathers of the industrial revolution, Bolton once made a lot of money, at least for the mill owners. The centrepiece of the town hall and adjacent arc of municipal buildings is properly grand, as is the old market hall, now a shopping arcade, all decorative cast iron and cascading light. The top floor smelled invitingly of popcorn and led to a cinema. Amongst these and many other gems, 1960s concrete units have muscled in, overlapping in a way that reminded me of Budapest, where European beauty and Soviet brutalism butt up against one another.

I mentioned this to my friend who'd come along for the day, suggesting that perhaps Bolton was the Budapest of the North. She politely replied that she couldn't see it, herself. She was a little nervous, having never busked before, but the sun was shining and the street had a busy hum to it.

We picked a spot on the pedestrianised street heading down to the bus station. My friend was subdued to begin with, and played within herself, but slowly she found her voice and together we started to enjoy the music in the sunshine. The staff in the cake shop next door were clearly enjoying it and came out with a tray of free samples, which boosted our confidence no end. One shopper recognised me and said he'd been following my *Busk England* blog. Fame at last!

The market has moved to a new market hall a short walk away from the town centre. We went there to explore and find some lunch. It's as good a food market as you'll see, with plenty of everything on sale. One butcher was proudly advertising 'Beef Trips'. I bought a pork pie and a packet of Uncle Joe's Mint Balls.

We took our lunch and wandered back to the main square. One of the big municipal buildings advertised an aquarium, which seemed so unlikely we had to visit it. In the basement about a dozen tanks are set into a room, containing a modest but apparently singularly valuable and rare collection of tropical freshwater fish. A man was carefully hoovering fish-shit from the bottom of a tank into a horrible bucket. He was humming to himself and seemed to be happy with his lot in life. I ate my pie and looked at the rays and catfish. Bright coloured and exotic, from the mountains of New Guinea, the cloud forests of Peru, the heart of Madagascar. I wondered how they felt about living in Bolton. The displays all looked a bit care-worn, although the fish themselves looked well. I was informed that the collection was started in 1941, and they have had notable success getting some of the rarest species to breed.

Back on the street, a man passed us. On his phone, moving at speed, we heard just a fragment of his frenetic conversation: 'Why the fuck's he got twenty boxes of washing tablets?'

Bolton was changing, adapting. The Old Three Crowns, once a huge town centre pub, has shrunk to half its original size, the other half having become a shop unit, now disused. A small pub sheltering meekly under a huge frontage. The Bolton timeball no longer operates since the shop beneath it closed. Previously, the large golden ball would rise up at 12:55pm, dropping down again at exactly 1pm. Nobody local paid it much thought, but I'd rather liked it, and was sorry to see it a victim of the economy. Some streets were showing the first signs of gentrification, an apologetic coffee shop here, a male grooming parlour there, not quite densely clustered yet to achieve critical mass and attract a breeding population of hipsters.

We busked again under an archway. The acoustics were nice and we had the best music of the day. Bolton is a tough busk, there are simply so many needy people, in every doorway. Some passive, some going from person to person, trying their luck. There were so many that they couldn't all find a spot at once, and would roam the streets, politely waiting for someone else to move on so they could grab a doorway. There seems to be an informal code of conduct, respecting each other's space, but moving on voluntarily every so often so everyone gets a go. Sometimes a police officer will come round the corner, and they'll desperately gather their few belongings together and stride urgently away with a haunted look in their eyes, the gently pacing officer displacing the homeless one hundred yards further up the street like a bow wave pushing ahead of a ship. Heartbreaking that those who could most use a bit of support from the tools of state instead considering it safer to run from them.

Such an atmosphere of desperation makes it hard to succeed as a busker. Your need is not greater than that of the rough sleepers of whom there are so many. I wondered why Bolton had such a large homeless population. There are rough sleepers in just about every town in England, but Bolton was exceptional. We had a final play on one of the side shopping streets, and a young Asian mother and her toddler came out of the apartment opposite to hear us play. It was a lovely moment.

On my third day in the town, a young rock band were setting up for a busk in the main square. I got a coffee and watched from a respectful distance back. I'd already had a busk myself, and made very little. Between the many rough sleepers and the numerous smartly dressed Jehovah's Witnesses and their free magazines on racks, hands were remaining in pockets, eyes down. My music had seemingly been a magnet for the more aggressive beggars to operate nearby, and I was getting nowhere. The band kicked off with 'House of the Rising Sun'. They were good, the singer was charismatic and sang the rock classics with a slick sense of purpose and a tremendous Lancashire accent. Sadly, they didn't seem to be doing much better than me. I gave them what little I'd made earlier.

Bolton has a good few statues, mostly to otherwise forgotten industrialists, 'Paid for by public subscription'. One of their most famous modern sons, Fred Dibnah, has a splendid statue by a plinthed mill engine further down the street. There are no statues of women in the town, other than the bare-breasted generic representations of woe on the war memorial. England is full of severe and oversized men looking down in death as they did in life. At least Fred is at street level and seems to be having a laugh with us.

Still the homeless came past, walking with steady resigned purpose towards nothing in particular, like the remnants of a routed army returning from a lost war to a country they no longer recognised and were no longer welcome in. I got talking to some, handing over a few pounds each time. The stories they told me were all alike. Some would admit to having problems – one told me 'A mate was keeping me off the drink, but then he moved on.' Others wouldn't, but each one of them had been renting from a private landlord who'd sold out. They'd then not been able to get anything else, unable to raise a deposit or provide proof of income. Bolton is on the edge of the economic miracle that is Manchester, and rents are rising, properties in demand, renewals and developments commonplace. Unable to satisfy the demands of a gentrifying housing market, a whole cohort of vulnerable people have fallen off the bottom rung, the supply of council houses utterly inadequate against this need. A rising tide lifts all boats? Not if they've got a hole in the hull. Ironically, it may well be Bolton having turned the economic corner that has precipitated this disaster. The money that's come from the rise of Manchester has left Bolton unaffordable to the weakest.

So why not leave? After a year of travelling round, I know if it happened to me I'd go straight to a provincial market town and try my luck. But that's easy for me to say. Every man I spoke to only knew Bolton. It's where they grew up, where they knew the streets, still knew a few friendly faces. Not only that but if you move you start at the bottom of the list again, a fate which acts as a terrible disincentive to use your initiative. I know from elsewhere that women and children are prioritised on the waiting lists, and the undersupply of accommodation and support is so severe that many of these men will never get near enough to the top for anything to happen. They are trapped in the only town they know, afraid to try anywhere else for fear of it being worse, and losing the only community they had left, each other.

The sheer numbers left everyone else poverty blind. I believe almost everyone is fundamentally compassionate, but when a single walk to the shop for a pint of milk presents you with more human suffering than you can ever imagine being able to help with, you are forced to ignore it and save your compassion for a problem you can actually solve.

Across the street, the Jehovah's witnesses had their stand. The headline this week was 'Who is God?' But they too seemed withdrawn, out on the streets with an obligation to save souls, but unengaged, too much to save here. I finished most of my conversations street sleepers with something like 'I wish I could do more', to which they all replied with 'Nah, you're alright mate.' And they meant it. There was an extraordinary lack of blame or jealousy. Just a sadness and a will to get through the day in the hope that their luck might change tomorrow.

The man in the coffee shop offered a warmer view. An unexpected Cockney voice, he said he'd been here ten years, having met a Bolton girl, opening his shop three years ago. 'I love it up here. It hit rock bottom, but it's coming back nicely.'

I left, for the first time down on my busking over three days. What little I'd made I'd given away, and more. Bolton is a beautiful industrial town that doesn't have all the answers right now. It's rapidly becoming a better place if you're riding the wave, and worse if you're not. The best food market in the North West, lovely architecture and open spaces, Manchester just down the road, plenty of culture, countryside within easy reach. But the streets are a human tragedy without an obvious end.

Widnes

I WALKED into Widnes town centre, passing a skip which contained a fully decorated Christmas tree standing neatly to attention in the middle. A couple of doors down the road, a man was holding an animated phone conversation. He wore no top, in defiance of the cold, rainy morning. In one hand he held what I might term as his conversation phone. Another phone was sitting on top of a low wall loudly playing music through little tinny speakers. His remaining hand held a cigarette, with which he was conducting an imaginary orchestra as he spoke. I lingered beside the festive skip for a moment to enjoy this alternative prom.

The Widnes accent contains a strong twang of Scouse about it, although the average resident would certainly not consider themselves a Scouser at all, and be quite upset at the suggestion. There really are so many accents here on the M56/M62 corridor, where worlds collide. Scouse, Lancashire, Cheshire, Mancunian, and travel just a few miles over the border and you're into Welsh speaking territory. There's nowhere else in the country where so many profoundly different accents persist in such a geographically confined area. Perhaps it's because the flat spaces between the Pennines and the sea were basically empty till just a couple of hundred years ago, a void of just a few little villages in the great emptiness between the medieval power centres of Macclesfield and Lancaster. Damp marshland, not much use for anything. Until cotton and coal anyway, when the dampness was suddenly perfect for keeping the fragile threads together as they were spun on state of the art machinery powered by the coal that had been waiting for this moment, deep underground.

From Scotland, North Wales, Ireland and beyond came the workers, to tend the machines, empty the ships, and hew the fuel, their accents colliding together like strangely lumpen asteroids forming in an early solar system, in towns that once founded became immediately insular, too poverty ridden to travel, inwardly focussed. Enough work to survive, no money to move any further. The Wigan and England rugby league captain, Sean O'Loughlin, a Wiganer himself, has to be subtitled when interviewed in Australia because his accent is too impenetrable.

Widnes

Widnes has a different story though, one of chemicals. Growing on the banks of the already successful Sankey canal, an early attempt to bypass the worst lethal vagaries of the Mersey and within striking distance by water of Cheshire's vast salt extractions, it became the natural hub of the chemical industry.

I had a busk. There was one main shopping street with a couple of arcades running off it. Most of the shops were open, and finding the right spot wasn't easy. Across from me, several cafes had decanted their furniture onto the street, and the resultant coffee drinkers gave the town a relaxed, homely feel.

A man went past with a very large loudspeaker strapped to his back. He had long, untidy hair and a significant beard, and was lithe and stringy. In one hand he held a can of 'Relentless' and in the other he controlled a flawless sleek black-haired lurcher on a lead. His loudspeaker was playing R&B at top volume, and he leant forward in his stride to balance the weight of it. He was a one man carnival float, and we all stopped our day to watch him as he passed through, apparently oblivious. It is the modern thing to play your favourite music in the street, and today's devices are much lighter and more accessible than the ghetto blasters of my youth, but a full blown PA marked a new escalation.

I searched for some lunch. A group of older lads stopped me.

'Heard you playing back there. Good stuff.'

It turned out one of them played some traditional music himself and we knew a few of the same people. We chatted about Widnes for a bit. None of them seemed especially proud of it, despite being born and bred. Some towns, local people will defend to the last breath, others, the harshest critics come from within. I wondered what caused the difference.

'What advice do you have for someone coming to Widnes?' I asked them.

'Avoid the women, they're ugly', one replied immediately, to laughter. I didn't laugh, and their laughter dissolved. They stared at their shoes for a second, before looking at one another.

'Mind you', he continued thoughtfully, 'we're nothing special ourselves.'

'Tell you what,' said another, as the group rediscovered their confidence, 'You need to go and see Eddie Perve and play him a tune. You'll find him in the Derby pub. He's fat, bald and has no sense of humour.'

'Yeah, he'd like that', said another.

Was it a set-up? I replied that I'd consider it.

I bought a sandwich and a pie and ate them outside a solicitors that specialised in defending dangerous dog cases. Having no further reason not to, I went to the Derby, just a few doors down from where I'd been busking. It was a large, cavernous, and well attended town pub. I looked through the windows for characters who matched the description I'd been given for Eddie Perve. There were a number of candidates. I imagined myself walking in, considered how I might discover which one was the real Eddie, but none of the approaches seemed a good idea. Maybe it was for the best. I went back to my playing. Rain had emptied the streets somewhat, but the acoustic was good and nobody seemed to mind. They never do in working class towns. There's less of a sense of personal entitlement over the street.

Widnes is a town whose story can be told in bridges. These days it's administered as a unitary authority alongside Runcorn, the town on the South flank of the Mersey. Just two miles apart as the crow flies, the towns began life as foreign entities, in view, but quite unconnected from one another. The railway bridge provided the first link, along with a ferry that was later split into two legs by the construction of the Manchester Ship Canal, forcing passengers to disembark and scale a wall half way across the water. This ferry was then replaced with the Transporter bridge, the largest ever attempted in Europe. The two towns were linked for good by the Silver Jubilee Bridge that finally allowed the continuous flow of traffic when it opened in 1961. Slowly, two towns that had nothing to do with one another were linked together until in 1998 they became the twin centres of Halton, a unitary authority. It's a strange sort of marriage. A Lancashire town and a Cheshire town with very different histories co-existing across a great estuary.

Down at West Bank in Widnes, you can admire the bridges past and present. Past the chemical museum, 'Catalyst', and the rewilded Spike Island where the chemical industry first seeded, you end up beneath the massive feet of the railway and road bridges, and perhaps on the foundation of the now demolished transporter bridge. These surviving bridges feed in high above on ramps that lead up from the distant town centre, leaving West Bank a strange peninsular where once it had been a destination and transit point. A careworn Greenalls pub, the Mersey, sits forgotten at the end of the road, discharging occasional old men into the street for medicinal cigarettes, waiting for ships, ferries, transporter cars that don't come any more. In the silence of the place and the moment you're momentarily able to believe it's 1959 again, when this pub marked the centre of the hourglass though which every grain must pass.

I returned the next day to Widnes to carry on my efforts. The main street had a few other actors treading the boards today. One group were a bunch of rough lads aggressively handing out anti-bullying wristbands. Another group were gathered under an awning in the main street, wearing camouflage patterns and metal helmets.

'When was the last time you went paintballing?', they called at me cheerily as I went past. I couldn't think of a quick answer so I scuttled on. I busked again, outside a chip shop that was still dormant at this early hour. It was a quiet morning, the wet weather dampening off the street and suppressing the characters. A kind man brought me a coffee from across the road, two unexpected sugars already stirred in, just to be on the safe side, and then enthusiastically applauded each tune I played. It was a good morning, people were friendly, and I'd made £40 by lunchtime.

Outside the indoor market, the butchers shop had a loudspeaker broadcasting an entertaining monologue about the day's special offers, so I sat by it for a while, until sausages came round again and it became clear that it was a pre-recorded loop. The meats went round and round until they became familiar and comforting. Sold, I went inside for a pie before heading off to meet an old friend of mine, Kim.

Kim is Widnes through and through. Her ambition is to write a novel for Mills and Boon, a genre of which she has many hundreds of examples at home. We discussed the finer points of this style of writing as we walked round Spike Island, a huge area of post-industrial greenness between the Mersey and the first mile of the Sankey canal. Eventually, the conversation moved on to Widnes, and life in a chemical town.

'I didn't realise till recently that it wasn't normal to have chemical drills at school.'

'How did they work?'

'The alarm went off every Friday, and you all had to run inside the building, and shut all the doors and windows. Pretty much the opposite of a fire drill.'

Upon adolescence, one might turn to drinking, whereupon the pint of choice was the 'Fat Frog', a Smirnoff Ice mixed with an orange Reef, and topped off with lager, enjoyed at 'Top of the Town', a now closed night club whose sticky floors kept a tight hold of a loosely tied shoe. Widnes had calmed down a lot since then it seemed. There wasn't much going on for younger people now, who had to head into Liverpool or Manchester for a big night out.

Kim wanted to show me more of the wider district, and so we drove out to Fiddler's Ferry, now perhaps better known for the power station, dominating the landscape, reaching the end of its days, coal giving way to other forms of electricity. We drove right by the base of the cooling towers I remember seeing jut out from the Mersey plain like little piscine teeth, when as a youngster I'd push my bike from Macclesfield all the way to the top of Cheshire ridge to freewheel right back to town. They were the limit of my world then, the last marker on the horizon before the world bent and belonged to someone else. Cheshire was my county even then, although I'd never been yet to the other side of it. It's an accident of history that the transport links are North/South and I had no reason to ever visit Chester or the West of the County. But I knew it was mine, right up to the rising land of Wales and the cooling towers.

At Fiddler's Ferry the Mersey is at its narrowest, and rows of funny little boats are kept up on another small isolated section of the Sankey canal. Without a theme, they're like a packet of breakfast cereal where there's one of every flake ever manufactured. The countryside rolls off towards the ridge at Frodsham, lush, alluvial, charming.

'Why does everyone talk Widnes down?' I asked. Nobody had a good word to say about the place. Ask any Widnes resident and most would tell you it was crap. But it wasn't. Perhaps not the most exciting town, but the town centre is thriving, the shops are decent, and there is enough work for everyone to get a job who wants one. Widnes is doing alright.

'Perhaps it's the smell' said Kim. 'The chemical industry stinks when the wind blows the wrong way.'

'Nothing like as much as it used to.'

'I think we're just a town with low self esteem. In the 1980s we had the best rugby team in the world. We had Martin Offiah and Jonathan Davies. People were proud of it. The industry has slowly declined and the rugby team too. There's nothing to really be proud of anymore. People have retired on good pensions but nothing new happens.'

'But there's plenty of jobs, it seems okay?'

'We've got employment but does that make it a good town? There's no culture. The Brindley is the arts centre but that's in Runcorn.'

It was funny to think of Widnes, the chemical town, becoming Widnes the retirement centre. Eastbourne-upon-Mersey. I couldn't quite imagine the deckchairs down the riverside just yet.

Perhaps part of the problem is that being a unitary authority, there's one of everything for efficiency, and half of them are in Runcorn which is suddenly a pretty hard place to get to, now that the Jubilee Bridge is shut.

On the outskirts of Widnes, there's a sign pointing left to 'Household Waste and Trampoline Park', and then the route to the newest crossing, the Mersey Gateway Bridge.

We passed a beauty shop billboard that offered the surprising juxtaposition of 'Sun Beds and Nails'. It was the end of another day. Widnes had been interesting, but it was only half the story. I'd give Runcorn a go and see what life was like on the other side of the Mersey.

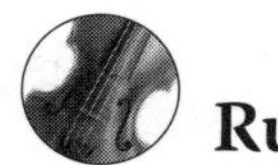

Runcorn

I BUSKED on what's left of the old high street in Runcorn. A man came striding by, stopped suddenly, stared at me frowningly, then looked down at his watch like I was a large and unwelcome wood carving that had emerged from a Swiss clock and refused to go back inside. Three doors down, a ginger and white cat was watching me too. A small boy tried to pick it up, but it slipped through his fingers like liquid. The boy then aimed a kick up its arse, but sensing this, the cat turned and faced him, daring him to kick it in the face. The boy gently lowered his foot and ran off.

Runcorn

Men in hi-vis jackets began appearing, a few at first, then more until there was a constant stream, coming from the right and departing back to the hive with packets of pasties and bakes. They peaked around midday, food time for people who start early, in this, the post-packed-lunch era.

A bald, smiling man emerged from the furniture shop next door. 'Are you intending to play there all day?' It was a polite question, without edge.

'Well perhaps another half hour before I get some lunch.'

'Ah lovely. I know we all have a living to make.'

'Aye.' There was a second of silence, as we both took a moment to appreciate the sunshine and the pleasant day.

'It's just, perhaps after lunch, you could make yours over there.' And he gestured to the other side of the road. Well fair enough. I did my half hour and had my sandwich.

Runcorn town centre is a shadow of its former self. The main street up to the canal basin is filled with substantial brick and stone built buildings, each with a chunky stone plaque hinting at a grand history. 'The Mersey Power Co. Ltd.' or 'Camden Buildings – 1810' and now home to a smattering of more modest tenants. Chinese takeaways, gas fitting shops, pizza. There are gaps, and the shrinkage of Runcorn's centre has left it spacious and slightly incoherent. By the canal basin, the fine old Waterloo Hotel, now without the passing trade has instead become a Buddhist Temple. Down the slope towards the Mersey, rows of brick built terraces have been pulled aside to make way for the feet of the bridges.

The expressway, the first continuous road link between Widnes and Runcorn, via the Silver Jubilee Bridge, cuts through and over the town, carriageway far above, its blocky concrete feet cleanly splitting apart rows of terraces. It's closed now, for the foreseeable, now the new bridge is open further inland, and there's a strange sort of silence about the area. An area that grew used to having no sound of its own above the roar of the traffic and hasn't yet found a new voice to fill the void. An abandoned teddy bear lay face down by a scruffy brick wall, amid the cigarette ends and dust. My ears focused on the few sounds there were. Drips from the closed road above me, and the cooing of the occasional pigeon, the ones who hadn't died in the netting that ran across the underside of the road. Presumably there to discourage pigeons, it had instead trapped and collected a great many carcases which were now in various stages of decay. Eventually, I suppose, a point must come where each has rotted down enough that it can fall through the net to the ground in a shower of desiccated lumps.

Out over the river on the bridge itself, even the workmen seemed subdued and at peace. Occasionally, the sound of a single percussion tool rang out, as if one workman had offended the gods and been doomed to the Sisyphean task of renewing this great structure alone and for all time.

Runcorn is a series of funnels to transport that is not there. The ferry long gone, same the transporter bridge, and the Silver Jubilee Bridge closed until further notice. Roads lead to the dead ends of open water and closed bridges. The silence from the infrastructure drew your attention to the few sounds there were. The singing of metal as an electric train crossed from Widnes, the clunk of track joints you might have heard at one time replaced by the sparking howl of the continuous welded rail, the song of metal lengths under tension.

I looked over the commemorative railings by the ship canal, causing a cormorant to honk and panic. Even going for a quiet walk here seemed like a thoughtless breach of the peace. Runcorn is again adapting to a shift in the course of its economic river.

Back in town I stuck my head in a charity shop. On a shelf were three 'Big Mouth Billy Bass' plaques in a row, the electronic singing fish that was briefly popular twenty years ago. Three was definitely much more fun than one, but I hadn't made enough to justify that kind of purchase, and I'd tried to learn my lessons after the rubber duck episode in Brighton. I wondered if they would ever sell them. It seemed optimistic. Fifteen years ago, I'd have started all three off and run out of the shop quick, but age has reduced my bravado and running speed.

I couldn't find a spot on the other side of the road, and the butcher made it clear he'd rather I didn't start up near his shop, in the way that only a smiling and terribly polite man in a bloodied pinny holding a large cleaver can do, so I thought it better to explore Runcorn a little more instead. Designated as a new town in the 1960s, Runcorn had suddenly doubled in size. The town hall was up the hill and I went to have a look. It looked like a New England colonial governor's mansion. Round the back was a modern bit covered in 'No Entry' signs and a stiff, ceremonial garden.

Even further into the hinterlands is Runcorn Shopping City. The traveller emerges exhausted from the jungle, having hacked their way through dense trees and creepers for weeks, or having followed their satnav off the ring road and down into one of the car parks. Set in a natural bowl in the ground, fully enclosed and surrounded by mature trees, the shopping city has all the feel of a lost fortress in the jungle, perhaps in decline, shabby, but still very much alive and populated. Buses come in and depart on raised roadways, two stories above the ground. They might as well be drawbridges. From inside one of the bus termini, I could see how the natives might mount a successful defence of their city against invaders from Warrington or other vaguely rumoured foreign entities, only to later succumb to a terrible disease to which they had no resistance.

In this concrete tree-top world, the 1970s had not ended, but had instead been allowed to develop and bloom until it reached its natural pinnacle. This was the ultimate shopping centre, the purest expression of the form I have ever seen.

The shops are all on the first floor, above the car parks and delivery bays. You rise up an unmarked escalator to a lobby which has a sign of pure poetry:

> This Entrance May Be
> Closed Earlier Than
> Normal
> On Occasions Depending
> Upon Circumstances.

The shops are arrayed in a large H formation, with busways at each corner, and elevated walkways leading to other parts of the new town, the police station, the courts, (now closed) and the council offices. I think we can, after five decades, judge the new town of Runcorn to be a success. Old men met and talked, sitting at oversize lawn furniture in the central plaza, the 'Community Square'. Some shops have been here so long they appear dynastic. Cafes and independents that have seen much come and go, and are rocks of stability to their customers.

I felt like I had when walking down the main street at Teotihuacan in Mexico, where an archaeological site was alive with people and pop-up shops. We get so bound up in the history that sometimes we miss the contemporary relevance of a place.

Our perception of place is so often linked to a contrived cultural sense of value rather than its actual utility, corporeal or spiritual. If a building is large, spacious and beautiful, we describe it as 'Cathedralesque'. The Cathedral is our reference point, our number one. But why? Is it the perceived spirituality of the place implying a higher value? Cathedrals today are simplified places, reduced to an uneasy duality of worship and tourism. They are no longer naturally the heart of a community at a human level. This shopping centre could claim a far broader remit of human utility, and was every bit as remarkable a construction, conceived and created as it was in the light of a new day dawning where the aspiration of giving the common person a decent life was the motor that drove the concrete revolution.

Could one find spirituality in Wilkos? Maybe not in the truest sense, but the pursuit of money, and the best means to spend it are as coherent a doctrine for today's society as the church's message has been in the past. Here in the heart of the concrete temple, Wilkos had a board outside the shop with this month's suggested gardening activities, from vegetables, to the lawn, to flowers. In the main square, staircases led to offices where anonymous security officers watched us and judged our actions. Those with the fob of admission are the priests of our time. At 4:45pm, these high priests travel to the inner sanctum to turn off the wifi so that the youths go home, their connection to divinity severed until tomorrow.

The one real problem with all this for me is that I couldn't busk. The whole property is privately owned, and I have far fewer rights here than on a public street. I am bound by their code of conduct, to behave, keep quiet, and buy stuff. And I must leave at closing time. Of course I could just not come, but as more and more of places we might wish to visit are on land owned like this, that becomes a harder thing to do. I have no right of way here, no right to busk, no right to just hang around if they don't want me here. Here those rights are left at the door of the temple like shoes. They're still yours, but you can't use them just now. The high street is a communal place, and the best of us understand that we should share it. The shopping centre is a monolithic space where we are subjugated by the act of our arrival. We are tolerated here, so long as we conform. The secular society took back rights from religion and handed them to citizens. One by one, we hand them back in return for a free parking space.

I left this concrete cathedral and drove across Runcorn to Weston Point, the residual docklands, where smaller, lesser ships heading up the Manchester ship canal unload their TEUs onto anonymous lorries that fan out across the North West. The Dockside pub was faded, the pub sign reduced by age and budgetary priority to an illegible oblong suspended above the pavement. Thankfully the dereliction and subsequent removal of neighbouring buildings had allowed them to paint 'DOCKSIDE PUB' in block letters down the openside wall. I lost my nerve and didn't go in. I should have done.

Halton doesn't really make sense. It's a unitary authority of two towns that feel really very different from one another, and the shifting fortunes of the bridges have currently left rather remote. The new bridge is a masterpiece, confidently spanning the Mersey where it broadens out, not needing to find a pinch point. But it links the broader region together, not the towns. The M56 and M62 are flanked by massive logistics depots where the requirements of the North of England are meted and doled in countless equal HGVs. The new bridge serves them, those trails of diesel-powered worker ants that run from nest to nest and feed and furnish every home. Widnes and Runcorn seem somewhat secondary considerations, having lost their bridge, for now at least. A marriage of convenience living on in unconnected wings of an over-large house, perhaps staring occasionally at one another from the distant ends of a preposterously long dining table.

But these are good places to live. There are jobs, friendly people, good shops, and if the culture seems a little lacking, Liverpool and Manchester are just down the road.

Welwyn Garden City

HAVING enjoyed Runcorn, I wanted to see more of our new towns. Some were existing towns that were expanded, others fresh creations. Milton Keynes is the most famous, but I picked Welwyn Garden City, partly because people kept telling me to, and partly because as one of the very first, it represented a grand experiment in town planning.

Making my way through the handsome boulevard of gardens that form the centrepiece of the town, I remembered reading that this was the place that inspired Milton Keynes. As claims go, this is perhaps on a par to being the band who inspired Coldplay.

The main run of gardens continues almost out of sight, the arterial road split either side of it, and thus diminished and subservient to the green space. Branching off to my left at the point where a grand fountain marks the junction, another run of gardens lead up to the combined shopping centre and railway station. This is the town centre, arrayed loosely around the greenery like a much loved and oversized woolly jumper. I sat on a bench and watched the world go by. A few benches along, a man enjoyed the simple pleasures of slowly releasing Rizlas into the gentle wind and watching them float away, one by one. A small boy ran up to a litter bin, regarded it fiercely for a second or two, declared it was 'A well laid trap!' and ran off.

This was Welwyn, then, peaceful, gentle, prosperous, uncanny and preposterously hard to place.

The gardens rang with the song of hedge trimmers and leaf blowers. Teams of orange-vested men combed down the rows of plump hedges, overlapping clatters and hums as council issue trimmers rose and fell to the same pitch. There wasn't much point busking with them at work, so I wandered, quite at peace in gentle sunshine. My notebook and fiddle case drew the attention of a man in a trilby, who announced himself as Justin. He was also writing a book about England, and had caught the train that morning out of London on a whim. He affected a false serenity, sitting on a bench with a studious calm that merely underlined an inherent restlessness. His was a semi-fictional epic and already 1,000 pages without end in sight. It was difficult to watch someone struggling so hard to convince themselves they were relaxed. I wondered to what extent I was looking in a mirror.

'I'm enjoying the journey' he told me, and I believed him. Even a park bench in a foreign town was too much like settling down. He moved on and I never saw him again.

The garden workers gradually arrived at the end of the final hedge and piled up on the concrete square before the shopping centre as if they'd fallen off the end of a conveyor belt, seemingly unsure what to do next. In the new found silence, I went for a busk, picking an odd corner between two walking paths. Welwyn is spacious to the point of being sparse, you end up playing into the great void if you're not careful. I learned to face the shops for the acoustic rather than stand in front of them. It went well. Schoolchildren found change, mothers stopped to introduce youngsters to music. A jogger extended his exertions to perform an astonishing Lycra-clad sword dance in front of me, the act of jogging clearly having erased any lingering self-consciousness.

Out of town insurance salesmen worked the street in small gangs, one a father and son combo, using the young lad to draw the attention of polite old ladies. It always looks like a confidence trick to me, even when it isn't. I'm immediately mistrustful of street sales, and concerned about the demographic they often seemed to target.

I made a decent £25 in a little over an hour at the end of the day and looked forward to the morning.

At 10am, my chosen spot was already occupied. A good sign – if the locals played there, that meant I'd judged well. A guitarist called Paul was at work, and he sang with a wonderfully melodious voice that filled the open space. I got a coffee and listened. He was making enough for his train fare and he'd be off. Maybe an hour? No pressure from me. The gardens ask you to amble about, from one semi-formal section to another. Residential roads branch off, with vast hedges square and fat from decades of careful maintenance.

Welwyn Garden City

New towns are odd places. It's the newness we hate, when the work is that of a designer, unsmoothed yet by the folk process of a thousand home-owners with different aesthetics, budgets, and priorities. A new new town jars the senses, and induces the same feeling of helplessness and unease that many find in IKEA or as I discovered in the strange village of Portmeirion in Wales, where beautiful though it may be, the collision of oddity and conformity left me feeling like I was wandering uninvited through the architect's mind, afraid to touch for fear of triggering some sort of chain reaction and getting stuck forever.

A single new house in an old town is immediately part of a warming diversity. A new estate, or whole new town is a great disconcertion, until enough people have lived in it to give it the natural diversity calmness craves. Here, the formal gardens and plantings are imperfect and crooked. Welwyn has bedded in. No two bits are quite the same any more, and that's as it should be. In perfect newness, you are the impediment, the unanticipated rogue element detracting from the design ideal. In a mature town, your oddness is just one among many, and not so likely to result in questions being asked, curtains twitching, officers of the state just 'checking' if everything is quite okay.

The humanising effect of time and countless cumulative little individual choices and acts of God have somewhat weathered the planned rigidity of the place and I liked it and felt unjudged. The long boulevard of gardens that split and lesson the roads, rendering them subservient to the walker were bright with birdsong. Catnip and lavender tumbled and bounced with countless excited bees. Roses were tidy and alert, and there, quietly tucked away, a woman sat sobbing on a bench.

I thought about asking if she was okay, but she'd hidden herself away and whatever her problems, it seemed unlikely to me that a big ginger bloke suddenly rocking up was going to be the answer.

Back in town, a traffic warden was writing a ticket for a BMW parked outside Costa on a double yellow line. A woman came running out: 'I'm sorry, I'm pregnant and I was desperate for the loo. Please don't give me a ticket!'

And much to my surprise, the traffic warden said: 'Ok, that's fair enough. Have a lovely day', and destroyed the ticket.

Everything was just so. Smartly dressed and well scrubbed school children walked past, oblivious to the world, unafraid of any danger, their noses buried in novels rather than phones. Even a beggar chose to address me formally; 'Excuse me sir, I don't suppose that there's any possibility that you could perhaps consider seeing if you could spare...' before arriving at the usual '...any change?'

It was all immaculate. The gardens in full summer bloom, full of pollinating insects, bright flowers, perfect hedges. Each shop a going concern with a decent hum of people. A kind and respectful populace making a good life for each other.

How I longed for a yob, a dickhead, a lager-drinking oaf with a foul mouth, a heavily tattooed man in a vest with a volatile dog on a string. How I wanted to round a corner and see a pile of discarded bin bags and broken bottles, and to hear a vulgar car drive by with the windows down, something loudly distasteful on the stereo and the stench of weed. But instead, another perfect day slowly unfolded before me.

Welwyn was not a town likely to spawn a musical genre, it seemed to me. I couldn't feel that sharp edge that demands art be made. I saw no sign of the counterculture, the unfeedable need to stir and provoke. But people are people, so where was it? I walked down another immaculate residential street and found myself imagining a different Welwyn within those private detached walls, where ever such nice people with perfect lives, successful children, diverse and fruitful pension portfolios, would close the door on another gentle, ripened day, and descend to colossal, perverted sex dungeons to exorcise the demon of repression. Consenting adults suspended in awful contraptions, hovering at the edge of sexual ecstasy, not quite able to reach the crossword puzzle. This person coming towards me, look at him in his nice jacket, almost certainly a massive pervert. There must be something, surely? Otherwise what's it all about? Where's the spark of human curiosity?

But as ever in my own wild fantasies, and within the limitations of my own experience, I was missing the point. I have a friend who lives in Milton Keynes. A creative, expressive, artistic friend, who needs her home to be a haven, with birdsong, walks in the trees and peace, so that recharged, she can get out there and be her vibrant self.

Welwyn is like being on retreat. A mere half hour from London on the fast train, it's a place of safety where folks can recharge their batteries in peace for another slog at it tomorrow. Where the elderly can retire in comfort and without worry. Where children can grow up safely, well educated, better able to choose where and when to push their boundaries as young adults away at university. The art will come, but perhaps elsewhere, and perhaps less destructively.

I had another busk, lasting nearly three hours till a very late lunch was enforced on me by fat summery drops of rain falling with weight from a humid sky. In that time I made £50 and saw plenty more of life. An old couple stopped by me for a chat. He was blind, having been a concert violinist and forced to give up due to no longer being able to read the page.

'But now I go to a folk group, and we improvise without the music. I'm learning again but I'm back in love with it.'

Were they happy in Welwyn? 'It's a good place. London is just half an hour. We're happy here.'

I wished them the best and decided not to ask if they had a sex dungeon. I paid in my coins at the bank. The young man behind the counter asked me about my music, and I asked him about life in Welwyn.

'It's quiet here', he said thoughtfully, smiling to think of it.

'Good quiet?'

'Yeah.'

I made my way back to my car. Outside a very expensive townhouse, a young man carrying a picnic hamper and immediately followed by his girlfriend headed towards a top level Jaguar sports car they were surely far too young to be able to afford. Remarkably, both of them somehow managed to look exactly like Jarvis Cocker.

On the edge of the town centre, an old grain factory was completing a transformation into an art and information hub. I left this dreamlike perfection of English good taste in the uncanny valley and moved on again.

Interlude: A Busker Miscellany

BUSKING is a strange thing to do. A performance to an ever changing audience who didn't chose to hear you play. You can brighten someone's day or fill someone with anger, often with the same tune. You're in a continual feedback loop with whoever goes by. It's the broadest possible audience, far more diverse and surprising than the self-selecting group who would chose to attend a concert. Even a year of busking isn't enough to see everything that could happen. That said, certain groups of people began to crystallise. Here are a few favourites.

The givers:

1) The walk-past: The walk-past will be striding along quite happily in their own little bubble only to suddenly find themselves enjoying the music. They start fishing for coins whilst continuing to walk away for as long as it takes to find them, which is often quite a long way, before awkwardly having to turn round and walk all the way back to drop them in your case.

2) The nonchalant flipper: The flipper decided well before they passed you that they were going to hand over a coin, and will eject it straight down into the collection without breaking stride or making eye contact.

3) The precise figure: This character will shake a bunch of coins into their hand, and stand in front of you, slowly calculating your exact worth to the penny before replacing the surplus coins in their cash bag. They frequently give 37p.

4) Projectile bike man: This terrifying figure will try to land a 50p into your case from some distance away and without slowing down. It's very much like watching a cruise missile attempting to enter a downstairs toilet window at 800mph. The mathematical calculations involved in this feat are far beyond our generous cyclist. This fellow, (It's always a man) will have to calculate the exact angle of release and the kinetic energy, whilst allowing for angular momentum and wind drag. They never manage it, and the coin goes feral, pinging off street furniture or your face, before hitting the ground on edge and rolling straight down the nearest grid. The cyclist will shrug and continue with their urgent journey.

5) The idiot: Despite the obvious pile of coins in the case by my feet, they will insist on trying to put them down the f-holes on my fiddle or into my moving hand or somewhere else totally inappropriate that would never have occurred to anyone but them. These people are particularly alarming if you've been absorbed in your music and not noticed them coming and you first become aware of them during an enthusiastic attempt to stuff 74p up your left nostril or down your flies.

6) The small child: This infant has been given a coin by a parent, and is now expected to make the arduous journey across the pavement, all on their own, towards the sweaty, bald fat man gyrating alarmingly for coins with his instrument. This clearly goes against the sort of advice small children would normally be given, and they will frequently stop to look over their

shoulders in scepticism. Some turn back. They are the ones who will make old age.

7) The paid conversation: This character regards their donation to the busking collection as a purchase of my time in whatever form they see fit. I have some sympathy with this, and enjoy a good conversation, but you won't get a lot out of me for 10p.

8) Husband / Wife combo: Wife will draw husband's attention to busker, husband will nod, pause, release a few small coins to wife, who is then permitted to proceed towards the busker for release. Thus completed, she will rejoin husband and their journey will continue.

9) Selfie man: This gentleman is generous, usually Asian, and will drop high value coins in the collection, before standing right next to you filming selfie videos with a huge grin on his face. He will often repeat this a number of times throughout the day.

10) 1p grandma: Slowly manoeuvring down the street, she will give you a warm, genuine smile, thank you for the beautiful music, before carefully and deliberately releasing a single penny, watching it land, and heading off satisfied in the knowledge of a job well done.

11) Other buskers: Buskers lock onto one another from a great distance, following chord fragments down passageways just as a St Bernard would seek an avalanche victim under a snowfield, appearing in your vision a respectful distance back, enjoying a deceptively nonchalant sausage roll and Subway coffee. They watch for a while, nod, and then give you 20p, which all true buskers know to be the minimum meaningful coin in the collection. Later, you will find their spot with similar cold calculation and return the exact same coin.

Of course, most people will simply walk past without getting involved at all, and that's fine. However, there is a second group who will get involved who are altogether less generous than the first. Let's meet them.

1) The bean counter: This character walks out of their way

with a determined stride to get a good hard look at your busking case. They stare at the coins within, counting them. The implied meaning is 'How much? Stealing a living! First thing I'll do when I'm in charge is ban the lot of them!' There's a jealousy and disapproval to their undisguised stare at your meagre earnings, made all the more pointless by the twin facts that they have no idea how long you've been there, and you've already removed quite a few coins.

2) Random object dude: This person prefers a quirky gift to currency. I've been given everything from fruit to poems to a gruelling memoir about a Japanese prisoner of war camp. A friend of mine busking one warm evening in New Zealand recently so impressed a drunk gentleman that he donated her his coat, phone, wallet, car keys, and shoes, before fleeing gloriously and uncatchably into the night.

3) Abuser: Thankfully rare, some people fly into unstoppable rage at the sight of a busker. I've always adopted a policy of moving on if asked, but it's rare to be asked politely. On the odd occasion where someone has a problem, they instead scream and bawl at me, hurling insults and threatening to call the police.

4) 'I own a Ukulele': This tedious character has no intention of supporting your collection, but instead wants to interrupt you to regale you with stories of a Ukulele they bought four years ago and intend to learn some time. Hints that they may wish to go away are deflected with the calm assurance of a player who intends to occupy the crease all day.

5) Geriatric conversation squad: If a group of old people meet their friends coming the other way right next to your pitch, you are doomed. The conversation is simply going to happen where they are right now, and you might as well grab a coffee or write that dystopian sci-fi novel because they ain't going anywhere for a while. To be fair, such conversations are usually joyous to overhear in the way that only old people talking far too loud with undisguised relish about their physical ailments can be,

and I don't resent them at all. It's hard enough being old, and at least being medically interesting must be some consolation.

6) Dog in training: It's a large puppy, cute and impossibly friendly with a frantic wagging tail, and it wants to wee lavishly in your fiddle case. Emergency manoeuvres must be taken.

7) The pocket panic-patter: The act of busking is to gently solicit money from those who pass by. For this person, there is no chance of that, but your unwelcome presence causes them to develop a pained look and to suddenly begin patting their body to ensure their wallet is still there, as if the mere act of playing a tune is enough in itself to dislodge the contents and draw them through the air into your case. 'That was a close one, it nearly got out', they think, as they march away with forced haste, one controlling hand on the fickle money.

8) The false count out: As they walk towards you, they begin counting coins into their hand until they've got to the amount you would be worth if you were any good. They then make eye contact, frown, and pop the coins back in their pocket as they stride past.

9) The near-miss asteroid: As NASA would undoubtedly tell us, these roaming objects present you with a double challenge. Firstly, you need to spot them, no easy task in the vastness of space, as they hurtle randomly and without relation to the predictable orbits of our familiar neighbours. Then, even if you spot one, how the heck to you stop it? Some people just have a direct path charted down the road, and the projecting neck of a fiddle isn't going to cause them to deviate. All that remains to be done is to take avoiding action. Aloof, their trajectory is fixed, and unnegotiable. A busker cannot close their eyes for fear of an extinction event.

10) Old Friend: These are the worst; 'Haha I thought you'd have made your first million by now! What went wrong?' Thanks mate. Although sometimes they do drop a coin in, or a hot sausage roll.

Workington

BY this time in the project, any hope of visiting places in a logical and sequential order had long since evaporated, and I found myself making some big jumps around the country to fit in the towns I really wanted to visit before the end. With the best will in the world though, Workington isn't really on the way to anywhere, so sooner or later it was just a matter of driving there and getting on with it.

I got up to West Cumbria early enough for a busk in Workington, a town I thought I knew well from over a decade ago, when as a naive young musician I'd headed up with my mate Gren Bartley to make our first professional album with Fellside Records. It had been hard work, and being nervous and inexperienced I'd struggled with the recording sessions. Paul Adams, running the show, had seen it all before, and seeing me flustered had pressed a respectably high value bank note into our hands and ordered us to get a pint. We set off into a gloomy and depressed former coal and steel town, where the few pubs that survived were populated by a smattering of unemployed and introspective men in string vests. Workington was going through hard times, and had an empty, haunted feel.

Thirteen years later, and a lot had changed. I parked my car in the canyon between the two sports stadia, Borough Park and Derwent Park, home to Workington Reds Football Club and Workington Town Rugby League Football Club respectively, twin examples of glorious lower league dilapidation. Plans for a new and modern ground for the clubs to share had recently fallen through yet again, and these venerable old heaps of corrugated iron would continue to be pressed into service, fighting back against the salt sprays that blow in from the harbour and corrode the steel pillars.

So far, so familiar. My favourite building in Workington has always been the oversize bus station, a towering shape made more impressive by the open space before it afforded by the demolition of neighbouring buildings. With a clear sight line at it from the junction, it looked like a slaughtered whale dragged up a ramp for butchery. It has a blue plaque that proudly notes that it was the first purpose built covered bus station in the UK, opened 1926. You get your civic pride where you can.

Workington town centre had changed massively, though. Where a smattering of shops had done their best to hold it together on dingy streets, now a smart new shopping zone had been built, airy and spacious and with a good vibe about it, aided by copious European money. A child in a buggy emerged howling from a cafe through the net of dangling chains like a big reveal on a makeover programme. I picked a spot on a pedestrianised T-junction and played. The sun shone and I did well. One young boy even gave me a fiver, which astonished me. Things had certainly improved in Workington if a schoolboy could spare that kind of cash.

I was facing the Lookout, a strange combination of clock and sculpture. Shaped something like a crane on top of a big stainless steel ball, the long arm rotates once per hour and gives the time against a series of markings on the floor, before periscoping on the hour to project images onto boards. It was running thirteen minutes slow, which troubled me. I'm all in favour of public art, but if you're going to make one with a practical element it should work properly. It looked to me like something of an overextension of ambition. I imagined it was probably hard to correct and it had just become simpler to let it run to its own timetable. Perhaps this dysfunction was intended, a disguised satire on West Cumbria, a place living in its own time. More likely there just hadn't been quite enough thought put into the time-keeping part of the design, which would have required both engineering skills and a sophisticated cultural understanding of how a minor public body might be likely to maintain it after the installation.

Workington

If I lived in Workington, I know for certain I'd be that guy who measured it every week, and wrote letters to the paper when it wasn't right, until everyone on the council hated me. Such objects bring out my obsessive side. At 4pm, or 3:47pm Workington time, I packed up and headed out.

Wonky timekeeping aside, the town centre redevelopment had been a success and Workington had the feel of a town getting back on its feet. My previous visits had coincided with the final end of the steel works and the lowest ebb of the economic decline. With a more diversified economy, things now seem to be improving.

But this was just a short visit, as I'd been invited to a really special event, the Cumbria – Rungwe Community Link Ceilidh.

Since 1987, there has been an exchange programme between West Cumbria and Rungwe, a rural district in South Western Tanzania. My friend Mary has been deeply involved in this for many years, and had invited me to the final night's celebrations at Calderbridge village hall. This invitation wasn't just for my benefit, as she'd organised a ceilidh and was short of a tune player to lead the music, a role I was glad to accept.

The exchange works on a two-year cycle, this year being the turn of a group of Tanzanians to come to West Cumbria for three weeks. The planning had been difficult. Getting visas for the group had been a particular challenge. Mary told me that the application forms effectively acted as filters to prevent poor people visiting the UK, as many of their demands were not easily achievable if you don't lead a rich, Westernised sort of life. Obligatory boxes like personal postal address were tricky to sort. But sort it they had, after the burning of much midnight oil.

Even having got the visas, the group had been questioned at great length and with some hostility at the airport. Valentino, one of the Tanzanian group leaders told me later; 'They had so many questions, why are you here, when will you leave, even though they knew the answers.'

The youngsters had certainly never made a journey like this before, a day across land before the flight, and tired and overwhelmed, were genuinely upset by their treatment.

'Then at last they let us through, we came round the final corner and Mary and everyone were waving Tanzanian flags and we were so happy.'

The ceilidh was a great success. We did a couple of British dances, then the Tanzanians would lead a couple of their traditional dances, in this case step dances, singing the music as they went with the kind of freedom that comes from being unafraid of a few imperfections. In our highly media saturated world, we're constantly surrounded by flawless, auto-tuned music and song, and the sound of voices raw and confident, just going for it, is now a rare one. In Tanzania, it seems, music is just what you make with your friends and family and there's no sense of judgement, perhaps as we might once have gathered round the piano. People here are often afraid to stick their head above the parapet and just play, fearful of falling short of an impossibly high standard. Music retreats from the commonplace and belongs to the specialist, its broad social function lost.

The Tanzanian group sang beautifully, full of passion and rhythm, and it was infectious. Everyone joined in, except the local teenage lads, who stood outside the circle with beers they were just learning to drink.

'Too cool to join in', I've heard it said of lads like this. The opposite is true. It's a very awkward and judgemental period, being a teenager, and most of these lads would have loved to join in and dance with freedom, but felt unable to. Not cool enough is the sadder truth.

Half time brought another highlight, as Mary introduced a gurning competition. Gurning is a big deal round here, with the world championships taking place in Egremont each September as part of the Crab Fair, an event that has been happening for at least eight hundred years. The gurning itself takes place through a horse-collar, or 'Braffin', and points are awarded not for the ugliest face, but for the biggest difference between faces before and during. Being naturally ugly is something of a disadvantage then, as the room for improvement is not so large.

We were lucky enough to have borrowed the genuine Egremont braffin for the evening and I felt a little buzz of excitement at being able to hold such a significant piece of English folk culture in my hands, and staring down at the aperture I allowed myself to imagine the countless appalling faces that must have leered back out of it over the years.

I rang my sister for advice. She'd entered the world gurning championships several years previously, and although an also-ran, she'd asked the judges for feedback on how to improve.

'Make a performance of it. Look the judges in the eye with your normal, smiling face, then turn away, compose yourself, and put your whole body into it. The best gurners use their body and the shoulders, arms.'

The judging panel was four teenage girls, two from Tanzania and two from the local area. There was no shortage of entrants. My turn arrived about half way through, and I gave it everything I'd got, using a lopsided face that years of petulantly spoiling family photographs had allowed me to perfect. I fell to my knees before the panel, and was awarded 4.5/5 and a provisional share of first place with one of the Tanzanian lads. Competitors came and went and nobody could beat that score, and I began to wonder if the prize might be mine, a 75cl bottle of Konyagi, the sweet gin-like spirit the Tanzanians like to pep their beer up with. Finally as the entrants dwindled, a young local lad called Jack was persuaded to put down his beer and show us how it should be done. With flowing blond hair and an easy smile, he looked a little like the young Robert Plant. He turned away and composed himself. There was a moment of pregnant anticipation before he violently turned back and advanced with menace upon the judging panel, a distressing figure of pure malice. Quite how anybody could suddenly have so many nostrils I am not sure, but this warped and disfigured horror lurched forward and the judges scattered whilst awarding perfect 5s.

I had a chat with him later on, outside for a spot of fresh air.

'They say it's a cultural exchange but really it's just an excuse for a piss-up.'

'Same difference', I thought to myself.

Jack was from Cleator Moor, where I'd intended to go the next day. 'The best pies are from Wilsons.' We agreed that whoever's pies you grew up eating were forever after the benchmark against which all other pies are judged. For me it had been Titterton's pies on Mill Street in Macclesfield, even though that butchers had been gone well over twenty years. I promised Jack I'd try one from Wilsons.

'What's the employment like round here?' I asked,

'It's either Sellafield or drugs to be honest', he replied, without offering an opinion which he was hoping for.

'Will you stay?'

'I'm not sure yet.'

I mentioned I'd be busking in Cleator Moor.

'Take your stab jacket', Jack replied casually, before heading off to a secret supply of beer for a refill.

In an otherwise perfectly normal village hall, a wall of big red posters detailed what to do should nuclear sirens go off. Just two miles away is Sellafield, a gigantic nuclear waste reprocessing plant, West Cumbria's kill or cure, forcing locals to accept the choice between the distasteful idea of processing and storing half of the world's nuclear waste, and mass unemployment. The plant provides thousands of well paid jobs and the area needs it, but as well as the safety concerns it's also an economic time bomb. Closure would hit West Cumbria with a fresh wave of depression just as it looks like overcoming the last.

From inside the hall the African voices cut through, a

powerful nasal singing tone. The ringleader of the music seemed to be a young woman called Martha. She knew the dances and had an energy that took the whole dance floor with her. I wanted to ask her more about it, but neither of us really had enough common language to make it work and in the end, she just offered me a fist bump, delivered with total commitment, a heavyweight blow from a 4ft 9in woman.

I later learned that she'd lost her mother young, and was fighting tooth and nail to get an education when much of her family would much rather she was married off as quick as possible. Freedoms and opportunities that seem automatic to some of us are incredibly hard won for others.

The night went on. Many cans were consumed. The bar was being run by 18-year-olds for whom this was their first attempt at such employment. I went to see what they were offering and found that all they had was lager and gin. I asked if they had any bitter, which caused some head scratching. Later they found me and told me they'd got a crate of John Smiths in specially, which I then felt obliged to drink.

West Cumbria doesn't get many visitors. Tucked right round the corner of the Lake District, far off the beaten track, not on the way to anywhere, the decline of industry has rendered this a forgotten corner of England. Yet it's one I feel I know very well. Many of my best friends are Cumbrians from this very part of the world, drawn to Manchester for work and excitement, and into my world by the music we have in common. I have friends from Whitehaven, St Bees, Cleator and Egremont.

The importance of exchanges like the Cumbria-Rungwe Community Link example is huge. Mary tells me that in many of the impoverished towns and villages, the kids have never seen a black person, and consider they could never go to London for fear of meeting one. Exchanges like this break that prejudice down in the nicest possible way, without criticising or excluding, but by creating opportunity for people to explore and learn.

Too many of our English interactions with the world, and especially former British Empire colonies, are patronising, and measured in terms of what we can do to 'help' or make things better. In this exchange, it is a meeting of equals, where both sides grow and benefit without cost to the other.

The midsummer sun finally set and both sides had danced enough. Things drew to an end. I took my can of John Smiths back into the building which was now deeply fragrant with the smell of teenage BO and took in the scene. Clusters of people were forming and re-forming, full of hugs, selfies, and the knowledge of a precious time come to an end. People young enough to still need to learn about that special kind of grief that comes from knowing that someone you've grown to love may be someone you never meet again. Tears happened outside, in private, a little later.

Cleator Moor

I'D had it in my mind to busk in Cleator Moor, right from the start of this project. It's just not like anywhere else I've been. A town few have even heard of, flung up in a few years to supply the iron industry and consequently not really between any two other places. You'd never end up here by chance, and few would choose to go. Disused railway lines converge on the town, viaducts lost under forests, embankments crumbling, sudden bridges, built to carry mineral trains now long scrapped. One line has become a cyclepath, a Lycra motorway that misses the town by a few hundred yards, and from which not one cyclist ever diverts to see Cleator Moor.

It feels like something of a ghost town now, like the gunslinger has come to town and everyone else has gone into hiding. The rows of handsome shop buildings around the main square are largely empty and hollow, save for the odd hairdresser. The two beautiful civic buildings in the square itself are being refurbished, and the library has temporarily moved out, leaving it even quieter than usual.

'You don't want to busk there – try Whitehaven instead, you'll do much better' was a common warning. I didn't care, and wasn't in it for the money today. I just wanted to get to know this fascinating little town better. My hosts Bob and Mary had supplied me with a couple of nuggets of information before I'd left that morning. The first was that Cleator Moor had been the scene of mainland Britain's last sectarian murder. The second was that in the ten minute walk from the old village of Wath Brow along the high street to the 19th century town of Cleator Moor the accent would change considerably.

This seemed unlikely to me – perhaps it might have been true in the 1850s when the Irish community moved to Cleator Moor and built their new town on the edge of Wath Brow, but surely not now, or if it did, just a subtle inflection here and there, only noticeable to the locals. I parked at Wath Brow and walked the few hundred yards to Cleator Moor, all one continuous urbanisation now, any border indistinguishable on sight. The accents at Wath Brow were as I expected, broad Cumbrian, a touch like the more famous Geordie accent to the untutored ear, but softer and more rounded.

Along the way you pass by the first of several chip shops. A colony of herring gulls lined the roof, waiting for opening time. Chip shops in West Cumbria open for just one hour at lunch time. Miss that and you'll go hungry. The birds knew this well and were alert and ready, like runners waiting for the starting gun.

I made it to Wilson's for my pie – which was excellent – and was addressed in a clear Irish twang by the butcher, who was tickled by the idea of someone busking in his town, and made me a free cup of coffee in solidarity. Outside, I was harassed by a small white dog, whose elderly female owner told it to 'Behave yer'sel'. Mary was right. In 2019, the town is still so static there's a considerable accent difference over the course of five hundred yards.

I busked in the main square by the bus stop. There was virtually nobody about, and what few people did come all got on buses for the bright lights of Whitehaven and Maryport. It didn't matter, sometimes it's fine to just play for the fun of it, and slowly a few coins did come, from old men who crossed the road specially and from children passing by. It was enough to buy lunch at least.

Across the way was a Chinese restaurant which proudly displayed an enthusiastic but cringingly patronising review in the window. 'Tommy (he has an unpronounceable Chinese name!) does the cooking.' 'I know it doesn't sound too exciting but it was surprisingly good!' I wondered what possible sequence of events could have brought a family from China to Cleator Moor. Alas, the restaurant was closed for staff holidays.

I headed back down to Wath Brow, past Sproaty's chippy, in search of my afternoon's entertainment.

Where the town finally finishes, butting up against Dent Fell, the last flat piece of land belongs to Wath Brow Hornets ARLFC (Amateur Rugby League Football Club). Normally thought of as a game for Lancashire and Yorkshire, Cumbria's deep love of rugby league has often gone unreported, with professional sides in Whitehaven, Workington, and Barrow, and numerous strong amateur clubs. Wath Brow are one of the best sides in the country, and were today entertaining Yorkshire rivals Siddal.

I am a passionate follower of rugby league, and have been since a very young age. My father took me to games all over the North West, starting at the age of six. I carried my own milk crate through the turnstiles so that I could stand on it to see what was going on. My passion for the game has only increased with age, as I've come to appreciate the significance that so many of the clubs hold for their communities. Played almost exclusively in northern, working class towns and villages, rugby league is frequently the one thing that these communities still have to feel proud of when so much else has been lost to the decline of industry.

I was joined by Bob, who'd cycled over from St Bees, normally a rugby union fan, but willing to give this other code a try for the day. We found a comfortable spot by the opposition dugout on the far side of the pitch and waited for the start of play. The feeling of community was strong around the ground, as a crowd of a few hundred assembled in the sunshine to enjoy the entertainment. Young girls in club shirts practised their tactical kicking in front of the goal posts. Older lads got in a couple of pints ahead so they wouldn't run out during the first half. All generations were represented, bringing family and community together, and a minute of silence was held for a departed friend.

Siddal started terribly, conceding a try within seconds. From the kickoff, they contributed to the wholesome family atmosphere by loudly shouting in unison: 'Smash the cunt!' as they charged after the ball. It seemed like a predetermined tactic to intimidate the opposition, but sadly for them they didn't seem to have a plan 'B', and having failed to 'smash' the 'cunt', looked somewhat bewildered and uncertain what else to do. Wath Brow were just too good, with flowing set moves, tough defence, and superior discipline.

It became a procession, and the Siddal dugout became an increasingly agitated place.

'You're all fucking bent, you three!' yelled the substitute to the referee and both his touch judges, leading me to wonder if a player can be sent off if he's not on yet.

Behind us, Ennerdale opened up into the West Cumbrian plain, wild open hillsides cascading down to this little impoverished but stunning corner of England, locked away behind the mountains and so rarely visited by the tourists who overwhelm Grasmere and Ambleside. Their loss.

I went for a wee at half time. A cancer awareness poster in the gents suggested that I 'Check my balls monthly', in the quaint belief there's a bloke out there who, if left to his own devices, doesn't check them hourly.

The second half continued much as the first, and I got chatting to an older lad who told me he'd had a professional trial with Workington Town many years ago. 'We played Salford, back when they were the best. Got stuffed! Loved it though.'

'How much were you on for a match back then?'

'£6 a game. Not much even then! But here's the thing, they never paid me, so when my trial was up and I wasn't signed, I went round to the director's house to get my money. Turned out he'd passed away two weeks prior. Never saw a penny!'

He saw the funny side now, forty years later.

'Look at them.' He said, pointing to the gaggle of tanked up lads who were ribbing the opposition players for every mistake, winding them up. 'At full time, you watch – they'll fuck off instantly. They act hard, but they're cowards! They'll be gone as quick as they can in case any of those players decide to take it up with them after the whistle.'

The whistle went and he was right, off they ran to the bar. Rugby league is the toughest of games, played by the bravest men and women. There's a reason why I've always preferred to stay in the crowd. With the win, Wath Brow went top, highest ranked amateur side in the UK, every player a local lad drawn from a village in a forgotten corner of England. It means everything to them and I can see why.

Watchet, Dunster and the Quantock Hills

I busked in Watchet on the edge of the harbour, looking out over the Severn estuary towards Cardiff and up the Bristol Channel. A small boy of about 5 years of age ran down the quayside and stood right in front of me as I played, staring right at me with a frown on his face and index finger jammed firmly up his right nostril, a pose he held for over a minute. 'A bright future ahead as a critic for this one', I thought to myself. Another child chased a herring gull round and round a nearby bench until his mother gave him 20p to drop in my case. The child simply weaponised it and threw the coin at the gull instead, and we all watched as it rolled over the harbour edge into the mud below. I imagined some future archaeologist uncovering it from the sediment, remarking at the placement and declaring it 'ritual'.

A lady came by with two boxer dogs, one ancient, gnarled and stoic, that calmly laid down near me; the other, barely full grown, nervous and agitated with the music.

'She's not heard a violin before', said the owner, encouraging the young dog to calm down. I stopped playing, and it crept out from behind her legs. I plucked a note, and the dog howled.

'She's got to learn.'

I played a few bars, and the poor animal produced a full-on river of piss. It seemed best to let it on its way before trying again. Once the dog was suitably far away, I played on. A regular at the bar along the quay arrived with a pint of beer for me. A young lad watched for a while and produced a fiver. It was a good session.

I'd picked a spot quite close to the statue of the Ancient Mariner, the fictional lead in Coleridge's epic poem, inspired by this very spot. Further along, another statue was seated looking out over the harbour, that of Yankee Jack, a noted mariner who definitely had existed. He was life-size and weathered, blending in with the landscape of the harbour. Another fiver came my way, this time from a lady who introduced herself as Margaret and said I should check out a pub called Pebbles as it often had live music on. I said I knew of it, as I was booked to play a concert there this evening.

'Oh', said Margaret. 'I suppose I'd better go then.'

Pebbles is a cider pub, snug and homely, and I'd been invited to play a few tunes and tell some stories from my trip so far. There was a PA system, but I found I didn't need it, as the audience comprising a mix of regulars and people who'd come down specially for the concert sat in perfect warm silence, and we had a great night. Ben, the landlord, insisted on showering me with hospitality, and when he saw I couldn't drink all the free cider, owing to needing to drive, chose a selection of his favourite bottled ciders for me to take away. It'd been a long day but a great start.

As I was about to leave, a man at the bar was suddenly keen for a word. 'You need to understand when you write about us, this is a town by the sea, not a seaside town. Understand? No fruit machines, no 'kiss me quick' hats.'

'Sounds like there's a gap in the market', I mused. He was scandalised.

I arrived at Watchet station bright and early the next morning. The bearded volunteer was just unlocking the building, and was concerned to see me parking in the station car-park. 'Are you travelling with us today?', he asked with scepticism.

'Yes, mid-morning if that's okay.'

'You'll need to buy a ticket.'

Clearly in my heavy metal hoodie, he did not take me in good faith as a real railway enthusiast, so I decided to raise the stakes a little.

'Do you still have the 7F?' This was one of a class of heavy freight locomotives built for the Somerset and Dorset Railway, one of which I knew to be owned by the S&D Railway Trust, who are based at Washford, the next station along.

'I'm not sure, I think so.' It was enough, and he left me alone. I went for an early morning wander around town before my train arrived. The atmosphere was different with the tide reaching the top. The tidal range is huge here, the second largest in the world, and the sea that had been distant and meek was now full and menacing, slurping restlessly at the harbour walls in opaque muddy thrusts.

Along the pier, evenly spaced, a row of fishermen with long and expensive rods cast out into the brown and chopping water of the estuary. One recognised me.

'Saw you in Pebbles last night. It was good. Sticking around today?'

'Reckon I'll catch the train to Dunster, and then back here late afternoon.'

'Good plan. You'll do well in Dunster.'

'Fishing any good today?'

'Not really, too choppy. Don't expect we'll catch anything.'

'So why bother?'

'Gets you out of the house and near the sea. On a good day you can catch dogfish, conger eels.' His view never left the estuary as we spoke.

Further along, three lads had rave music on loud from a portable speaker, and were working through a crate of Strongbow. They hadn't caught anything either, but were clearly enjoying the early morning, boogying away, rods set. They hollered at me as I went past with my fiddle case, but I gave them a breezy 'Good morning' and they ignored me as no fun. All each fisherman along the length had to show for the effort was a small pile of seaweed that'd been reeled in instead of fish.

I admired the determination to keep going, even though conditions were all wrong. The activity itself more important than the prospect of success. I'd had more than a few busking sessions that way. Back on the quay, the fishing rave was carrying clearly across the harbour, so I abandoned any ideas of a warm-up busk and bought my train ticket to Dunster. In the coffee shop I was recognised again.

'Nice gig last night. Took some pictures, let me know where to tag them.' I was small-town famous.

On the platform, a family were struggling to come down to the Somerset pace of life, still being stuck at London speeds. I overheard their frantic flow of words.

'I wanted the restaurant for 6:30 but they only had 5:30 or 7:30. What shall we do? Shall I try somewhere else or should we go tomorrow instead?'

I realised how I'd already slowed down. There's no hurry to be anywhere round here, and all times are approximate. It's not laziness; all the work gets done, just steadily and cumulatively, when the time is right, rather than to an arbitrary timetable. The family near me hadn't found the pace yet, and were still frantically tearing through life whilst Somerset gently smiled at them.

I was reading Tove Jansson's *The Summer Book*, a semi-fictional account of a little girl and her grandmother growing together on an island in the Gulf of Finland. The pacing was perfect for my setting and I enjoyed the gentleness of the writing and didn't care how long it took for the train to arrive.

'They picked out the stones that hadn't been worn completely round and threw them out into the water to make them rounder.'

Somerset is a good place to find time to read again.

Slowly, the platform came to life with expectation. Small boys still love steam trains. Why? Nostalgia can't account for it. Even their parents can't remember when steam trains were in regular use. One hard-to-reach child was withdrawn, not responding to anything his mum said to him. When the distant whistle of the train came over the hill, he sat upright and beamed. 'A train!' His mum beamed too.

Perhaps it's just that they are living, breathing things. A clanking, hissing event upon arrival, an expression of effort upon departure, the smell of steam oil, nutty and sweet, and the shower of black bits that get in your eyes when you try to look out of the window. A cumulative, society wide belief that they are important and somehow quintessential. I'm smitten, for sure, and have largely resisted the temptation to turn the whole project into a train-spotting session. But this one was going where I needed to go, so why not hop on and get a face full of smudges?

'The funniest thing,' said the station master to me, as the train came into the platform, all shining brasses and action, 'is watching people look for the push buttons on the carriage doors.'

Increasingly, station staff have to go up and down the platform, helping people deal with slam door coaches. Nobody knows now how to lift the window up and out of its socket and reach out to the turn-handle.

'They'd be stuck on all week if we didn't help.'

At Dunster, we all dutifully watched the train on its way like good tourists, before starting the walk into the village. At the station, the staff have adopted a robin, and it lives amongst the period suitcases with a bowl of food and a bowl of water, hopping between perches. It looked rough, with bald patches and scars, like a boxer who should have retired ten fights ago but doesn't know what else to do with their life. Sometimes other robins come to fight it and the station master chases the invaders away with a broom.

Dunster itself is pretty and it knows it. A broad main street leads up to the castle driveway. I busked outside knick-knack shop that was closed for the day. A concerned shopkeeper from down the road came to see me.

'You can't do that, you'll be in awful trouble.'

'Really, why?'

'Well, it's not allowed, is it?'

'Busking? Unless there's a specific bylaw forbidding it, then surely it's okay?'

'You could go in there, that'd be okay', she said, pointing at the Yarn Market, a beautiful covered building, owned by the

National Trust, and the one place where I knew for certain I couldn't legally busk.

'I prefer it here. Seriously, it'll be fine. Look, if the problem is that you'd rather I wasn't busking, but you're too polite to say so, then I'll just move on. I don't want to annoy anyone.'

'Oh no, it's fine, I just don't want you getting in trouble.'

I assured her that I knew the busking laws pretty well and I continued. Sometimes the street was silent and the sound rang all up and down, and sometimes rows of cars came along and the sound of exhausts and tyre noise dominated instead. A long line of motorbikes came by, parking up at the top of the village. The black-leather clad drivers gathered in front of the yarn market for a team photograph before dispersing into the many tearooms for lunch.

I made £20 in the first hour, but it died right down during the next half hour as the sun reached its zenith and the flow of people congealed, so I went for lunch. Round the corner of the castle hill is another street with a few shops, a sort of emergency backup town centre in case the first one needed an overhaul. Right at the bottom was a rough looking pub, quite out of keeping with the picture postcard loveliness of the rest of it. The landlord had a world weary approach, and lunch was rough-hewn baguettes and catering chips served by an awkward youth. The next table was taken by a family from Birmingham who couldn't get over how long a drive it had been to get down here for their holiday.

I could hear a parrot, so pretending to go to the loo, I sought it out in the back yard and taught it a funny noise.

Dunster had used up its appeal to me. All very pretty but not much life to it. If you like a Ye Olde Teashop or buying original oil paintings, then you could get a morning out of it but that's it. It's a place that trades on how it looks. Watchet was a place that traded on who it was and what you might do, and that was more interesting. In Dunster, I'd been met with bemusement when I'd busked. It just wasn't the done thing. It's always the same with these slightly faux places. All morning I'd felt like I was winding them all up but that they were too polite to ask me to go away.

As I walked back to the station, a man stopped his car across the road from me and wound down the window.

'Are you heading to Minehead?'

I recognised him as another one of my audience from last night's gig.

'No, back to Watchet.'

'Want a lift?'

This was a kind offer, but I had a return ticket for the steam train, so I said I'd rather catch that.

'No problem! I'll see you back in Watchet then!'

Back in Watchet, I busked again on the quay. The ancient mariner looked down at me like I was making an already bad day worse. My fan arrived. It was a bit odd to find busking turning into a little concert, so I tried to pretend he wasn't there and just played as normal. After a while he bought me a coffee.

A small ginger girl with freckles and stacks of confidence sat on the wall next to me and kicking her heels against the stones told me I was better than her music teacher.

At 5pm, I took my loot to Pebbles and swapped it out for a few bank notes.

I was staying as a guest of Halsway Manor, National Centre For Folk Arts, who'd invited me down for a few days. Rachel showed me round. We headed to the apple tree, a local variety, the Quarrenden, down at the bottom of the formal lawn. It was speckled with hundreds of ripening red apples.

'It's probably the most wassailed apple tree in England', Rachel told me. 'No wonder it does so well.'

I helped myself to a windfall, warm from the sun, and looked back at the manor, framed by trees against the sheer sides of the Quantock hills. It's a place that wears its seasons well, now in the deep greens of late summer. Soon the autumn golds and reds will flush the landscape and garland the manor, before falling to bare branches and exposing the jet black bodies of the rooks who live within.

About two miles down the road is the small village of Crowcombe, and I headed out of the evening to see if I could meet the locals. The footpath was clear and easy in the fading light, and I noted the fallen tree for my journey back. The Carew Arms is at the far end of this slender village, the pub long and lanky too, with a skittle ally and a dining room stretching away from the bar. The door to the bar wouldn't open, so I gave it a beefy shove and sent a young fellow on the other side flying. It was his sister's birthday and he was barring the door whilst the cake was brought and she was outside, not expecting a strapping lad like me to suddenly stride in from the darkening wilderness, full of determined, thirsty purpose.

The rest of the pub was quiet. It's the dining trade that keeps the lamps burning these days, and most diners were fed and leaving, so I sat at the empty bar with Rachel's copy of *The Rime of the Ancient Mariner* and read it, trying not to look too much like a twat reading poetry at the bar. Not having much of a classical education, I'm mostly familiar with this work from Iron Maiden's version on Powerslave, their fifth studio album. It's quite a poem, though, full of emptiness and endless misery. I admit I struggled with the meter, which was relentless and unchanging, forcing in some pretty desperate rhymes to make it all fit. I couldn't help but feel it would have made a better story than a strict tempo poem. But I hardly know enough about poetry to be a critic. I think I'll stick with Iron Maiden.

Without a great deal else to do in an emptying pub, the barman struck up conversation with me, asking me why I was in town. He was from Georgia in the US, having ended up running the bar in a rural Somerset pub by a series of events and coincidences. I explained my journey and interest in the English character. A regular, perhaps my age, had joined me along the bar with a pint of lager, and the landlord threw the point over to him, asking; 'What do you think of yourself as an Englishman?'

This was heavy philosophy for a bloke who'd come out for a quiet pint and his eyes bulged in fear at the enormity of the question. Before he could answer, his phone suddenly rang in his hand.

'Thank fuck for that!' he said, answering it.

The landlord had some stories to tell. He'd worked with horses in the States.

'It costs a lot to dispose of a dead horse. We knew a man with a ranch who'd allow you to bury them on his land for half what the professionals charged. You turned up with the dead horse, took the mechanical excavator into the land and picked a spot. He'd got so many buried you usually had to dig four or five holes before you found a spot without one in already. There were thousands buried out the back there. Imagine the trouble if they develop the land some day.'

He was a passionate supporter of gun rights.

'Hey, I carry in the States. It's saved my life. Ran out of gas in a bad part of town. I was filling up, and this man was walking round my truck, saying 'So you're pretty rich then?' I was like, 'no, not me', and he pulled a knife on me anyway. Well I had my gun and I held him there till the cops came. He's in jail now and I'm alive. Problem is they just want to take the guns off people without involving us in the decision.'

'The thing we see though,' I said, to find if there were limits to his position, 'are those really big guns, the semi-automatic stuff. Do you really need to have all those?'

'Aw yeah, I don't see why anybody needs to carry more than, say, twelve rounds. But they need to talk to the NRA and groups like that. If they just try to take the guns, there'll be violence. You can't do it by just banning them. Everyone needs to be involved.'

If anything summed up my journey around England, it was perhaps this scene. You think you're going for a pint of cider with West Country folk, and you end up in a discussion about the Second Amendment with an American. Everything is so jumbled up, people from all over searching for the spot in England that suits them best. Quintessence can be bought into for a little while. England, still the same hills, villages, towns, as a complex river of life flows through. Every time you think you're within reach of the 'real' England, something totally left-field happens that reminds you of how cosmopolitan and international we are. And yet, England bubbles along beneath, quite unreadable and aloof.

I made my way home in darkness, leaving the last house of the village behind and along the footpath in the trees. Truly dark now, I enjoyed letting my eyes find the rough shapes of the land round me. We forget how good we are at the dark, and how even a sliver of moon becomes enough to paint the world anew when we've truly let our eyes adjust. My frame cast a broad shadow on the hedges. Crickets sang, and the night became friendly and welcoming, a new space to share.

As I carefully made my way up the track, I startled a horse at a gate, who had clearly not been expecting anyone at this time. It humphed and reared and circled the field in protest, before standing in front of a distant gate on the brow of a small mound, staring back at me, silhouetted and impossible to scale against the star filled sky and between two walls of foliage. I said hello, hoping to reassure it I was friendly. It watched me with suspicion, and I watched the horse, a colossus against a secret sky, and time passed without measure. A shooting star came through, right above the mound and the moment was complete, watchful horse and skyline just shapes, but more powerful for being reduced so.

The thing about shooting stars is how common they are. But we forget to look, smearing the urban skies with the marmalade orange of sodium and staying indoors. The night has become a place avoided and reduced, where the imaginary bad things pool up in unlit corners. Those few moments when we see the shooting stars, lying on our backs among the vines and turf with someone we love, or on a solo adventure through the night, it proves it's not the stars that are rare, but our taking the time to see them. It's the most beautiful show of all, and it goes almost unwatched.

The moment lingered, and I became aware of the warm and physical presence of second horse much nearer me and lost to my eyes in a hollow that kept the darkness rich. It had its arse to me and was untroubled by my arrival. It let off soft equine farts from time to time. The moment had lost its magic and I finished the walk back to the manor, cursing the security light that ruined my night vision, robbing me of the safety and connection to the land it had brought.

In the morning, I'd planned to walk the Quantock Hills, where Coleridge and Wordsworth had walked as they overdosed their way to the birth of romantic poetry. Rachel, as ever my guide for the area, had sorted me a map and drove me to Nether Stowey, across the hills, as a starting point. As we arrived, she had a moment of concern, and double checked that I knew how to read a map. Clearly she had suddenly had visions of me wandering off into the woods, falling at last into the fairy kingdom and passing into legend, before bursting from the leafy verges decades later, entirely covered in hair and bellowing something unintelligible about pastry.

I assured her I'd be alright, and piled off into the countryside, round the castle mound and into the woods. Wordsworth and Coleridge had been full of opium on their wanderings. I was full of sausages. I'd have to do my best. The gentle hills came and went and added to something greater. The thick summer air balanced dragonflies on the wing, common darters, southern hawkers, common hawkers, rising over hedgerows that felt urgent with life. Lambs came to gates and pressed their faces through in expectation of remembered bottles. Higher up, the trees rose and met above and the world became mottled light falling on a pick and mix ground of twigs and decomposition. A tractor stormed through, towing a grain holder, and I had to step back from the track.

I left the track and took the path up further, surrounded by a gentle wildness. A single and momentary ray of light, permitted by the movement of a single leaf far above, picked out a floating jewel before me. It was a glimpse of a web, strung from two trees ten feet apart, and built by a spider the size of my little finger nail. How this creature had conceived such a magnificent plan I couldn't work out, let alone the logistics. I tried to photograph this spider, hung across my path and so far from the anchors of the land and the trees, but the camera wouldn't focus, only seeing the distance. A gentle reminder that a special moment shouldn't be captured and carried home like some cheap trinket. Alerted to the net across my way, and being prey too big to stick, I crashed my way around the outside on the rough ground instead and wished the spider well with its day. The presence of the web suggested I must be the first to come through today.

Every day this Quantocks world is born anew, and each traveller will find their own unique story to share, if they look carefully enough. The glittering citrines of woodland predators, disguised in dappled shade. I caught the stench of a stinkhorn mushroom and found it, dishevelled and declining behind a mound, phallic and foul. Ground dwelling spiders dug into a bank, lining nests with cones of silk, funnelling lunch inwards.

The top of the hill was still under tree and sky, and the banks of the ancient hill-fort were harder to spot, smoothed by the loam of millennia. But the shapes are there, the walls tracing the logical rim of the summit. It's a strange slice of life, between the earth and under the canopy, where the twisted and narrow trunks reach up from poor soil to grab what light they can, the lower part of the tree barren and wasted, and each view a spaghetti of greying wood, where the modern mind, grown in cities and used to regular shapes and good order tries to find a symmetry that cannot ever quite resolve.

Clouds of flies rose from puddles as I came through, and unsure what to do next, they sank down again to wait for the next disturbance. I crossed through the valley to the next ridge. Here, cars were parked and people of all sorts were making brief excursions from the safety of the vehicle to the worrisome edge of the wild. One family were on bikes and I heard the father speak with that voice that tries to exude control of the situation but manages instead to sound petulant: 'I'm simply trying to resolve the issue.'

Another family, Asian, had gone far enough. 'I'm not walking another step away from the car. The ground is no good and I'm tired', said the frustrated patriarch, sitting down where he was.

Clearly the ridgeway was not the calming outdoor space it might have been. It's only the great escape if you don't bring your problems right along with you for the ride. Up here, beyond the rounded tops of the Quantocks you can see the nuclear power station at Hinkley Point, an inexhaustible outcropping of jumbled cranes and grey concrete, as hard to scale as the horse had been in the blackness of the night. I wondered what the great poets might have made of it. Perhaps Wordsworth would have turned his back and drawn inspiration instead from Exmoor, still mostly untouched, whilst Coleridge would have said nothing of it, but let it return as an echo, a nightmarish visitation, feeding off the discord.

Wild horses stood docile in groups of two or three, and I was able to walk right up to them. Clouds of flies thrived on their juices, rushing for the eyes, clambering up over each other to drink where the liquid pools up in the corner. The horse has no defence and must suffer them in thousands every midsummer, wretched and countless.

The ridgeway continued, and at Halsway post it split. I ate my lunch beneath a kestrel. It's a landscape that encourages an interest in smallest details, where you get on your hands and knees to look a spider in the eye inside its burrow, and the widest vistas, from nuclear seaside to Exmoor tops, where you yourself are the little detail being boggled at by buzzards and kites. The Lake District is only about the big. The small is gone, industrially farmed out of existence. It is a big, beautiful, broken landscape. The Quantocks marry the infinite with the microscopic and everything between. A painter with a giant canvas couldn't catch it all, and the finest magnifying glass would always leave some passionate and essential detail undiscovered. It is a world of infinite perspective, where each can find their own moment.

I scrambled down the steep bank to Halsway and returned the map, before visiting the lucky Quarrenden tree for supplies for my route north. In Watchet, I tried one more busk, with it being market day. The town crier recognised me, having, almost inevitably, been to my gig at Pebbles, and announced me with gusto to a public who didn't care. It failed as a spot, too busy, the melancholy magic of the quiet harbour gone, the anonymity shattered. Yankee Jack was marooned between a fudge stall and a wood carver, oddly decontextualised and clearly bemused with his situation. I left Watchet and the Quantocks for the long drive home to plan my final expedition.

Hull

HULL was to be my last destination. I'd chosen it for two reasons. First, this was where I learnt to busk, sixteen years ago when I was dating a woman at university here. I really had no money at all, and always busked for my train fare home. The people of Hull never let me down, and so there seemed a pleasing circularity in bringing it all to an end here. But there was a second reason for coming to Hull. My paternal grandparents had grown up here, on opposite sides of the city, surviving the Second World War as teenagers, un-evacuated and exposed to the blitz that hit Hull so hard. There would be bits of my family history scattered around to find.

I re-acquainted myself with my former busking pitch. I think it was a Woolworths when I'd last been here, but was now three smaller shops, so I picked the disused entrance to a closed down Marks and Spencers opposite and picked up where'd I'd left off those years before.

Whitefriargate has lost its sheen now, with so many closed shops. It's half empty, and much of what remains is popup or cheap remainders. People head through on their way, rather than being engaged in the act of shopping. A lady came past and shouted something derogatory. I ignored it, but another shopper found a coin for me and apologised on Hull's behalf.

'I think she might have a few issues. Don't worry about it.' She said. 'Hey, all those notes, if it was a guitar I'd called you a fretwanker!'

'But I don't have any frets, so I guess that makes me a...'

'A wanker!' she concluded for me gleefully, 'Yes, but it's good stuff. Don't be so hard on yourself.'

I made a respectable £25 in a couple of hours and wandered around towards the river Hull, the dividing line between East and West Hull, a navigable trench, sweeping in ancient pre-city arcs under so many colourful lift bridges. The Manchester Arms had a sandwich board outside that proudly announced that this pub was 'The home of Shit on the Grass', without making it clear if this was a band or a cocktail, or something else altogether. I didn't go in to enquire further.

A bedraggled man barked 'What time is it?' at me as I walked along the riverside walk.

'3:45pm', I answered.

'Fuck me, wasn't sure if it was morning or afternoon.'

I met my host for the trip, Steve, in HOME, a dinery and bar he runs on the Beverley Road. After a bite of dinner, we decided to take a walk through the industrial fringe of the River Hull and possibly visit a couple of bars along the way.

Veering off Beverley Road, you pass a number of tanneries as you head towards the river. They stink, big old brick buildings where huge drums tumble slowly, over and over, and a tangible white mist of stench sits in the hollows between the walls. At the end of the street is a Jewish graveyard, disappearing into the brambles, gravestones hidden in trees. A sign, rising from the thicket gives the name of the road, 'Air Street'.

The Hull is still fringed by industry all along. With tall concrete slabbed walls and fences, the area is known as the bankside gallery, and graffiti artists have coloured every suitable surface. It's a semi-formal arrangement now, and certain buildings have signs on saying things like 'Listed building, no art please!' Banksy left a picture here, on a disused and raised drawbridge, now covered in a stiff and see-through plastic sheet to protect it from the elements and the jealous.

We made it to the Whalebone, a pub on the verge of surviving its context. I love pubs like this, where the world that spawned them has gone, demolished, redundant, redeveloped, and suddenly they're the only remnant of a time past, decontextualised and strange, surrounded by modernity. The Baltic Fleet in Liverpool is a fine example, a sailor's pub left architecturally lost amongst the contemporary urban accommodation that sprouted with such vigour when the warehouses came down. Or the Peveril of the Peak in Manchester, all green glazed tiles, a two-storey city pub from another age, base out of alignment with the footprint of the huge new buildings all around, a subtle clue to the ever-shifting flow of the city streets.

Hull

The Whalebone is half way there. Industry is on the way out here, but the Whalebone persists, and perhaps even thrives, a rare bright light in this dusk, a glowing beacon of life amidst the lifeless ruined brick and graffiti sprawl of post-war industrial Hull, bombed out and rebuilt on the cheap to get the place going again. Development is coming. Further down towards the Humber, warehouses and industry have become flats and museums, quirky bars, and the wave is slowly lifting itself upstream. There's an outlier, a single warehouse already flats, developed ahead of time by some forward-thinking Hull resident with the cash to do it and finger to the pulse of the city, surrounded by factories and garages, recycling centres and scrapyards. The air smells of processes, and the views are of rubble and the gentle end of eras, but when the wave reaches this street, somebody stands ready to cash in.

'My mate bought an old mill and rented it out to artists for a while.' Said Steve.

'They bloody love a mill, artists.'

'They do.'

'It's like catnip to them, they just can't resist one.'

The garages and scrapyards will turn into popup bars, little kitchens, galleries, squats, then houses, then flats and trendy pubs, and finally the artists and free spirits that arrived as the first colonisers will be economically and socially displaced and move further upriver and the area will become boring again, as achingly dull people evict the cultural life that drew them here, wanting to feed off the vibe without the slog of adding to it themselves. The next fifty years were already determined for this street. And the Whalebone would sit there through it, an unbroken link to a past that will seem far away and mysterious.

The Whalebone is a homely place, good beer, clean and considerately lit, tidy but busy with sporting mementoes and history, including framed photographs of Clive Sullivan, Hull's most famous adopted son, the rugby league player who led

Great Britain to victory over Australia in the 1972 World Cup. He played for both the city's clubs, bridging the divide that rugby league represents, and was the first black man to captain any British sporting side. It says a great deal about Hull's openness that their greatest sporting hero was a black Welshman who moved to the city to try his hand at the northern code. He died of cancer aged just 42.

We tried another pint a couple of streets on, at a big, lonely sort of place called 'The County'. It was 9pm and already the landlady was closing the curtains, peach and lilac patterns than matched her clothing so well that when she stood in front of them, she entirely disappeared from sight. There were two darts boards at opposite ends of the bar, suggesting at least the historical existence of both an 'A' and a 'B' team. Such numbers seemed hard to believe on a night like this. We took our pints of Chestnut Mild ('Tastes of nowt!') to the back of the room and watched as the landlady flitted between following the 1980s crime drama on the TV over the bar and feeding pounds into the fruit machine, during the adverts. All around the deep picture rail were huge vintage chocolate tins, a reminder of how large Roses and Quality Street used to be before the era of austerity shrank them to their current tragic sizes, a sort of economic island-dwarfism effect.

It was too melancholic to stay here for long, so we found the Ye Olde White Hart instead, which had rather more life about it, including a man having a loud phone conversation about the history of Formula One. He continued without break during our time in this pub, and I started to entertain the suspicion that the person on the other end of the line didn't quite hold the same interest level. The pub was ancient and wood panelled and somewhat worn out. The door to the toilets suddenly took you into a long white panelled corridor lit by fluorescent tubes and so out of keeping with the rest of the establishment that I wondered if I'd been abducted by aliens.

Hull

We concluded our adventure in Dive, a bar a little out of town, set up by a couple of young lads who'd wanted a bit of autonomy in the pub business. So many of the pubcos have exploitative models of tenancy that any smart youngster looking to run one has generally concluded it's better to set up as an independent, and unable to buy out the larger houses, there's been an explosion of little bars all over the country. They probably don't make any more money here, but at least it's theirs to do as they please, without the pubco accountants working out exactly how much rent to chisel them for this year. It's a microcosm of the wider economy, really. Without the same career progression and security of the old jobs market, if you're in the service sector and have a bit of youthful ambition, you might as well do your own thing, be that coffee shops, hairdressers, bars.

Steve was doing what all good landlords do, keeping a polite eye on the competition. It was a dive too, but that made sense. Nail a bar together out of chipboard and paint it, get a smattering of mismatched furniture off freecycle and just get the place going. Make a point of getting to know your customers, build it up as time and money allow, but just get trading. You can't afford perfection.

The lad behind the bar was controlling the music through a tablet and I asked him if the system took requests.

'No.' He answered, having clearly weighed me up, probably correctly, as the sort of person who would probably ask for something daft or unsuitable.

There were two young women at the bar next to me, towards the end of a good night out.

'I'd better go home, I have to lead a yoga session 8am tomorrow morning', said one, somewhat worse for wear, and stumbling out.

'Good luck with that!' I said, and I meant it.

They were replaced by a skinny and heavily bearded man

who ordered a Guinness. He was full of opinions, but very hard to follow. Later on Steve said; 'He was a musician, you know.'

'What did he play?'

'Vibes.'

'Of course.'

The next morning I walked back down the bank of the Hull. The tanneries were still at it, fire doors open for ventilation. Dereliction was being torn down, machines with claws reducing the spent parts of the city to rubble and scrap. Buddleia is the flower of Hull. It lives in every crack in the brickwork, grows through crumbled brick and concrete. Pushes out of stock left fallow for too long in padlocked yards. It finds a way high up in unwashed gutters on careworn warehouse and mill, and even in the Autumn of the year, the scent is in the air, mixing with the many other smells of the city.

Hull is a city of smells. It doesn't stink; that's too easy a denigration. It smells of processes, natural and industrial. Chemicals, solvents, pollen, and a fresh layer of mud dropped on the ebb tide. Once it smelled of fish as well, but that industry is dead, never to return, the trawlers no longer passing right across the face of the city to the Hessle Road, returning from what was regarded as the most dangerous job in the world. It produced outspoken, clear headed people, like Lillian Bilocca who in 1968 led a successful campaign for mandatory safety improvements on trawlers. Her actions saved many lives and she was rewarded by being blacklisted from the industry, never working with fish again, being in some sense perhaps scapegoated for the rapid decline in the trawling trade in the decade that followed.

Outsiders still perceive Hull as a city of fishing, even though that's now long gone. It's changed hugely since I was a regular visitor, becoming far more bohemian and cultural. Being city of culture in 2017 certainly helped, although it's proving hard to keep that momentum up.

Hull

Hull has a bit of everything. The road followed the ancient curve of the river, and I came upon a nest of skips, arranged like occasional tables, as if a Feng Shui expert had fulfilled a brief and departed.

In town I chose to busk on King Edward Street, wide and spacious. After a slow start, I began to do okay. I was then interrupted by a street sweeping machine. He'd passed me by yesterday as well, a once round Whitefriargate, but it seemed the centre of town was his focus. Up and down he went, the rowdy drive-on hoover, sometimes on the far side of the street, sometimes coming right at me and veering round my case at the last second. 'They must pay him by the ton,' I thought to myself as he came by yet again, spoiling a good tune.

As he went round the corner for a while, I resumed my playing. Two heavily armed policemen came by, with large guns slung across their fronts, pacing slowly, a little distance apart.

'You having a good morning?' said one to me, with measured professional politeness. I didn't know how to answer, their weaponised presence disconcerting, so I just blanked him. Not out of rudeness, but I found I couldn't hold a conversation like that with a man carrying an automatic weapon. Why were they here? Did they know something I didn't, or is this just how things are now? Far from reassuring me, they troubled me a great deal. The sweeper returned again, roaring past the other way. Hull must have the most diligently swept streets in England.

I bought some lunch and gently meandered towards the old Fruit Market part of town. This had been a ghost town fifteen years ago, recently abandoned, empty at night, frontages of a different age and uncertain future. Now it had been redeveloped, and I looked forward to seeing it brought back to life. It was a disappointment. Like a film set it looked great from certain angles, but entirely false when you knew where the joins were. It was stiff and inorganic, a vision foisted upon a street full of history, as insincere as the highbrow shops that filled it, empty and over-priced. The only one that looked like any fun was called 'Dinosaur experience' but it was closed, intriguingly, for 'Staff training'.

At least the Minerva was still there, the last pub before the Humber. It had been an outpost of welcome sanctuary, beyond the forgotten town, warm, almost cramped, but homely. It hadn't changed at all, and looked out over the estuary, its back to all the nonsense behind. On the pavement outside was a worn brass plaque with the single word 'Haddock' on it. I couldn't find any others.

Back into the city, I stumbled upon the minster, somehow hidden away in an old part of town, squat and tucked under the wind. A lady was leaving and finding herself walking alongside me asked about my fiddle. I said I was a busker.

'You should try outside the minster in a bit, there's a lovely concert on later, lots of people going.'

I said I'd consider it.

'It'd be good to hear. Now why don't the homeless play something like you do?'

I flashed white hot. I am rarely an angry man, but a year of pent up frustration suddenly boiled over. Several times previously I'd been given this ludicrous equivalence between my busking and the plight of a rough sleeper, and on each occasion I'd been so surprised and shocked I'd not had the words to explain the difference, playing what I should have said over and over in my head after the event and wishing I'd been erudite at the time. This time, then, I was ready and angry, I stopped dead in the street and fired back.

'The homeless? Where are they going to get an instrument from? How are they going to get the years of tuition? How are they going to find the energy when they're sleeping out in this weather? When their fingers are cold and sore?'

'Well, they could bang a drum or something', she replied,

surprised I'd not taken the initial intended compliment as expected.

'They're starving and dying on the streets, and you want them to bang a drum before they're worth your charity? What a complete and utter lack of empathy. Disgusting.'

'There's no need to be like that', she finished, heading into a shop she didn't need to go in to get out of my way.

I watched her head in. There exists a large group of people for whom such misfortune could surely never happen. They have good friends, families, second chances, safety nets, strong networks of support and care. And some of them draw the mistaken conclusion that therefore rough sleeping could only occur to someone who deserved it. They must be lazy, taking the piss, irredeemable.

They've made mistakes, the people I've met on the street, often big ones. They have problems that are hard to solve. But then I think of the times when a relative or friend has held out a hand and stopped me making a mistake, or where the support of those around me allowed me a second chance, a recovery, and I count my lucky stars it's not me there. I came from the right sort of family, had the sort of background that saw mistakes as learning opportunities rather than insurmountable failings that dog you for the rest of your life. Had this woman ever sat down and talked to the homeless? I guessed not. But I was being unfair, bringing my entire trip's experience to bear on a lady who'd only meant a compliment and just not really thought it through. I'd perhaps have held similar views myself once.

The whole conversation replayed in my head as I set up for another play. I was soon cheered by a skateboarder who dropped off a bag of cheese quavers as he raced past. The street sweeper was still at it. Such devotion to duty. Maybe he was just incredibly passionate. Perhaps his mates had to find him at 5:30 and say 'Come on Dave, that's enough for one day, let's go for a pint now.'

A rough sleeper came by, smiled, and dropped off a smattering of copper coins. It was enough to break your heart.

Rain ended it. It had been coming for a while, you could taste it, hurrying across the plain of East Yorkshire, a freshness driving dust and tiredness before it. Fat drops came all in a hurry and I packed down. I'd made £40 across the day, enough, perhaps. I handed dollops of it to the needy as I headed out again, back up the Buddleia road, past the gravel warehouse and back to my accommodation.

That night I played a concert for Steve in HOME. It was a strange sort of thing, as the place was sold out with diners who regarded the entertainment as a nice extra. 'When's the singer on?' I heard, more than once, thinking 'They'll be disappointed!' But it worked, people bought into it, questions were asked.

A few of us ended up back at Steve's later. He's been putting on gigs in the city for decades and has had dozens of artists of all styles pass through.

'You'll be sleeping in a bed that once had Mr Methane in it', he told me.

'Something to live up to', I replied.

On my third day, I headed out for other parts of Hull.

Bransholme was the vast new estate built after the war to replace the housing that had been demolished in the bombing. The shopping centre was busy and basic, and I bought a very old fashioned heavy woollen jacket for £3 from a charity shop. There were no modern shops at all, no fancy coffee shops or eateries. It was a shopping street from the 1990s, still thriving. I was on my way to visit the estate my grandmother had grown up in, back in the 1930s and through the war. We'd visited it together a few years ago, me driving her over the M62 in my knackered green Ibiza with flame decals down the side, an unlikely pair of fellow travellers. She'd made a packed lunch and we set out to see the world of her youth. The estate had been tired and run down, but we found her old house, and the fellow had let us see the back garden which still contained her air-raid shelter, a sturdy brick built unit. I found it an emotional artefact to encounter, to think that my grandmother as a child had sat in there so many nights, waiting for the all clear. It'd brought back memories for her too and she told me a great story.

'One night the siren went off, so we went to the shelter. My grandparents lived next door so they shared the shelter with us. Dad was at sea. Then an incendiary bomb landed in the back garden, so my granddad ran out and buried it with his spade. In the morning, it turned out it had landed in the potato patch and cooked them all!'

It was a remarkable story that blended the horrors of war with the mundanity of life carrying on.

I arrived on the estate to find it missing. The whole lot had been demolished, save a small number of single houses boarded up and graffitied. The streets, the lights, the speed bumps, the signs were still there, but the plots were flattened and grassing over, an open expanse.

It'd been a smart new estate in the 1920s, built for the growing population of Hull, better homes for working families, but time and expectations had changed and it had grown tired and too worn out, and the council had ultimately demolished the lot. A few had resisted, refusing to leave. It must have been strange and fearful to see every house around yours torn down and the closed world of the estate opening up into a new urban parkland. Most had given up now, and only two showed signs of life, the other half dozen or so gutted and boarded and awaiting the final blow.

A bus wended through the silent streets, following a ghost route. Small children and their teachers were collecting conkers from the mature trees that lined the edge of the estate.

'Yeah, they demolished them this year, in waves', one teacher told me. 'Started in about March, most recent just a couple of months ago.'

Elsewhere in the desolation, two lads from the demolition contractor were repairing the pavement.

'Council are making us mend it after the demolition. No idea why. It's fucking shit.'

'Will they be redeveloping it?' I asked.

'Don't know, probably. They're waiting for the ground to settle down.'

Leaving the lads to their labours, I walked all round it again, taking far more photos than I normally do. It was compelling, bizarre, uncanny. I wondered how my grandma would feel to know her road had been demolished and erased. How would I break it to her? Eventually I rang up.

'Oh yes, it was knocked down earlier this year wasn't it?' Even at 89, she doesn't miss much.

Our trip here those years before had finished at the chapel at Marfleet where she'd married, and never returned to until that day. The church is surrounded by gently humming industrial estates, an island of an older Hull where the beeping of reversing lorries carries gently through the foliage of the graveyard. I took one more look here, with the gravestones of ancestors in the mosses, and quietly declared my trip a done deal. There would always be another town and city to visit. There was so much more I could have done, but it felt like time to stop, here before the front of the church, with the warden keeping a worried eye on me through his window across the road.

Conclusion

A BOOK like this calls for a clear narrative. I set out to get to know my own country better, a country whose politics, priorities, and obsessions had surprised me so very much. Who are the English? What matters to us? What unites us? Having explored well over fifty varied corners of England during the course of the adventure, the need for a satisfactory narrative now calls upon me to answer these questions with clear, reassuring answers. This is the part where I should reveal the common threads, the deep quintessential Englishness that binds a country together beneath the surface.

But I cannot.

What does a Durham coal mining village have in common with a Cotswold village? What does Bradford have in common with Truro?

I could have carried on for another year, found another fifty places, and I don't believe I'd be any nearer to the answer. I'd just have another fifty Englands. England is too varied, too jumbled up. It is defined not by what unites us, but by our many differences, cultural, social, economic, geographic.

It's easy to point at ethnic diversity, something England has a-plenty, but even within what one might clumsily term the 'Anglo Saxon' constituent there are also vast differences. Parts of England remain defined by their industrial past, others by incoming communities, yet others sit within the orbit of London. Retirement communities fill rural villages. Drifters head West and open coffee shops. England is full of people living lives that they would consider to be quintessentially English, and yet many have little to no overlap. I will not submit to the lazy narrative satisfaction of confecting a false and comforting conclusion that we're all alike and pulling the same way.

What strikes me further is how so many of us, myself perhaps included, consider our personal experience of being English to be somehow definitive and representative. We don't know our neighbours. We travel abroad on package holidays to Spain, but no longer know Blackpool or Skegness. Business travel within the country is identical Travelodges and motorway service stations, creating a superficial sense of uniformity and preventing exposure to the real undercurrents. Our only real collective common ground is to be found in the mundanity of life – trading estates, daytime TV, nuisance calls, doctors' waiting rooms, the consequences of drug abuse as they play out on the streets.

Englishness doesn't really mean anything specific. It has no binding, singular politics. Our dominant culture is American, our economy featuring pockets of both immense wealth and devastated communities. I spent over a year playing English music on the streets, and most people who spoke to me didn't even recognise it as English, often assuming it to be Irish. We are, quite simply, a nation with no clear sense of identity.

People yearn for identity, though, and fill empty vessels with it. Poppies and football teams, flags and political movements, the NHS. Each a cast-iron example of Englishness to the perpetrator and a bewildering misappropriation to the onlooker, who no doubt has their own cultural totems to defend.

And so it's a mess. The line on the map that defines England as being different from all the places round it demands also a uniformity of purpose and value within. But we are jumbled up, confused, and strangely insular, jumping to personally tailored dog-whistles that offer simple solutions to complexity.

How could this be resolved?

The twinning schemes that run between places in different countries look like a good model to examine. Why not replicate that within our own country? Link communities with vastly different stories. Much of what seems to me to go wrong with politics and policy comes from a failure to imagine that other people live in very different circumstances. We each consider our version of being English to the authentic one, and that our advantages and difficulties are similar to those of other places. It's hard to show empathy to people you haven't met and whose circumstances are an unknown. My trouble in Easington came from a total failure to understand what it was to live in a community like that and how their experiences gave them a totally different set of priorities and values.

Conclusion

English politics is consumed by an unhelpful tendency to simplify us into a single group of people, with identical priorities and values. Talking about the 'English' like they are indivisible will never produce results that satisfy more than one constituent part. Even coming at the problem regionally will only help a little. Great extremes exist within a few miles of each other. Rich and poor within sight across a valley floor. Top down politics will rarely serve a kaleidoscope nation well, whilst community-based initiatives so often make little sense in the bigger picture. An ex-mining town has more in common with another ex-mining town at the other end of the country than it does with its market town neighbour six miles away.

Does that lead to the inevitable conclusion that we are still a nation dominated by class division? Perhaps it does, although the traditional brackets are virtually useless now. The children of the middle class often have no money, and prefer a life of lived experience and art over wealth and possessions. You only really find the traditional working class in towns with no work.

But another, more human conclusion would be to remember that for over a year I travelled round England with my fiddle, playing tunes and surviving thanks to the kindness of strangers. I was taken in for meals, given places to stay, shown things of interest, and was sustained by the generosity shown to my busking collection.

I saw the seasons go right round in their circle, played through the heart of winter and earned the warmth of the summer. It wasn't a chore, but a pleasure. The very variety that makes England so hard to pin down also makes it infinitely fascinating. No two places were the same. I feared repetition, I ended up not knowing when to stop.

'The most enjoyable book about British folk music out there...' - *Songlines magazine*

'...a very, very funny and informative book. If you like good writing and folk music then you will love this.'
– *Norma Waterson*

All the Wrong Notes

Adventures in Unpopular Music

By Dave Hadfield

For almost 50 years, Dave Hadfield has followed the genres of music that grabbed his youthful heart and mind. Now, in ALL THE WRONG NOTES, he has written not just a musical memoir, but a personal and social history of the last half-century. Like a Zelig with a finger in his ear, he has been where folk music has happened and describes it, affectionately but warts-and-all, in a way it has never been described before.

Hadfield's sure ear for quirks and eccentricities produces unique takes on major figures like Bob Dylan, Ewan MacColl and Leonard Cohen. It celebrates the foot-soldiers and their role in keeping left-field music alive. Humorous and provocative in equal measure, ALL THE WRONG NOTES is the key to a fascinating world of music.